# Judaism in Five Minutes

# Religion in 5 Minutes

Series Editors
**Russell T. McCutcheon**
University of Alabama
**Aaron W. Hughes**
University of Rochester

**Published**

*Religion in Five Minutes*
Edited by Aaron W. Hughes and Russell T. McCutcheon
*Atheism in Five Minutes*
Edited by Teemu Taira
*Buddhism in Five Minutes*
Edited by Elizabeth J. Harris
*Hinduism in Five Minutes*
Edited by Steven W. Ramey
*Indigenous Religious Traditions in Five Minutes*
Edited by Molly Bassett and Natalie Avalos
*Pagan Religions in Five Minutes*
Edited by Suzanne Owen and Angela Puca
*The Old Testament Hebrew Scriptures in Five Minutes*
Edited by Philippe Guillaume and Diana V. Edelman
*Yoga Studies in Five Minutes*
Edited by Theodora Wildcroft and Barbora Sojková

**Forthcoming**

*African Diaspora Religions in Five Minutes*
Edited by Emily D. Crews and Curtis J. Evans
*AI in Five Minutes*
Edited by Katherine Chiou, Lawrence Cappello, and Nathan Robert Loewen
*Ancient Religion in Five Minutes*
Edited by Andrew Durdin
*Chinese Religions in Five Minutes*
Edited by Ben Van Overmeire and James Miller
*Christianity in Five Minutes*
Edited by Robyn Faith Walsh
*Islam in Five Minutes*
Edited by Edith Szanto
*Jainism in Five Minutes*
Edited by Steven M. Vose
*Mormonism in Five Minutes*
Edited by Daniel O. McClellan
*New Religious Movements in Five Minutes*
Edited by Lukas K. Pokorny and Franz Winter
*The New Testament in Five Minutes*
Edited by James Crossley and Robert J. Myles

# Judaism in Five Minutes

Edited by
Sarah Imhoff

SHEFFIELD UK   BRISTOL CT

Published by Equinox Publishing Ltd.

UK: Office 415, The Workstation, 15 Paternoster Row, Sheffield, South Yorkshire S1 2BX

USA: ISD, 70 Enterprise Drive, Bristol, CT 06010

www.equinoxpub.com

First published 2025

© Sarah Imhoff and contributors 2025

All rights reserved. No part of this publication may be reproduced or transmitted in any form or by any means, electronic or mechanical, including photocopying, recording or any information storage or retrieval system, without prior permission in writing from the publishers.

British Library Cataloguing-in-Publication Data

A catalogue record for this book is available from the British Library.

| ISBN-13 | 978 1 80050 697 8 | (hardback) |
|---|---|---|
| | 978 1 80050 698 5 | (paperback) |
| | 978 1 80050 699 2 | (ePDF) |
| | 978 1 80050 718 0 | (ePub) |

Library of Congress Cataloging-in-Publication Data

Names: Imhoff, Sarah, editor.
Title: Judaism in five minutes / edited by Sarah Imhoff.
Description: Bristol : Equinox Publishing Ltd, 2025. | Series: Religion in 5 minutes | Includes bibliographical references and index. | Summary: "Judaism in Five Minutes provides an accessible and lively introduction to common questions about Jews and Judaism, with a focus on Jewish communities, textual traditions, practices, rituals, laws, holidays, and life-cycle events. As with other volumes in the Religion in 5 Minutes series, this volume is suitable for beginning students and general readers through a series of general questions, succinctly answered by experts in the field"-- Provided by publisher.
Identifiers: LCCN 2025001685 (print) | LCCN 2025001686 (ebook) | ISBN 9781800506978 (hardback) | ISBN 9781800506985 (paperback) | ISBN 9781800506992 (pdf) | ISBN 9781800507180 (epub)
Subjects: LCSH: Judaism.
Classification: LCC BM43 .J82 2025 (print) | LCC BM43 (ebook) | DDC 296--dc23/eng/20250304
LC record available at https://lccn.loc.gov/2025001685
LC ebook record available at https://lccn.loc.gov/2025001686

Typeset by Scribe Inc.

# Contents

Preface   xi

**Texts**

1. Why are texts sacred to Jews?   3
   *Brian Hillman*

2. What is the Torah?   6
   *Laura Carlson Hasler*

3. What is the Talmud?   9
   *Sara Ronis*

4. What is midrash?   12
   *Sarah Imhoff*

5. What is Kabbalah?   15
   *Brian Hillman*

**Laws and Rituals**

6. What is Jewish law?   21
   *Yonatan Y. Brafman*

7. What is a rabbi?   24
   *Sarah Imhoff*

8. What is Hanukkah?   27
   *Jodi Eichler-Levine*

9. What happens during Passover?   30
   *Laura Yares*

10. What does kosher mean?   33
    *Nora L. Rubel*

11. Why don't Jews eat pork?   36
    *Jordan D. Rosenblum*

12. Do Jews drink alcohol? 39
    Jordan D. Rosenblum

13. Why do Jews circumcise boy children? 42
    Alison L. Joseph

14. What is a bar/bat mitzvah? 45
    Rachel Kranson

15. Why does gender matter in Jewish law? 48
    Ronit Irshai

16. What does it mean to be Hasidic? 51
    Sam Shuman

17. What do Jews do on the Sabbath? 54
    Adrienne Krone

18. Can Jews get tattoos? 57
    Chaim McNamee

19. Why is the name of God important? 60
    James A. Diamond

## Groups and Beliefs

20. What are the differences among Reform, Conservative, Reconstructionist, and Orthodox Judaism? 65
    Joshua Shanes

21. What are the differences among Ashkenazi, Sephardi, and Mizrahi Jews? 68
    Max Daniel

22. What is Karaite Judaism? 71
    Meira Polliack

23. What languages do Jews speak? 74
    Sarah Bunin Benor

24. What does it mean to be a secular Jew? 77
    Jennifer Caplan

25. Do Jews believe in God? 80
    Elias Sacks

26. Can you convert to Judaism? 83
    Michal Kravel-Tovi

27. Can Jews marry non-Jews? 86
    *Samira K. Mehta*

28. How do Jews think about non-Jews? 90
    *Ishay Rosen-Zvi*

29. What do Jews think happens after you die? 93
    *Matthew J. Suriano*

30. What do Jews believe about the messiah? 96
    *Martin Kavka*

31. Are there angels and demons in Judaism? 99
    *Sara Ronis*

32. Who are crypto-Jews? 102
    *Sasha M. Ward*

**Judaism and Other Religions**

33. Why don't Jews believe in Jesus? 109
    *Adam Gregerman*

34. Was Jesus Jewish? 112
    *Meira Z. Kensky*

35. Did Jews kill Jesus? 115
    *Eric Vanden Eykel*

36. Was Paul Jewish? 118
    *Elias Sacks*

37. Why do Jews and Christians disagree if they read a lot of the same Bible? 121
    *Benjamin E. Sax*

38. What are Jewish-Christian relations? 124
    *Jessica Cooperman*

39. Who are Messianic Jews? 127
    *Yaakov Ariel*

40. What is the relationship between the Bible and the Qur'an? 130
    *Shari L. Lowin*

41. What is Judeo-Islamic civilization? 133
    *Liran Yadgar*

42. Who was Moses Maimonides? 136
    *Alan Verskin*

## Jewish Difference

43. What is antisemitism? 141
    *Jeffrey I. Israel*
44. Are Jews White? 144
    *Sabina Ali*
45. Are Jews European or Middle Eastern or something else? 147
    *Aziza Khazzoom*
46. What is the relationship between Blacks and Jews? 150
    *Henry Goldschmidt*
47. Is Judaism a religion or an ethnicity? 153
    *Jeffrey I. Israel*
48. Does Judaism pass down through the mother? 156
    *Deena Aranoff*
49. Can you tell if you're Jewish from your DNA? 159
    *Rachel B. Gross*

## Holocaust

50. What is the Holocaust? 165
    *Helene Sinnreich*
51. What role did race play in the Holocaust? 168
    *Mark Roseman*
52. How did Jews resist during the Holocaust? 171
    *Sean Sidky*
53. How do Jews commemorate the Holocaust? 174
    *Laura Levitt*
54. Is it OK for art, films, or novels to depict the Holocaust? 177
    *Sean Sidky*
55. How do Jews think about God and the Holocaust? 180
    *Barbara Krawcowicz*

## Zionism and Israel

56. What is Zionism? 185
    *Jacob Beckert*

57. What is anti-Zionism? 189
   Shaul Magid
58. What is the role of Judaism in the State of Israel? 192
   Alexander Kaye
59. How is ancient Israel related to the State of Israel today? 195
   Rachel Havrelock

**Judaism and Social Issues**

60. What are Jewish ethics? 201
   William Plevan
61. What does Judaism say about social justice? 204
   Aryeh Cohen
62. What's the connection between Jews and feminism? 207
   Steven Kaplin
63. What does Judaism say about the climate crisis? 210
   Dustin Atlas
64. How do Jewish traditions portray trans and
   nonbinary identities? 213
   Joy Ladin
65. What does contemporary Judaism say about sexualities? 216
   Jonathan B. Krasner
66. How do Jewish traditions approach disability? 220
   Andrea Dara Cooper
67. What's the deal with Jews and comedy? 223
   Jennifer Caplan
68. Where do stereotypes about Jews and money come from? 226
   Samuel Hayim Brody
69. What does Jewish tradition say about war? 229
   Geoffrey D. Claussen
70. How have Jews approached slavery? 232
   Jonathan K. Crane
71. What do Jews think about abortion? 235
   Samira K. Mehta

   Index 239

# Preface

Judaism is both an ancient religion and a modern one. Religious Jews draw on texts from antiquity, such as the Hebrew Bible, the Mishnah, and the Talmud. Judaism includes rituals whose earliest forms date to antiquity, and Jews also participate in religious practices that date to the twenty-first century.

Judaism is traditionally a descent-based religion, so being born into a Jewish family is the most common way of becoming Jewish. But it also allows for conversion into the community as well as departure from it. For most of history, Jews have lived alongside practitioners of other religions, and Judaism has had particularly close interactions with Christianity and Islam—two traditions that share some textual traditions and narratives but also diverge in significant theological ways.

The essays in this volume provide a window into the internal diversity of Judaism. Its origins date to the ancient Israelites in Southwest Asia—sometimes called the ancient Near East—and Jews moved across Europe, Africa, Asia, the Americas, and Australia over the centuries. In those locations, Jews often spoke the local languages and sometimes intermarried with non-Jews. In these geographically dispersed communities, differences emerged in some kinds of practices, such as the groupings we now refer to as Ashkenazi, Sephardi, and Mizrahi. Differences in theologies also emerged and even led to divisions in Jewish communities with the emergence of modernity, resulting in the labels we see today, such as Reform, Conservative, and Orthodox, or Zionist and anti-Zionist.

As a quick look at the table of contents will suggest, this book acknowledges that Jewishness is particularly complicated because it is not exclusively religious. Some Jews neither believe nor practice Judaism but nevertheless maintain a strong identification as Jewish. The content of this Jewishness can be ethnic, cultural, linguistic, or lineage based. The scholar of religion knows that these things are often still entangled with religion, even when individuals call themselves nonreligious.

These essays are written by scholars, but they are meant for a curious, nonscholarly audience. Many are inspired by the questions our students have about Judaism. In recognition of the fact that short essays cannot tell the whole answer to any of these questions, each chapter concludes with suggestions for further reading, both essays from within this volume and published works beyond it.

Sarah Imhoff, Indiana University Bloomington

# Texts

# 1
# Why are texts sacred to Jews?

## Brian Hillman

The Jewish tradition is often characterized as "text-centered." This means authority is manifested in textual sources, and consequently, those who can read, interpret, and apply texts are highly valued in normative Jewish societies—those that see themselves as following halakhah (Jewish law).

The earliest and most authoritative text in the Jewish tradition is the Hebrew Bible. Composed over centuries (roughly between 1000 and 100 BCE) in the ancient Near East, the Bible is accorded divine authority. Because the Pentateuch (first five books of the Bible) narrates direct divine revelations to the Israelites, it is the most sacred and authoritative part of the scriptural tradition that includes the Prophets and later writings. Gradually, the notion of divine authority of the entire Pentateuch and, consequently, its immaculate nature developed.

The destruction of the Second Jerusalem Temple in 70 CE fundamentally altered how ancient Israelites worshipped Yahweh, the deity. As Yahweh could no longer be worshipped at a centralized temple (with its attendant tithes and sacrifices), Israelites had to access the deity through other means. The Pharisees, forerunners of the rabbinic movement that would come to construct normative Judaism, greatly valued their own interpretations of the Hebrew Bible and the teachings of their predecessors. Consequently, they were well suited to weathering the destruction of the Temple because they privileged texts and tradition over Temple ritual and physical space. Through the rabbis of late antiquity, the Jewish tradition transformed from being Temple-centric to text-centric.

After the failed Bar Kochba Revolt from 132 to 135 CE, the rabbis formalized their teachings. The first prominent rabbinic text, called the Mishnah, redacted around 200 CE, includes topically organized compendia of legal, ethical, and ceremonial teachings of esteemed rabbis with meticulous attribution. The rabbis developed an expansive notion of "Torah" grounded in the myth that Moses received both a Written Torah (i.e., the Pentateuch) and the Oral Torah (i.e., the Mishnah and

Talmud—the rabbinic expansion of the Mishnah redacted in Palestine and Babylonia in late antiquity). Thus, the Mishnah and Talmud are taken to be the continuation or extension of the revelation of the Hebrew Bible, authenticated by their direct connection to an authoritative tradition. Most fundamentally, Jewish texts are sacred due to their rootedness in divine revelation and connection to an authentic tradition.

The study of this tradition became a central religious act, reflected in the Mishnah's statement that the study of Torah is equivalent to all the commandments (*m. Peah* 1.1). Reflecting an understanding of the difference between biblical and Rabbinic Judaism, the Talmud (*b. Eruvin* 63b) teaches that the study of Torah is superior to the Temple sacrifices. With a Written Torah and an Oral Torah that clarifies and explains the perennial relevance of the former, an expansive notion of "Torah" developed in Rabbinic Judaism. Texts considered to be part of, or vehicles for, the Jewish tradition were deemed categorically distinct from other purely human-generated texts and hence sacred.

Over the centuries, more texts entered into this orbit of "sacrality" determined by having a connection to the original moment of revelation where the sacred resides. Different Jewish communities accord sacredness to a wide range of texts, including legal compendia, such as *Shulḥan Arukh* by R. Yosef Caro (1488–1575) and its glosses by R. Moses Isserles (1530–1572), mystical texts such as the Zohar (the central text of Kabbalah), prayers, and other writing by esteemed rabbis. Due to the centrality of texts, Jewish communities have tended to emphasize literacy and education, especially for men.

The sacredness of texts is reflected in how Jewish people treat these texts as physical objects. Many prominent Jewish ritual objects have textual components. A Torah must be handwritten in a specific manner on properly prepared parchment to be considered kosher for sacral use. The mezuzah, an ornate box affixed to a doorpost following a biblical injunction in Deuteronomy 6:9, contains biblical verses on parchment that must also be written in the proper manner and maintained.

How Jewish communities dispose of their holy texts also reflects their sacredness. As the name of God is understood to be holy, Jewish communities usually buried these texts or housed them in a storeroom called a genizah rather than destroying the divine name. The practice came to include other pieces of writing in Hebrew, as the sacredness of the Hebrew Bible was thought to extend to its language. Considering why texts are sacred to Jews gives rise to related questions, including the following: What is a Jewish text? Can a Jewish text be written in any language? Can a sacred text be written by someone considered a heretic by some Jews?

## About the author

**Brian Hillman** (he/him) is an assistant professor in the Department of Philosophy and Religious Studies at Towson University in Towson, Maryland. His research focuses on modern Jewish thought, Jewish mysticism (Kabbalah), and religion and popular culture. His writing has appeared or is forthcoming in the *Journal of Jewish Identities*, *Jewish Studies Quarterly*, *Religious Studies Review*, and the *Jewish Book Council*. He also serves as the managing editor for the *Journal of Jewish Thought and Philosophy*.

## Suggestions for further reading

*In this book*
See also chapters 2 (What is the Torah?), 3 (What is the Talmud?), and 4 (What is midrash?).

*Elsewhere*
Halbertal, Moshe. *People of the Book: Canon, Meaning, and Authority*. Cambridge, MA: Harvard University Press, 1997.

Hayes, Christine. *What's Divine About Divine Law? Early Perspectives*. Princeton, NJ: Princeton University Press, 2015.

Holtz, Barry W., ed. *Back to the Sources: Reading the Classic Jewish Texts*. New York: Simon & Schuster, 2006 [1982].

de Lange, Nicholas. "The Authority of Texts." In *Modern Judaism: An Oxford Guide*, edited by Nicholas de Lange and Miri Freud-Kandel, 243–253. Oxford: Oxford University Press, 2005.

Scholem, Gershom. "Revelation and Tradition as Religious Categories in Judaism." In *The Messianic Idea in Judaism and Other Essays on Jewish Spirituality*, 282–303. New York: Schocken, 1971.

# 2
# What is the Torah?

## Laura Carlson Hasler

"Torah" sometimes denotes the first five books of the Hebrew Bible: Genesis, Exodus, Leviticus, Numbers, and Deuteronomy. This torah is the "T" in the anagram Tanakh (a Jewish term for the Hebrew Bible as a whole) and is sometimes used interchangeably with the word "Pentateuch." (To avoid confusion, I will use "Pentateuch" to refer to that discrete five-book collection as attested in the Masoretic Text [MT]). But torah can also refer to the Hebrew Bible as a whole. In fact, the term "torah" also has many connotations. It sometimes functions as a proper noun (what we might refer to in English as Torah with a capital *T*) referring to a specific textual collection. The contents of that collection, however, might vary widely. The term sometimes also serves as a generic noun, such as in biblical texts, where it is translated as "teaching," "instruction," or "law" (e.g., Prov. 1:8; Lam. 2:9), or in Hasidic communities, who may refer to "the rebbe's torah" to connote a leader's teachings.

"Torah" can refer to a particular text or textual collection. Within the Hebrew Bible, Moses calls upon his audience to obey "*this* torah" (Deut. 30:10)—that is, the contents of the book of Deuteronomy in particular. Ezra-Nehemiah's references to torah seem to have something *like* the Pentateuch in mind but do not neatly conform to it. For example, Nehemiah 8:15 resembles but is not the same as MT Leviticus 23:40. While these biblical authors may have had a specific text collection in mind when referring to torah, it is apparently not identical to any single known "Torah" that has survived today.

Later documents from the Second Temple Jewish community at Qumran also deploy the term "torah" to refer to non-Pentateuchal texts. The Temple Scroll, an adapted version of Exodus and Deuteronomy written in the second century BCE, describes itself as "torah." Similarly, the Samaritan Pentateuch, perhaps also penned in the first century BCE, claims the title of torah. It contains important differences from what would become the MT Pentateuch. The Samaritan version of Deuteronomy attests, for example, to the place that YHWH "has chosen" (e.g., SP Deut. 12:5) instead of the place YHWH "will choose" after the Israelites cross the Jordan (MT Deut. 12:5). This small but consequential change in tense indicates that the divinely appointed place of worship is Mt. Gerizim and *not* Jerusalem's Mt. Zion.

When books like Ezra-Nehemiah and Malachi, among others, refer to torah, they often refer to it in conjunction with one of two important figures: the Torah of Moses (e.g., Ezra 7:6; Mal. 4:4) or the Torah of YHWH (e.g., Ezra 7:10). The phrase "the Torah of Moses" is sometimes taken to mean that Moses wrote this collection. But this phrase, like "the Torah of YHWH," may aim to convey a looser affiliation than direct authorship. These attributions may instead reflect a figure believed to be a (more abstract) source or even a recipient of this teaching's dispensation at Mt. Sinai/Horeb.

The first five books of the Hebrew Bible came to be known as Written Torah. A larger anthology of instruction, known as Oral Torah, was committed to writing in the wake of the Second Temple's destruction in the first century CE. Oral Torah also traces its origins to Moses at Sinai (cf. *m. Avot* 1:1). This body of law is traditionally thought to have passed down orally from Moses to Joshua and then on through subsequent teachers until its eventual textualization in the Mishnaic and Talmudic collections. In general, we can say that torah *tends* to mean a body of instruction that is tied to Moses at Sinai, though exactly what that instruction might contain and when it was believed to be committed to writing can vary widely.

## About the author

**Laura Carlson Hasler** is an assistant professor of Jewish studies and religious studies at Indiana University, Bloomington, where she holds the Alvin H. Rosenfeld Chair in Hebrew Bible. She is the author of *Archival Historiography in Jewish Antiquity* (Oxford, 2020), which was awarded the Manfred Lautenschlaeger Award for Theological Promise in 2021.

## Suggestions for further reading

### In this book
See also chapters 3 (What is the Talmud?) and 4 (What is midrash?).

## Elsewhere

Anderson, Robert T., and Terry Giles. *The Samaritan Pentateuch: An Introduction to Its Origin, History, and Significance for Biblical Studies.* Atlanta, GA: Society of Biblical Literature Press, 2012.

Collins, John J. *The Invention of Judaism: Torah and Jewish Identity from Deuteronomy to Paul.* Oakland: University of California Press, 2017.

Hayes, Christine. *What's Divine About Divine Law? Early Perspectives.* Princeton, NJ: Princeton University Press, 2015.

Najman, Hindy. *Seconding Sinai: The Development of Mosaic Discourse in Second Temple Judaism.* Boston: Brill, 2002.

Sommer, Benjamin D. *Revelation and Authority: Sinai in Jewish Scripture and Tradition.* New Haven, CT: Yale University Press, 2015.

# 3
# What is the Talmud?

## Sara Ronis

In the wake of the destruction of the Second Temple in 70 CE, a new Jewish group emerged in Roman Palestine called "the rabbis." These rabbis were a male scholarly elite who created and transmitted an enormous body of oral tradition. These oral traditions explained biblical laws, offered short explanatory stories, and organized the rabbis' world into a series of lists and principles—a rich Oral Torah to complement the Hebrew Bible, or Written Torah.

In the second and third centuries CE, a group of rabbis associated with the Jewish leader Rabbi Judah the Patriarch and his household began to organize these oral traditions into a unified whole called the Mishnah. Written in Hebrew, the Mishnah is divided into six thematic "Orders": *Zera'im* (Seeds, i.e., agricultural laws); *Mo'ed* (Holidays); *Nashim* (Women, i.e., laws relating to marriage, divorce, and personal status); *Nezikin* (Damages, i.e., civil law); *Kodashim* (Holy Things, i.e., the laws relating to worship at the Temple when the Temple stood); and *Tohorot* ("Pure Things," i.e., issues relating to biblical purity and impurity). Each order is subdivided into tractates (sixty-three in total), which focus on a particular theme.

The rabbinic movement was found across two major empires in late antiquity: the Roman Empire (today much of the Mediterranean world) and the Sasanian Empire (at its height, stretching from modern-day Armenia to Tajikistan), centered in the province of Asoristan or Babylonia (today Iraq). By the mid-third century, the rabbis in both the land of Israel and Babylonia saw the Mishnah as an authoritative body of teachings. Its authoritative status required it to be fully understood. And that led each rabbinic community to create a new and even larger body of explanations, interpretations, and discussions of the text of the Mishnah together with other traditional teachings: a Talmud. Both the rabbinic communities in the land of Israel and Babylonia created Talmuds, but when people today refer to "the Talmud," they are referring to the Talmud of the rabbinic community of Babylonia.

A mix of Hebrew and Aramaic, the Babylonian Talmud contains discussions of the Mishnah but also functions as an encyclopedia of Babylonian rabbinic knowledge from the third through seventh centuries CE. Its genre is sui generis, containing accounts of legal proceedings, biblical interpretations, medical knowledge, and extensive debate and discussion. Put together by its redactors or editors, the Talmud reads as an extensive intergenerational discussion and debate or the minutes from a very long and particularly engaged class discussion. The editors juxtapose numerous statements attributed to named rabbis from different time periods, weaving them together into a multivocal discussion. The Talmud rarely offers conclusions to the discussion, instead modeling ways of thinking about earlier traditions and their relationship to the contemporary world. The Talmud is aimed at an internal rabbinic audience and constructed holistically, assuming a detailed degree of rabbinic knowledge throughout.

In the medieval period, an extensive campaign by the heads of the rabbinic academies of Babylonia led to the widespread Jewish acceptance of the Babylonian Talmud as *the* classical work of rabbinic literature and the foundation of Jewish legal thinking moving forward. Medieval and early modern Jewish law codes often rooted their rulings in the text of the Talmud, and even when the Talmud does not discuss the specific issue that a particular rabbinic thinker is trying to address, jurists often found helpful analogies in the Talmud, which offered a framework through which to approach a topic.

In medieval Europe, the Talmud became the subject of disputations staged between rabbis and Christian theologians. In one of the first such disputations, in Paris in 1240, the Talmud was "found guilty" of blaspheming Christian doctrine, and more than twenty cartloads of Jewish manuscripts were burned. This event was only one of many in which the Talmud served as the subject of debate between Jews and Christians over Jesus as Messiah and the Jews' stubbornness in rejecting what medieval Christians saw as the obvious foreshadowing of Jesus in the Hebrew Bible.

Despite this difficult history, or in part because of it, the Talmud remains the foundational rabbinic text for Jewish law and practice today. Though traditionally available only to educated Jewish men, the twentieth century saw the Talmud become more available to women and a wider swath of the Jewish world. Initiated by the Hasidic rabbi Meir Shapiro in the early 1920s, the practice of Daf Yomi (reading a folio per day until one completes the entire Talmud in an entire seven-and-a-half-year cycle) has made the Talmud popular with a larger segment of the Jewish world, spurring the rise of accessible translations, Talmud newsletters, and podcasts.

## About the author

**Sara Ronis** is an associate professor of theology at St. Mary's University, Texas. She holds a PhD in ancient Judaism specializing in the Talmud from Yale University and a BA in Near Eastern and Judaic studies from Brandeis University. Her research interests include rabbinic subjectivity and definitions of personhood, constructions of gender and authority in rabbinic literature, and rabbinic imaginings of and encounters with the other in late antiquity. She is the author of *Demons in the Details: Demonic Discourse and Rabbinic Culture in Late Antique Babylonia* (University of California Press, 2022).

## Suggestions for further reading

*In this book*
See also chapters 4 (What is midrash?) and 7 (What is a rabbi?).

*Elsewhere*
Hayes, Christine Elizabeth. *The Emergence of Judaism: Classical Traditions in Contemporary Practice*. Minneapolis: Fortress Press, 2010.

Kraemer, David Charles. *A History of the Talmud*. New York: Cambridge University Press, 2019.

Stemberger, Günter. *Introduction to the Talmud and Midrash* (2nd edition). Translated by Markus Bockmuehl. Edinburgh: T&T Clark, 1996.

Wimpfheimer, Barry S. *The Talmud: A Biography*. Princeton, NJ: Princeton University Press, 2018.

# 4
# What is midrash?

## Sarah Imhoff

Midrash is creative textual interpretation that draws on biblical texts. The word can refer to two things: At its broadest, it denotes the genre of inquiries, speculations, imaginative exegesis, allegorical readings, line-by-line commentaries, and even new stories related to the Bible; its more specific meaning denotes the set of texts of this genre that gather and record rabbinic interpretations of the Bible from about 200 to 1000 CE.

The specific set of midrashic collections from antiquity largely began as oral traditions passed down through elite groups of Jewishly learned men, often called "the rabbis." These collections largely do not have a single identified author or compiler, though they do often name the rabbi who taught each interpretation as they introduce it. Some of these early collections, such as the *Mekhilta de Rabbi Ishmael* (interpretations related to the book of Exodus, associated with the school of Rabbi Ishmael) and the *Sifra* (interpretations related to the book of Leviticus), collect rabbinic interpretations that include extended discussions of halakhah, or Jewish law. For that reason, they are often classified as midrash halakhah. Nevertheless, these collections too contain innovative interpretations and extrabiblical stories of biblical characters. Most of the textual collections categorized as midrash halakhah bring together traditions from the earlier centuries (first to early third century CE).

The majority of midrashic collections, however, are often categorized as midrash aggadah—or narrative midrash—because they do not contain lengthy legal interpretation. These stretch to the eleventh century. Some of these, such as *Bereshit Rabba* (interpretations related to the book of Genesis), are ordered according to the biblical text itself. *Bereshit Rabba*, then, begins with a series of rabbinic stories that riff on, interpret, or ask questions about the first line of Genesis, usually translated as "In the beginning, God created . . ." One asks when the angels were created. Another one explains that God looked into the Torah and used it as a blueprint to create the world, just as an architect uses plans to build a house. Yet another says that there were actually six items that preceded God's creation here at the beginning of Genesis, and then it tells the story of each.

Others, like *Vayikra Rabba*, collect sermons about the biblical text (in this case, the book of Leviticus). These sermons hinge on a quotation of a line from Leviticus, but throughout, they draw individual verses from all across the Bible. Sometimes these verses are even juxtaposed to imagine that one verse from, for example, the Psalms actually explains the answer to a question raised by a verse from Leviticus. This juxtaposition is called intertextuality, and it is a style of interpretation that appears throughout many rabbinic texts.

Sometimes scholars also divide midrashic collections into exegetical ones (those whose primary genre seems to be interpretation of biblical texts, such as *Bereshit Rabba*) and homiletical ones (those whose primary genre seems to be sermons, such as *Vayikra Rabba*.) Of course, sermons are also interpretations, and both genres use textual citation, interpretation, and intertextuality.

Midrashic collections are not exclusive; that is, we can find the same sermon, story, or interpretation in more than one collection. We can even find some of these in one of the Talmuds. *Vayikra Rabba*, for example, includes teachings or interpretations that also appear in *Bereshit Rabba*, the Jerusalem Talmud, and the Babylonian Talmud.

The tradition of creativity in textual interpretation continued even after these classical rabbinic collections. In the sixteenth century, for example, Jacob ibn Habib and his son Levi ibn Habib collected the narrative portions of the Talmud and put them together with new commentaries into a new compilation called *Ein Yaakov*. Another medieval example, *Midrash Tehillim*, was written in two pieces: Midrashim on Psalms 1–118 appear in the first, older section, and midrashim on Psalms 119–150 were added later in the medieval period (although scholars do not agree about exactly where or when the addition took place.)

Today, Jews continue to write midrash to offer creative interpretations of scripture. For example, women have offered feminist midrashim, such as those retelling the story of Lilith, originally portrayed as Adam's first female partner, who demanded equality and then was punished by becoming a demon. In Judith Plaskow's rendering, after her punishment, Lilith waits just outside the Garden of Eden for the time when she and Eve can build something together.

## About the author

**Sarah Imhoff** is the Jay and Jeanie Schottenstein Chair in Jewish Studies in the Borns Jewish Studies Program and a professor in the Religious Studies Department at Indiana University, Bloomington. She is the author of *Masculinity and the Making of American Judaism* (Indiana University Press, 2017) and *The Lives of Jessie Sampter: Queer, Disabled, Zionist* (Duke University Press, 2022).

## Suggestions for further reading

### In this book
See also chapters 3 (What is the Talmud?) and 62 (What's the connection between Jews and feminism?).

### Elsewhere
Bakhos, Carol. "Recent Trends in the Study of Midrash and Rabbinic Narrative." *Currents in Biblical Research* 7(2) (2009): 272–293.

Neusner, Jacob, and Alan J. Avery-Peck. *Encyclopaedia of Midrash: Biblical Interpretation in Formative Judaism* (2 volumes). Boston: Brill, 2005.

Plaskow, Judith. "Midrash Three: Genesis 1–3." In *Taking the Fruit: Modern Women's Tales of the Bible* (2nd edition), edited by Jane Sprague Zones, 23–25. San Diego, CA: Woman's Institute for Continuing Jewish Education, 1989.

Porton, Gary. *Understanding Rabbinic Midrash: Text and Commentary*. Hoboken, NJ: Ktav, 1985.

# 5
# What is Kabbalah?

## Brian Hillman

Kabbalah is often described as Jewish mysticism. This is fitting insofar as Kabbalah purports to deal with matters that transcend normal human consciousness and the terrestrial world.

Kabbalists distinguish between the transcendent, unknowable aspect of God (which they call *eyn sof*, "without end") and the components of divinity that are revealed to humans, generally understood as divine attributes. Called *sefirot*, these attributes constitute the inner workings of God in the cosmos. They are organized in a descending arboreal structure, with the highest *sefirah*, *Keter* (the crown), at the head and the lowest, *Shekhinah*, connected to the physical world. Shekhinah is understood as feminine and described as giving birth to the world of humans. God thus has both male and female aspects. The divine energy flows from the highest sefirot to the lowest. The Jewish people, with their covenantal relationship with God, are responsible for regulating the flow of divine energy. When Jews sin, they disrupt the flow of divine energy in the sefirot, which can have significant consequences for life on earth.

Traditionally, Kabbalistic ideas and texts have been closely guarded by a small cadre of intellectual and pious elites, partly out of fear that Kabbalistic teachings, if misunderstood, could spell personal or cosmic disaster. Scholars locate the origins of Kabbalah in twelfth-century Provence (present-day France). The most influential Kabbalistic text, the Zohar, appeared in Castille (present-day Spain) at the end of the thirteenth century. The body of the Zohar is structured as a commentary on the Torah. Like the rabbinic commentary on the Mishnah, called the Talmud, the Zohar is written in a colloquial Aramaic. The Zohar narrates the peregrinations of the third-century sage Rabbi Shimon bar Yohai and his students. They roam the land of Israel while discussing the esoteric secrets of the Jewish tradition. Rabbi Shimon occasionally reveals profound Kabbalistic ideas that even his disciples can hardly contemplate. For example, he reveals the nature of the soul and the notion that the Torah, as written, is but a garment of the primordial Torah that exists in nonphysical form. Although many traditionalist Jews accept the attribution of the Zohar to Rabbi Shimon, most scholars attribute the bulk of the texts that form the Zohar to Rabbi Moses de León (ca. 1240–1305).

Around the time of the Zohar's first printings in the mid-sixteenth century, a revolutionary Kabbalistic movement was underway in Safed in present-day Israel. In Safed, Rabbi Isaac Luria (1534–1572) developed influential ideas such as the *Zimzum*—the idea that God self-contracted prior to creation to make room for the physical world and *parzufim*, or clusters of sefirot, that constitute the cosmos. Regarding Zimzum, the newly created physical "vessels" could not contain the pure light of divinity and shattered, casting "sparks" of holiness into the physical world. Lurianic Kabbalah emphasized the role of Jews in restoring the broken divine realm through lifting the sparks to their origin through holy acts.

Kabbalah continued to spread throughout the Jewish world, including North Africa, Italy, and Eastern Europe. It was used to justify and then explain the popular messianic claimant Sabbatai Zevi (ca. 1626–1676), a Jew from Smyrna who gained a considerable following before converting to Islam while imprisoned by the Turkish sultan. Both before and after his apostasy, Sabbatai Zevi engaged in antinomian behavior, reportedly pronouncing the true name of God and marrying a Torah scroll. Some Jews still considered him to be the messiah for centuries following his death.

Despite concerns that the dissemination of Kabbalah would lead to another messianic heresy, Kabbalah continued to develop in Italy and North Africa, and a mass movement grounded in Kabbalistic teaching began in eighteenth-century Eastern Europe. Rabbi Israel ben Eliezer, known as the Ba'al Shem Tov (1698–1760), initiated this movement, which came to be called Hasidism. He taught proximity to a charismatic leader (*Zaddik*) as a pathway to communion with God and encouraged the joyful performance of one's duties in life as a religiously significant activity. Some forms of Hasidism consider all things to be a part of God, a view often described as pantheist or panentheist. After the Holocaust, the largest Hasidic groups can be found in America and Israel. One Hasidic group, the Chabad movement, engages in outreach among Jews worldwide to build Jewish community and perform the commandments, an activity that, understood kabbalistically, affects the sefirot.

Kabbalah has wended its way into popular culture and consciousness through Chabad; through the "Kabbalah Centre," an organization that blends New Age religious ideas with Kabbalah and has prominent celebrity adherents such as the musician Madonna; and through the Jewish

Renewal movement, which offers a non-Orthodox progressive Judaism based on Kabbalistic ideas.

## About the author

**Brian Hillman** (he/him) is an assistant professor in the Department of Philosophy and Religious Studies at Towson University in Towson, Maryland. His research focuses on modern Jewish thought, Jewish mysticism (Kabbalah), and religion and popular culture. His writing has appeared or is forthcoming in the *Journal of Jewish Identities*, *Jewish Studies Quarterly*, *Religious Studies Review*, and the *Jewish Book Council*. He also serves as the managing editor for the *Journal of Jewish Thought and Philosophy*.

## Suggestions for further reading

*In this book*
See also chapters 16 (What does it mean to be Hasidic?), 20 (What are the differences among Reform, Conservative, Reconstructionist, and Orthodox Judaism?), 30 (What do Jews believe about the messiah?), and 50 (What is the Holocaust?).

*Elsewhere*
Elior, Rachel. *The Mystical Origins of Hasidism*. Oxford: Littman Library of Jewish Civilization, 2006.

Giller, Pinchas. *Kabbalah: A Guide for the Perplexed*. London: Continuum, 2011.

Idel, Moshe. *Kabbalah: New Perspectives*. New Haven, CT: Yale University Press, 1988.

Scholem, Gershom. *Major Trends in Jewish Mysticism*. New York: Schocken, 1995 [1941].

Wolfson, Elliot R. *Through a Speculum That Shines: Vision and Imagination in Medieval Jewish Mysticism*. Princeton, NJ: Princeton University Press, 1994.

# Laws and Rituals

# 6
# What is Jewish law?

## Yonatan Y. Brafman

Jewish law is often identified with a specific set of rules and practices or the texts that discuss them, but it is better to take a cue from the Hebrew term *halakhah*, which is popularly associated with the grammatical root for "to go" or "to walk." Halakhah is concerned with divine commands that guide the Jewish way in the world. More directly, it is the human effort to implement commandments ascribed to God.

The commandments span the entirety of human life, ranging from religious ritual to interpersonal ethics; state law, including civil and criminal statutes; and political institutions. And thus, so does halakhah, since it is the human determination, interpretation, and application of these divine commandments.

Halakhah is expressed and developed through texts and oral traditions, including the Hebrew Bible and early rabbinic writings, such as the Midrash, Mishnah, and Gemara. Later rabbinic literature mainly consists of three genres that have a cyclical relation with each other: commentary, codes, and *responsa*. Commentary involves the analysis of an earlier text. The Gemara, for example, is arguably a (very) digressive commentary on the Mishnah. Taken together, they are referred to as the Talmud. In turn, the Talmud has inspired a plethora of commentaries.

The growth of commentary around a halakhic text attests to its authoritative status, yet it is unhelpful for practical guidance. Consequently, rabbis have written codes that cut through the thicket of interpretation and concisely state halakhic rules. Central examples are Moses Maimonides's *Mishneh Torah*, Jacob ben Asher's *Arba'ah Turim*, and Yosef Karo's *Shulḥan Arukh*. Yet these codes are never final for two reasons. First, due to their generality, they cannot be applied directly to specific circumstances. Rabbis thus compose *responsa* that offer guidance to individuals in their particular situations. Second, when a code attains authoritative status, it becomes subject to commentary, which often draws on the decisions of *responsa*. With the accumulation of commentary, it becomes necessary to promulgate a new code. And the cycle repeats.

For example, how are Jews obligated to give charity? Deuteronomy 15:7–8 says, "If, however, there is a needy person among you, one of your kin in any of your settlements in that land that your God is giving you, do not harden your heart and shut your hand against your needy kin. Rather, you must open your hand and lend whatever is sufficient to meet the need." The Talmudic rabbis understood this to entail the obligation to give charity to the poor. Later rabbinic literature such as the *Shulḥan Arukh* then specifies who is owed charity, the order of priority among poor persons, and the amount that they are owed. *Responsa* might then discuss questions like whether the required percentage of charity refers to pretax or posttax income.

Halakhah historically developed while Jewish communities possessed varying degrees of autonomy and thus differing opportunities to live by Jewish law. This had several effects. First, halakhah is highly decentralized. Codes are not promulgated by an authorized institution but become authoritative by being the object of commentaries and being cited in *responsa*. Likewise, recognition as a halakhic decisor is conferred not by holding an office but by being acknowledged as an expert by rabbinic peers. Second, historically, local rabbinical courts could enforce compliance with their decisions through both physical coercion and social sanctions, yet they were also subject to non-Jewish political authorities. This led to the development of the principle of "the law of the kingdom is the law." This principle conferred halakhic legitimacy on non-Jewish rulers and non-Jewish laws, sometimes even when they conflicted with halakhic rules.

The emergence of the nation-state in modernity fundamentally changed the status of Jewish law. The modern state claims sovereignty, which involves the supremacy of its law over other norms and a direct relation with individuals within its territory. Semiautonomous Jewish communities were dissolved, and Jews were, haltingly, granted citizenship.

In most countries, Jewish law could continue to function in the lives of Jews, but with two significant changes: It was now classed as exclusively "religious," and obedience to it was wholly voluntary. Halakhah was now about the relationship between the individual and God as well as interpersonal ethics, whereas civil and criminal law and especially political institutions were the domain of the state. Contemporary Jewish denominations can be described in relation to this settlement. Reform Judaism acknowledges that Jewish law is no longer obligatory, even as it recommends various religious rituals that derive from it. Conservative and Orthodox Judaism both recognize the continuing normativity of Jewish law, though they differ over how it should be interpreted and applied.

The State of Israel presented an even more complicated situation for Jewish law. Classical halakhah did not countenance a Jewish state where law was secular or established by a parliament (Knesset). While some Orthodox thinkers and activists tried to establish a constitution according to Jewish law, they did not succeed. Others wanted to develop a secularized "Hebrew Law" out of the sources of halakhah by distinguishing among its religious, ethical, civil, criminal, and political elements; however, this movement has had only a limited impact on Israeli legislation and jurisprudence. Israeli law has been more influenced by Ottoman and British precedents that granted religious courts jurisdiction over issues of "personal status." In this truncated domain, which includes religious identity, marriage, and divorce, halakhah remains enforced for Jewish Israelis. This is not, however, a continuation of the historic role of halakhah in Jewish communities: It derives its authority not from divine commandments but from the laws of the Knesset, and it became centralized in a manner unprecedented in Jewish history.

## About the author

**Yonatan Y. Brafman** is an associate professor of modern Judaism in the Department of Religion, with a secondary appointment in the Department of Literary and Cultural Studies, as well as a member of the Program in Judaic Studies at Tufts University. He is also an affiliated scholar at the Brodie Center for Jewish and Israeli Law at Yale Law School.

## Suggestions for further reading

*In this book*
See also chapters 1 (Why are texts sacred to Jews?), 2 (What is the Torah?), 3 (What is the Talmud?), 4 (What is midrash?), 20 (What are the differences among Reform, Conservative, Reconstructionist, and Orthodox Judaism?), and 58 (What is the role of Judaism in the State of Israel?).

*Elsewhere*
Adler, Rachel. *Engendering Judaism: An Inclusive Theology and Ethics.* Boston: Beacon Press, 1999.

Batnitzky, Leora, and Yonatan Y. Brafman, eds. *Jewish Legal Theories: Writings on State, Religion, and Morality.* Waltham, MA: Brandeis University Press, 2017.

Kaye, Alexander. *The Invention of Jewish Theocracy: The Struggle for Legal Authority in Modern Israel.* New York: Oxford University Press, 2020.

Saiman, Chaim N. *Halakhah: The Rabbinic Idea of Law.* Princeton, NJ: Princeton University Press, 2020.

# 7
# What is a rabbi?

## Sarah Imhoff

The word "rabbi" comes from the Hebrew word *rav*—literally, master or great one—which designates a revered teacher. In many Semitic languages, *rav* functions as a title or as part of a title for an officer, chief, or leader in both religious and nonreligious offices. Although from antiquity to the present, a rabbi has been a communal authority on Judaism, the role of rabbi within Jewish communities has changed over time.

The role of rabbi as an ordained religious leader first crystallized in the first century CE among Hebrew- and Aramaic-speaking Jewish communities. During that time, the title referred to religious scholars who read and interpreted the Bible and Jewish legal texts and traditions. The phrase "the rabbis" or "the sages" often appears in the Mishnah, Talmuds, and other texts from those periods; that phrase refers to the particular group of men who taught and handed down interpretations of these texts orally, which were subsequently collected and written down. It is from this group of scholars across those centuries that we get the collective term "rabbinic literature," which refers to the Mishnah, Talmuds, and midrash.

In late antiquity, however, the men called rabbis were not closely associated with synagogues. Different—even competing—male authorities preached and facilitated gathering, ritual, and prayer at synagogues, which were simultaneously becoming central Jewish institutions. The rabbis, in contrast, taught in small scholarly circles, study houses, and academies. Although we do not know the precise details of the process, conferral of the title rabbi depended on an adult male completing extensive study with these rabbis if they deemed him an authority on Jewish law and texts, especially the Talmud.

In the medieval period, rabbis continued to function as scholars and interpreters as well as increasingly as judges and deciders of Jewish law for the larger community. Some of these medieval rabbis, such as Rashi (ca. 1040–1105), wrote commentaries; Rashi's commentaries on the Torah and the Talmud are still read by Jews today. Others, such as Maimonides (1138–1204), wrote philosophical works and Jewish legal compendia, which Jews today also read. Although medieval rabbis often functioned as judges within the Jewish community, the role of rabbi was not a paid profession as such.

In the modern period, rabbis have become much more closely associated with synagogues, congregations, and pastoral care, though this still varies across time period, geography, and the religious orientation of the Jewish community. In the eighteenth and nineteenth centuries, many European rabbis taught in *yeshivas*, where they focused on teaching reading and interpretation of the Talmud to Jewish boys and young men. Rabbis across the Jewish world continued to serve as interpreters of religious texts and judges of *halakhah*, or Jewish law, for their communities, often writing *responsa*—or halakhic opinions in response to a question—and adjudicating disputes within members of the Jewish community.

Today, many rabbis function within Jewish congregations. They are often hired by synagogues, where the congregation expects them to organize religious services, conduct weddings and funerals, provide comfort and counseling, perform public outreach, run educational programming, manage budgets, and carry out other synagogue-centric tasks. In Conservative and especially Orthodox communities, the rabbis offer halakhic advice, and in all Jewish communities, they function as religious authorities on Jewish texts and their interpretations. Some rabbis work outside of congregational settings, such as those who work as chaplains, in schools, at foundations, or in communal organizations. Many Orthodox communities still have yeshivas, now including some separate institutions for women.

There are two main paths to becoming ordained a rabbi today. The most common path is through an institution, such as the Hebrew Union College (Reform) or Jewish Theological Seminary (Conservative) in the United States. Each institution has a program of study and official benchmarks and standards a student must meet before receiving ordination. These programs typically take five to six years and include the study of Hebrew, Jewish texts, liturgy, Jewish philosophy, and other topics. The less common route to ordination is a path sometimes referred to as "private ordination," in which a person studies texts and tradition in a sort of master-disciple relationship with an ordained rabbi, who then confers the title. This path is more common among Hasidic communities, and it is largely considered outside the bounds of acceptability for Reform and Conservative institutions.

Different branches of Judaism now have different rules for who may be ordained. The Reform, Conservative, and Reconstructionist movements all allowed women to be ordained in the 1970s and 1980s. The 1980s marked the opening of Reform and Reconstructionist rabbinical programs to gay and lesbian rabbis, and Reform, Conservative, and Reconstructionist movements now all accept lesbian, gay, bisexual, trans, and nonbinary rabbis. Within Orthodoxy, the ordination of women is still contentious, with some institutions educating women in rabbinic tracks and allowing them to use official titles (such as *rabba* or *maharat*) and others denying that halakhah allows women to be ordained. Similarly, different Orthodox communities have different interpretations of whether and how gay and lesbian rabbis should be recognized.

## About the author

**Sarah Imhoff** is the Jay and Jeanie Schottenstein Chair in Jewish Studies in the Borns Jewish Studies Program and a professor in the Religious Studies Department at Indiana University, Bloomington. She is the author of *Masculinity and the Making of American Judaism* (Indiana University Press, 2017) and *The Lives of Jessie Sampter: Queer, Disabled, Zionist* (Duke University Press, 2022).

## Suggestions for further reading

*In this book*
See also chapters 3 (What is the Talmud?), 4 (What is midrash?), 6 (What is Jewish law?), 16 (What does it mean to be Hasidic?), and 20 (What are the differences among Reform, Conservative, Reconstructionist, and Orthodox Judaism?).

*Elsewhere*
Freud-Kandel, Miri. "Women in the Synagogue." In *Tois Pasin ho Kairos: Judaism and Orthodox Christianity Facing the Future*, edited by Nicholas de Lange, Elena Narinskaya, and Sybil Sheridan, 53–64. Lanham, MD: Lexington Books / Fortress Academic, 2023.

Nadell, Pamela Susan. *Women Who Would be Rabbis: A History of Women's Ordination, 1889–1985*. Boston: Beacon Press, 1999.

Wasserman, Mira Beth. "Rabbis and Their Others." In *A Companion to Late Ancient Jews and Judaism: Third Century BCE to Seventh Century CE*, edited by Naomi Koltun-Fromm and Gwynn Kessler, 259–275. Hoboken, NJ: John Wiley and Sons, 2020.

Shanks, Hershel. "Origins of the Title 'Rabbi.'" *The Jewish Quarterly Review* 59(2) (1968): 152–157.

# 8
# What is Hanukkah?

## Jodi Eichler-Levine

Hanukkah is a festival of memory, violence, and abundance; it is an American dream about an ancient uprising. This eight-day winter celebration is a Jewish holiday with ancient origins that has become vital in the modern world. Why?

In 164 BCE, a group of Judeans rededicated the Jerusalem Temple after sacrifices to Zeus had been performed there under the aegis of the Greek ruler Antiochus IV Epiphanes. In one telling, this was a belated celebration of the fall harvest festival Sukkot, delayed due to military strife. Headed by brothers Judah and Jonathan, the Hasmonean family took on military and then religious leadership in this decade, beginning a period of limited Judean self-rule at a time when this territory was usually dominated by a major empire. But contrary to popular belief, the Hasmoneans were ultimately quite engaged with Greek culture.

This minimalist historical reconstruction is different from "The Hanukkah Story" as it appears in children's books and cartoons today. *That* story goes more like this: Ancient Jews were religiously persecuted by their Greek overlords. A band of rebel brothers, headed by Judah Maccabee (Judah "the Hammer") led an uprising against them. After victory, the Jews rededicated their holy temple with a small cruse of oil that miraculously lasted for eight nights. They celebrated God's miraculous deliverance from the hands of their enemies.

The power of this legend has a long imaginative reach, though it comes from sources appearing decades or even centuries later, including texts like 1 and 2 Maccabees (ca. 134–63 BCE), the writings of Josephus (ca. 75–94 CE), and the Talmudic tractate *Berakhot* (ca. 500–600 CE).

Hanukkah rituals vary globally. Most commonly, Jews light candles on each evening of the holiday, adding one light each night until there are eight lights (plus one extra). Unlike on major Jewish holidays, work is permitted during Hanukkah.

During Hanukkah celebrations, food abounds. One medieval custom encouraged eating dairy in honor of Judith, a heroine who defeated the enemy general Holofernes by making him thirsty from salty milk or cheese. He drank too much wine, and she beheaded him. (Appetizing!) Some European Jews ate goose for Hanukkah, imitating their neighbors' Christmas feasts. Foods fried in oil are also featured. Potato latkes (pancakes), now popular in North America, were a late addition, coming only after the colonization of the Americas. The earliest fried pancakes were probably made of cheese—an Italian Jewish tradition. One finds fried chicken with couscous in Morocco, pakoras (fried vegetable fritters) in India, and *sufganiyot* (jelly-filled doughnuts) in contemporary Israel.

Hanukkah has long been a commercial holiday. Early modern Amsterdam, for example, had mass-produced *hanukkiot* (Hanukkah lamps; familiarly called menorahs). Chocolate *gelt* (money) and the gambling game of dreidel (a spinning top) also emerged in this era. Hanukkah became a blockbuster in the modern Western Hemisphere, in part because of its adaptability for children. In the United States, this celebration of the Jewish past became "a means to try to ensure the Jewish future by impressing youngsters of its importance," writes historian Dianne Ashton.

US Jews have used Hanukkah to make themselves legible as both Jews and Americans. In a 1912 speech, US Supreme Court Justice Louis Brandeis said that the "struggle of the Maccabees" was "part of the eternal world-wide struggle for democracy." During the Cold War, this sort of interpretation took on an extra layer as the religious faith and liberty of the Maccabees was contrasted with the religious repression and (perceived) atheism of the Soviet Union. It was also evident in immigrant Hanukkah pageants. Artist Mae Rockland Tupa recalled a production where each child dressed as the Statue of Liberty; their collective torches formed a Hanukkah lamp as they recited lines from Emma Lazarus's "The New Colossus."

At the turn of the twenty-first century, Hanukkah reached new cultural turns in *The Hebrew Hammer* (2003), a satirical film based on the blaxploitation genre of the 1970s, and in an episode of *The O.C.* about "Chrismukkah," a hybrid of Hanukkah and Christmas. Chrismukkah has become increasingly common as blended, multireligious families celebrate their hybrid traditions.

The satire and playfulness of these examples demonstrate precisely why Hanukkah practice endures. It might seem ironic that a story didactically used to decry assimilation is the site of recent Christmas-inspired trends like ugly Hanukkah sweaters and matching dreidel pajamas. Some Jewish gatekeepers bemoan these developments. But since Jewish culture has in fact been a hybrid affair since the time of the Maccabees, what could be more fitting?

## About the author

**Jodi Eichler-Levine** is the Berman Professor of Jewish Civilization and a professor in the Department of Religion, Culture, and Society at Lehigh University, where she works at the intersection of Jewish studies and North American religions. She is the author of *Painted Pomegranates and Needlepoint Rabbis: How Jews Craft Resilience and Create Community* (UNC Press, 2020) and *Suffer the Little Children: Uses of the Past in Jewish and African American Children's Literature* (New York University Press, 2013).

## Suggestions for further reading

*In this book*
See also chapter 9 (What happens during Passover?).

*Elsewhere*
Ashton, Dianne. *Hanukkah in America: A History*. New York: New York University Press, 2013.

Eichler-Levine, Jodi. "The Curious Conflation of Hanukkah and the Holocaust in Jewish Children's Literature." *Shofar* 28(2) (Winter 2010): 92–115.

Mehta, Samira K. *Beyond Chrismukkah: The Christian-Jewish Interfaith Family in the United States*. Chapel Hill: University of North Carolina Press, 2018.

Schwartz, Seth. *Imperialism in Jewish Society, 200 B.C.E. to 640 C.E.* Princeton, NJ: Princeton University Press, 2001.

Solis-Cohen, Emily. *Hanukkah: The Feast of Lights*. Philadelphia, PA: Jewish Publication Society of America, 1937.

# 9
# What happens during Passover?

Laura Yares

What do Harry Potter, Seinfeld, William Shakespeare, and Lego have in common? You can buy a Passover Haggadah (pl. Haggadot) themed around each one. There are thousands of different editions of the Passover Haggadah—the ritual text used to celebrate the Passover seder. Across generations, Jews have reimagined the Haggadah's story in light of their contemporary questions—and their popular culture interests too.

The commandment to celebrate Passover is outlined in Exodus 12–13. It includes instructions to refrain from eating bread for one week and to make the first and last days of that week into a holiday of feasting and celebration. The Torah defines Passover as a commemorative event, a remembrance of a communal story that once, Jews were slaves in Egypt, but through divine intervention, they became free. The name Passover—or *Pesach* in Hebrew—is commonly interpreted to refer to the "passing over" of Israelite homes by the angel of death, who struck down the firstborn sons of Egyptian families in the story recorded in Exodus to compel Pharaoh to release the enslaved Israelites. The prohibition of eating bread commemorates their subsequent escape from Egypt, undertaken in such haste that there was no time for bread to rise.

The core rituals of Passover in the biblical era included slaughtering a lamb at the Temple in Jerusalem and eating the roasted meat with unleavened bread and bitter herbs. The Passover seder celebrated by most Jews today, however, differs significantly from these biblical precedents. After the Temple was destroyed in 70 CE, a group of Jewish scholars reimagined celebrations of Passover, creating an elaborate set of rituals for the home. Jewish celebrations of Passover have thus changed significantly since the era of the Temple and since the time of Jesus, who is described as celebrating Passover in the New Testament. Jesus did not celebrate Passover in the way that Jews do today, not because he was not Jewish, but because the Passover Haggadah had not yet been written. The earliest texts similar to today's Haggadah appear in prayerbooks written in the ninth and tenth centuries CE.

The word Haggadah comes from the Hebrew verb "to tell." Haggadot are, essentially, elaborate scripts for telling the Passover story, with songs, jokes, debates, trivia, and symbolic foods to make the narrative interactive and evocative. The rabbis who compiled the earliest Haggadah modeled their text on the Greco-Roman symposium, a storytelling feast featuring multiple food courses and many cups of wine. Throughout the centuries, Jewish communities have elaborated the Haggadah's story of freedom from tyranny utilizing images and themes from their own cultures. Early modern European Haggadot, for example, employed scribal text artistry and images of royal courts to depict the battle between tyrannical Pharaoh and the Jews who sought to escape enslavement. These illustrations indicate not only that Jews imagined their religious rituals utilizing the popular aesthetics of their day but also that Jewish scribes who wrote Haggadot likely trained among Christian scribal artists. Wine stains and food smears, meanwhile, show that these elaborately decorated texts were not conserved as precious relics but were used by generations of families.

The weeklong Passover holiday formally begins with the ritual Passover seder. Yet in many Jewish homes, preparation for Passover begins days earlier with thorough cleaning to ensure that no crumbs of *hametz* (leavened bread) remain. Some families change out their dishes and cooking utensils for a set designated as "kosher for Passover," meaning that they are never used to prepare meals containing leaven. Different customs around what foods are considered "kosher for Passover" can be divisive—some Jews may consider refraining from eating bread products as keeping kosher for Passover; others may stringently adhere to strict dietary rules. A wide repertoire of Passover recipes, meanwhile, illustrates the rich cultural diversity of Jewish life and the culinary imprint of the many cultures in which Jews have lived. Matzah ball soup and brisket are treasured Passover dishes for Ashkenazi Jews, while Mizrahi Jews might serve fish stew or grape leaves stuffed with rice.

For many Jews, Passover is a time for families to gather, eat, and celebrate their cultural traditions. The story of emancipation celebrated in the Haggadah also inspires many Jews to reflect on Jewish commitments to social justice and the importance of working toward a more equitable and liberated world. Ideas from the Passover Haggadah are thus frequently invoked when Jews gather to protest, rally, or work toward justice, transcending their original designation as a script for a holiday meal.

## About the author

**Laura Yares** is an assistant professor in the Department of Religious Studies at Michigan State University. She is a scholar of Jewish history, religion, and culture in North America, with particular research interests in education, gender, and material culture. She is the author of *Jewish Sunday Schools: Teaching Religion in Nineteenth-Century America* (North American Religions Series, New York University Press, 2023). Her newest book, a contemporary ethnographic study of learning in the context of Jewish cultural artistic sites, will be published by New York University Press in 2025.

## Suggestions for further reading

*In this book*
See also chapters 7 (What is a rabbi?), 8 (What is Hanukkah?), and 10 (What does kosher mean?).

*Elsewhere*
Bradshaw, Paul F., and Lawrence Hoffman, eds. *Passover and Easter: Origin and History to Modern Times.* Notre Dame, IN: University of Notre Dame Press, 2000.

Epstein, Marc Michael. *The Medieval Haggadah: Art, Narrative, and Religious Imagination.* New Haven, CT: Yale University Press, 2011.

Ochs, Vanessa L. *The Haggadah: A Biography.* Princeton, NJ: Princeton University Press, 2020.

# 10
# What does kosher mean?

## Nora L. Rubel

It is a popular misconception that *kosher* means food that is clean or blessed by a rabbi. The term technically means "fit" or "suitable" and can be used for various categories of objects. The most common use of the term refers to food that is appropriate for Jews to eat. *Kashrut*, therefore, refers to the dietary laws Jews observe in their daily lives. Food that is prohibited is termed *treif*, literally meaning "torn."

The majority of Jews today do *not* keep kosher, but those who do observe kashrut keep it for a variety of reasons. Primarily, kashrut is kept because God commands it in the Torah. Some Jews see it as a way of remaining distinctive as a people, honoring those who came before them, or creating a cultural Jewish space in a non-Jewish world.

Based on biblical principles, Judaism prohibits the consumption of fish without scales and fins (thus banning shellfish and bivalves), birds of prey, and bugs. Mammals who do not have cloven hooves and don't chew their cud—most notably pigs but also camels and rabbits—are also forbidden. These rules are primarily found in Exodus and Leviticus, and they are expanded upon in the Mishnah and Talmud. All fruits, vegetables, nuts, and grains are permissible and considered *pareve*, best defined as "neutral." Fish that is acceptable is also considered pareve.

These rules outlining kashrut are relatively straightforward, but the implementation and practice are far from it. For example, animals deemed kosher require a specific form of ritual slaughter (*shechita*) and must be drained of all blood because the consumption of blood is strictly forbidden. Most kosher animals must be salted and soaked to remove any residual blood.

Some permitted animals have certain parts of the body that cannot be consumed, such as the hindquarters of cows. The Torah also directly prohibits the "boiling of a kid in its mother's milk," a commandment interpreted in the Talmud as forbidding the consumption of milk and meat products at the same time—going so far as to require different dishes, pots and pans, cutting boards, and utensils for meat and dairy. Meat and dairy cannot even be present on the same table. Jewish law also prescribes waiting between eating meat and dairy, although the length of time is a matter of debate. Pareve foods can be eaten with meat or dairy, although some Jews avoid eating fish with meat in the same dish.

Because bugs are prohibited, fruits and vegetables must be washed and inspected thoroughly. Many strict observers avoid vegetables such as broccoli and cauliflower because they are so difficult to fully cleanse of bugs.

Another level of kashrut is *glatt kosher*. Glatt means "smooth" in Yiddish and refers to a mammal's lungs that are smooth, meaning free of any defects that might render the meat treif. In the contemporary period, many use the term "glatt" to refer to a higher standard of kashrut, although this is not quite accurate. *Cholov Yisroel*, Jewish milk, stems from older practices where farmers might mix the milk of nonkosher animals with cow's milk. In order to protect one's kosher integrity, some Jews prefer to buy milk only from Jewish farmers. This, like glatt kosher meat, is a more stringent level of kosher observance.

Wine has its own rules of kashrut. While the process of making kosher wine is much like making all other wine, it must be produced, handled, and watched over by observant Jews. Wine is seen as particularly important because it is regularly used in Jewish ritual.

Keeping kosher during the holiday of Passover requires an added set of rules. During Passover, Jews may not consume any items that include wheat, rye, barley, spelt, or oats (or foods that may have come into contact with these forbidden grains). Instead of leavened bread, Jews eat *matzah*.

Historically, keeping kosher used to be a shared responsibility of the homemaker and the *shochet* (ritual slaughterer). The shochet was responsible for providing kosher meat, and the woman of the house was responsible for maintaining the ritual purity of the kitchen, ensuring the absence of nonkosher ingredients and supervising the separation of milk, meat, and the vessels that they are contained in. In the twentieth century, kashrut also became the responsibility of corporations. In the 1920s, kosher supervision began to occur with processed and prepared foods found in supermarkets. A stamp attesting to the product's kashrut is called a *hechsher*.

The term "kosher" is also used in colloquial language. For example, "something's not kosher here" means that something doesn't seem right. And while this use is slang, it actually is a correct use of the term, which means "suitable."

## About the author

**Nora L. Rubel** is the Jane and Alan Batkin Professor in Jewish Studies and chair of the Department of Religion and Classics at the University of Rochester. She is the author of *Doubting the Devout: The Ultra-Orthodox in the Jewish American Imagination* (Columbia University Press, 2009) and coeditor of *Religion, Food, and Eating in North America* (Columbia University Press, 2014) and *Blessings Beyond the Binary: Transparent and the Queer Jewish Family* (Rutgers University Press, 2024). She is currently completing a monograph entitled *Recipes for the Melting Pot: The Lives of The Settlement Cook Book*.

## Suggestions for further reading

*In this book*
See also chapters 9 (What happens during Passover?) and 11 (Why don't Jews eat pork?).

*Elsewhere*
Fishkoff, Sue. *Kosher Nation: Why More and More of America's Food Answers to a Higher Authority*. New York: Schocken Books, 2010.

Horowitz, Roger. *Kosher USA: How Coke Became Kosher and Other Tales of Modern Food*. New York: Columbia University Press, 2016.

Rosenblum, Jordan D. *Forbidden: A 3,000-Year History of Jews and the Pig*. New York: New York University Press, 2024.

# 11
# Why don't Jews eat pork?

## Jordan D. Rosenblum

Leviticus 11 and Deuteronomy 14 enumerate various animals valid (kosher) or invalid for ingestion. In the category of domesticated quadrupeds, all kosher animals must *both* chew the cud *and* have split hooves. The Hebrew Bible specifically singles out some domesticated quadrupeds that possess one, but not both, of these criteria. Camels are not kosher (no split hooves), and neither are pigs (they do not chew the cud). Pigs are thus not kosher because God says so. But at least in the Hebrew Bible, they are no more nonkosher than any other nonkosher animal, such as the camel.

This begins to change in the Second Temple period. In the Books of the Maccabees, which recount the story of Hanukkah, we learn far more about the pig than about the miracle of oil. We learn about an old man named Eleazer and an unnamed woman and her seven sons. Both Eleazer and the woman are made a sinister offer by Antiochus IV Epiphanes: Submit to his authority and eat the pig, or abstain from pork and suffer a gruesome martyrdom. Both chose the latter. What emerges here are two themes that develop and expand over time: first, that the pig is the most nonkosher of all the biblically nonkosher animals, and second, that to eat pig is to reject Judaism and embrace another religion or authority.

Rabbinic literature developed these notions further. For the rabbis, the pig comes to represent not only the other but one other in particular: the evil empire of Rome. Like Rome, whose law courts make it seem outwardly just, the pig masquerades around with split hooves, seemingly kosher. But inside, they are both corrupt, devoid of justice / have ruminant stomachs. Text after text stigmatizes the pig, connects it to Rome and foreign rule, and refuses to even refer to it by name; instead, it is called "that thing."

In the medieval period, the pig became a powerful symbol of oppression utilized by non-Jews against Jews. In Germany, Jews were forced to take the "Jewish Oath" before testifying in court. Part of this ritual requires that the Jew stand on a sow's skin. Germany is also home to the *Judensau*, a vulgar image in which Jews are depicted suckling from the teats of a sow and, in many versions, drinking its urine and eating its excrement. These images develop out of animal allegories for vices, in which the pig represents greed. The connection is made between greed and Jews, and then pigs and greed, and then it devolves into the vulgar and dehumanizing image of the *Judensau*. Germany was not the only country in medieval Europe to use the pig to mock Jews. A famous example comes from Spain, where Jews were forced by the Inquisition to either flee, be martyred, or convert to Catholicism. Those who did convert were suspected of practicing Judaism in secret and were referred to by the derogatory term "Marrano." And what is the etymology of Marrano? Pig.

In the modern period, we continue to see non-Jews mock Jews by means of the pig. Behind this rhetoric (noticeably used to violent ends by the Nazis, for example) was an attempt to dehumanize Jews by means of their presumed diet. Jews, however, had multiple and complex relationships with the pig. Many Jews refused to eat pig and viewed this rejection of pork as significant for their identity and beliefs. Other Jews embraced eating pig, such as early twentieth-century Jewish communists in Russia who joined collective pig farms to demonstrate their allegiance to the communist cause and their rejection of their religious identity. The latter demonstrates another development that we see over time: Jews who continue to identify, in a variety of complex and complicated ways, as Jews who choose to eat pig to establish a transgressive Jewish identity, but a Jewish identity nonetheless. These conflicting identities play out across the globe and have proven especially tricky in Israel, where secular and religious law often conflict in regard to the pig.

In sum, there are many reasons why some Jews do not eat pork. And there are reasons why some Jews do. Not all Jews do the same thing. The pig has a complicated Jewish history, and some Jews choose to eat—or not eat—the pig for various reasons, all of which inform, and are informed by, their notions of Jewish identity and practice.

## About the author

**Jordan D. Rosenblum** is the Belzer Professor of Classical Judaism at the University of Wisconsin–Madison. He is the author of four books, most recently *Forbidden: A 3,000-Year History of Jews and the Pig* (New York University Press, 2024) and *Rabbinic Drinking: What Beverages Teach Us About Rabbinic Literature* (University of California Press, 2020). He has also coedited four books, including *Feasting and Fasting: The History and Ethics of Jewish Food* (New York University Press, 2015) and *Animals and the Law in Antiquity* (Brown Judaic Studies, 2021).

## Suggestions for further reading

*In this book*
See also chapters 10 (What does kosher mean?) and 42 (Who was Moses Maimonides?).

*Elsewhere*
Barak-Erez, Daphne. *Outlawed Pigs: Law, Religion, and Culture in Israel.* Madison: University of Wisconsin Press, 2007.

Fabre-Vassas, Claudine. *The Singular Beast: Jews, Christians, and the Pig.* Translated by Carol Volk. New York: Columbia University Press, 1997.

Rosenblum, Jordan D. *Forbidden: A 3,000-Year History of Jews and the Pig.* New York: New York University Press, 2024.

# 12
# Do Jews drink alcohol?

Jordan D. Rosenblum

After surviving a worldwide divine flood, Noah disembarked the ark and did something that—according to the Hebrew Bible—had never been done before: He planted a vineyard (Gen. 9:20). Once those grapes ripened, Noah made the world's first wine. Subsequently, Noah was the first person in the world to engage in three related (and, in descending order, less than exemplary) practices: "He drank of the wine and became drunk, and he uncovered himself within his tent" (Gen. 9:21). In the span of two biblical verses, Noah goes from planting the world's first grapes to being the first person ever to get drunk and naked!

This biblical story shows both sides of the story of alcohol: It can lead one to rejoice or regret. These opposing emotions dominate Jewish discourse on wine for the ensuing millennia. For example, the rabbis make wine a central part of rejoicing rituals. From the rituals that mark the beginning and end of the Sabbath (Kiddush and Havdalah, respectively) to the four cups of wine consumed as part of the Passover seder, wine is a key component of Jewish ritual. In fact, wine receives its own special blessing. While one blesses grapes with the generic fruit blessing of "Blessed are You, Lord, our God, King of the universe, Who creates fruit of the tree," before drinking wine one recites the blessing "Blessed are You, Lord, our God, King of the universe, Who creates the fruit of the vine." Compare apples; when whole, one recites the former blessing, and when in juice form, one recites the generic blessing: "Blessed are You, Lord, our God, King of the universe, by Whose word everything came into being." At the same time, the rabbis acknowledge that drinking too much wine can lead one astray. Just as often as they praise wine, they suggest moderation. Even at the one moment where some traditions suggest overindulgence might be meritorious (the Jewish holiday of Purim), there are traditions that suggest that one should be careful not to go too far.

The rabbis of late antiquity also had a fear associated with wine: namely, that idolaters libate wine. To libate wine is to pour some out prior to drinking as part of the worship of an idolatrous deity. This fear led the rabbis to enact a series of prohibitions against consuming wine prepared by non-Jews and regulating non-Jewish interaction with wine prepared by Jews.

In the medieval and modern periods, these various themes played out in important ways. On the one hand, there is a need for Jewish communities to have access to wine for ritual purposes. On the other hand, they wish to regulate both their own consumption and their wine-based interaction with non-Jews. Thus, Jews would often make wine for themselves or their community (a notable example is the famous medieval rabbi Rashi, who is reputed to have been a winemaker). As a common medieval and early modern occupation for Jews was running inns and taverns, they would serve this wine to customers too. The fact that they were controlling the production and serving of wine allowed for rabbinic regulations to be enforced. Further, a piece of both internal and external lore became further entrenched: While Jews could make and serve wine, they did not drink it. The fact that they consumed wine for ritual purposes was ignored (as was the fact that, from Noah until today, we have plenty of evidence that there were always at least some Jews who imbibed too much).

The association between Jews and sobriety was embraced in the 1800s and early 1900s, when, especially in the United States, the Christian temperance movement sought to extol Jews as exemplars of temperance. However, when they discovered that Jews did in fact drink wine for ritual purposes, they quickly switched to antisemitic canards. During Prohibition, the Volstead Act allowed Jews to make and consume a limited amount of wine for ritual purposes. Interestingly, the membership rosters for many synagogues suddenly became quite ecumenical and diverse, as some sought to use this loophole to procure "ritual wine."

To circle back to our generative question: Do Jews drink alcohol? After acknowledging that we cannot make any simple statement that applies to *all* Jews at *all* times, the evidence suggests that for millennia, most Jews drank at least some alcohol—though often for ritual purposes and not to the point of inebriation. Though we also cannot ignore that some Jews, either from time to time or on a daily basis, followed in the footsteps of their ancestor Noah.

## About the author

**Jordan D. Rosenblum** is the Belzer Professor of Classical Judaism at the University of Wisconsin–Madison. He is the author of four books, most recently *Forbidden: A 3,000-Year History of Jews and the Pig* (New York University Press, 2024) and *Rabbinic Drinking: What Beverages Teach Us*

*About Rabbinic Literature* (University of California Press, 2020). He has also coedited four books, including *Feasting and Fasting: The History and Ethics of Jewish Food* (New York University Press, 2015) and *Animals and the Law in Antiquity* (Brown Judaic Studies, 2021).

## Suggestions for further reading

*In this book*
See also chapters 6 (What is Jewish law?) and 10 (What does kosher mean?).

*Elsewhere*
Davis, Marni. *Jews and Booze: Becoming American in the Age of Prohibition*. New York: New York University Press, 2012.

Dynner, Glenn. *Yankel's Tavern: Jews, Liquor, and Life in the Kingdom of Poland*. New York: Oxford University Press, 2013.

Rosenblum, Jordan D. *Rabbinic Drinking: What Beverages Teach Us About Rabbinic Literature*. Oakland: University of California Press, 2020.

# 13
# Why do Jews circumcise boy children?

## Alison L. Joseph

The Jewish ritual to circumcise baby boys begins with the commandment to the patriarch Abraham in Genesis 17. God tells Abraham to circumcise himself, his offspring, and all of his household as a sign of the covenant. While Abraham was ninety-nine years old at the time, the command is that "throughout the generations, every male among you shall be circumcised at the age of eight days. As for the homeborn slave and the one bought from an outsider who is not of your offspring, they must be circumcised, homeborn and purchased alike. Thus shall My covenant be marked in your flesh as an everlasting pact" (Gen. 17:12–13). For this reason, the Jewish ritual is called, in Hebrew, *brit milah*, "covenant of circumcision" (or, colloquially, according to the Ashkenazic pronunciation, *bris*).

As Abraham is often viewed by Jewish tradition as the first monotheist and the first Jew, this is a significant event. Perpetual circumcision is Abraham's condition of the covenant in which God promises to make Abraham "a multitude of nations" and to give him everlasting possession of the land of Canaan (Gen. 17:4, 8). A physical marker of belonging, it is also imbued with theological meaning. It is interesting to note that Genesis 17 is not the first iteration of God's promise to Abraham, but here the addition of the requirement for circumcision makes it conditional (Gen. 12, 15).

While it is well documented that circumcision was practiced by other ancient peoples, in the Hebrew Bible, circumcision is seen as an important identifier of Israelites. To join the Israelites and even to partake in some of their rituals, circumcision was a requirement for belonging, although this is not to be confused with proselytizing. For example, even resident aliens had to undergo circumcision before they could be allowed to partake of the covenant-feast of Passover (Ex. 12:48).

In the Hebrew Bible and subsequent Jewish literature, labeling someone or some group as uncircumcised becomes a stand-in for identifying them negatively as "non-Israelite." This is particularly clear in the case of the Philistines, a perpetual enemy of Israel. The Philistines are widely known for the champion Goliath, who King David first challenges, "Who is that uncircumcised Philistine that he dares defy the ranks of the living God?" (2 Sam. 17:26). The term becomes synonymous with *tame*, meaning "unclean" (e.g., Isa. 52:1).

During the Hellenistic period (fourth to first centuries BCE), circumcision also became a physical obstacle to assimilation, despite how Hellenized Jews behaved. At this time, some Jews attempted epispasm, a surgery undertaken to undo circumcision, to allow them to more fully participate in Greek life, including the sporting events of the gymnasia, which were performed naked. During his reign from 175 to 164 BCE, Antiochus IV Epiphanes passed many edicts that forbid Jewish and other non-Greek practices. These persecutions, which compelled the Maccabees to organize a revolt against Antiochus, included prohibitions against circumcision, Torah study, and observance of Shabbat, among others. These prohibitions were lifted when the Maccabees were victorious over the Seleucids and reestablished Jewish sovereignty in the land of Israel, lasting more than a century.

In contemporary times, circumcision of boys on the eighth day is still practiced by most Jews, although Jewish law provides exceptions for medical circumstances that may require delay until a baby boy is older and/or stronger. Today, some Jews have rejected the practice as medically unnecessary or harmful, but this group is a small minority. Traditionally, the responsibility for circumcising a son belongs to the child's father, but he can appoint a proxy to fulfill this commandment for him. As such, most circumcisions are performed by a *mohel*, someone with ritual training in circumcisions. The ceremony is usually done at home or in the synagogue. Hospital circumcisions, unless required by medical restrictions, are not usually accepted according to Jewish law. General practice for conversion to Judaism still requires circumcision, in addition to a rabbinic court and immersion in a ritual bath. If a man has already been circumcised before his conversion, a ritual of drawing blood from the penis (*hataphat dam*) is performed as part of the conversion process.

Many Jewish communities, including Ashkenazi, Sephardi, and Mizrahi Jewish communities, have also created parallel celebrations of a girl's birth that do not involve circumcisions, such as naming ceremonies or celebrations of the birth of a daughter.

## About the author

**Alison L. Joseph** is the director of Digital Scholarship and associate professor of Bible at Gratz College. She is the author of numerous publications, most notably *Portrait of the Kings: The Davidic Prototype in Deuteronomistic Poetics* (Fortress, 2016) which received the 2016 Manfred Lautenschlaeger Award for Theological Promise. She received her PhD in Hebrew Bible and Jewish studies from the University of California, Berkeley, and her MA in Jewish studies from Emory University. She also holds undergraduate degrees from Barnard College and the Jewish Theological Seminary.

## Suggestions for further reading

*In this book*
See also chapters 2 (What is the Torah?), 3 (What is the Talmud?), 6 (What is Jewish law?), and 15 (Why does gender matter in Jewish law?).

*Elsewhere*
Hirsch, Emil G., et al. "Circumcision." JewishEncylopedia.com, accessed November 19, 2024. https://jewishencyclopedia.com/articles/4391-circumcision.

Marcus, Ivan G. "Birth, 'Bris,' Schooling." In *The Jewish Life Cycle: Rites of Passage from Biblical to Modern Times*, 30–81. Seattle: University of Washington Press, 2004.

Mark, Elizabeth Wyner, ed. *The Covenant of Circumcision: New Perspectives on an Ancient Jewish Rite*. Hanover, NH: Brandeis University Press, University Press of New England, 2003.

# 14
# What is a bar/bat mitzvah?

Rachel Kranson

Bar, bat, and b'mitzvah celebrations mark a Jewish child's entrance into religious maturity, generally at the age of thirteen. Colloquially, these terms can refer to either the child undergoing this transition or the ceremony itself. For instance, it is common for American Jews to say that they are "going to a bat mitzvah"—referencing the event—and also to comment that "the bat mitzvah did a great job"—remarking on the child participating in the ritual.

In most contemporary American Jewish congregations, there is no meaningful difference among bar, bat, and b'mitzvah ceremonies other than the gender identity of the celebrant. Bar mitzvah (son of the commandment) is the term used for a boy, while bat mitzvah (daughter of the commandment) is used for a girl. In recent years, synagogues have employed a number of gender-neutral phrases for nonbinary Jewish children coming of age, including b'mitzvah (in the commandment), bnei mitzvah (children of the commandment), and simchat mitzvah (celebration of the commandment). In most congregations, no matter their gender, these children mark their religious maturity by publicly chanting from the Torah or *Haftorah* (prophetic writings), offering a speech based on the section of the Torah they chanted, and then celebrating with a party. In certain Orthodox congregations, only boys read from the Torah, while bat mitzvah girls contribute a learned speech before the party in their honor.

The bar mitzvah represents the earliest of these coming-of-age ceremonies, as public chanting from the Torah was reserved for boys and men until the twentieth century. The first iterations of bar mitzvah rituals date back to the medieval period, though the experience was not formalized until the sixteenth century in Central Europe. At that point, boys denoted their new position as full-grown members of their religious community only through the synagogue-based rituals of publicly reading from the Torah or Haftorah for the first time and, beginning in the seventeenth century, delivering a speech that demonstrated their religious knowledge.

They would then assume the full array of religious practices, which included wearing ritual garments such as *tefillin* (phylacteries) during times of prayer and joining a *minyan* (prayer quorum) three times a day. Eastern European, Sephardi, and Mizrahi Jews did not host official bar mitzvah ceremonies until the eighteenth and nineteenth centuries.

The bar mitzvah had become a firmly established practice by the early twentieth century. Throwing a party after the synagogue rites became commonplace in the American context. While clergy over the years insisted that the synagogue-based rites ought to be most important, for many American Jews and bar mitzvah celebrants, the postsynagogue revelries emerged as an equally crucial component of the milestone.

Clergy have not always been supportive of these coming-of-age ceremonies. In fact, the leaders of the Reform movement of American Judaism tried to eliminate the bar mitzvah in favor of the rite of Confirmation for older teenagers. By the middle of the twentieth century, however, it had become clear that most American Jews preferred the bar mitzvah and would not give up the practice. The question of how to include girls in the ceremony therefore grew more pressing.

Judith Kaplan celebrated the first American bat mitzvah in 1922. Her father, Rabbi Mordecai Kaplan, founded the Reconstructionist movement, a denomination of American Judaism that values ritual innovation. By mid-century, many US synagogues began to introduce bat mitzvah rituals into their services. There was little uniformity across congregations. Often, girls would celebrate their milestones on Friday nights instead of during the more popular Saturday-morning service reserved for boys. Sometimes, girls would commemorate their milestone as a group instead of as individuals. Many congregations did not allow girls to chant directly from the Torah scroll.

The emergence of the feminist movement and its call for gender equality led to parity between bar and bat mitzvah ceremonies in most US synagogues by the 1970s. In Reform, Conservative, and Reconstructionist synagogues, a commitment to gender egalitarianism ensured not only that girls would have the same opportunities as boys to read from the Torah at age thirteen but also that they would regularly participate in synagogue rituals and leadership for the rest of their lives. Orthodox communities began to mark the bat mitzvah milestone in the late twentieth century—at the age of twelve rather than thirteen and with different rituals from the bar mitzvah. By the end of the twentieth century, this fairly recent American innovation of the bat mitzvah had become nearly ubiquitous among Jewish people around the world.

## About the author

**Rachel Kranson** is an associate professor and director of Jewish Studies at the University of Pittsburgh, Pennsylvania.

## Suggestions for further reading

*In this book*
See also chapters 20 (What are the differences among Reform, Conservative, Reconstructionist, and Orthodox Judaism?) and 62 (What's the connection between Jews and feminism?).

*Elsewhere*
Hyman, Paula E., and Carole B. Balin. "Bat Mitzvah: American Jewish Women." In *Shalvi/Hyman Encyclopedia of Jewish Women*, Jewish Women's Archive, last updated June 23, 2021, accessed November 19, 2024. https://jwa.org/encyclopedia/article/bat-mitzvah-american-jewish-women.

Joselit, Jenna Weissman. "Red-Letter Days." In *The Wonders of America: Reinventing Jewish Culture, 1880–1950*, 89–133. New York: Hill and Wang, 1994.

Marcus, Ivan G. *The Jewish Life Cycle: Rites of Passage from Biblical to Modern Times*. Seattle: University of Washington Press, 2004.

Stein, Regina. "The Road to Bat Mitzvah in America." In *Women and American Judaism: Historical Perspectives*, edited by Pamela S. Nadell and Jonathan D. Sarna, 223–234. Hanover, NH: Brandeis University Press, University Press of New England, 2001.

# 15
# Why does gender matter in Jewish law?

## Ronit Irshai

The field of Jewish studies, and especially scholarship about Jewish law, traditionally ignored gender. It was not just that women and femininity were not independent research topics and that femininity and masculinity were viewed as rigid categories but also that issues related to the body and sexuality were seen as unworthy of attention and foreign to the project of Jewish studies.

Gender studies radically changed this. Its strongest impact was on the hermeneutical tools of halakhic research, where it subverted the conventional notions of gender categories. In many cases, halakhic conversations assumed that different rules applied to men and women; that is, men tend to have more religious obligations, responsibility, and authority. Yet this new scholarship asked about the very formation of the categories of "men" and "women" and the ways modern Jewish law and scholarship established them as essential, stable, and binary, as if these were the only possible readings of premodern halakhic texts and ideas.

Those critical tools include paying attention to gender, dismantling essentialism, and using genealogy to demonstrate the unnecessary directions halakhah has taken, even according to its own methods and values. Dismantling essentialism diversifies our understanding of rabbinic culture and writings, expands the hermeneutical horizons of previous and current halakhah, and especially, critiques the ways modern halakhah understands femininity and masculinity and their (un)equal role in the social order.

"Essentialism" refers to the idea that the world order as created by God entails the existence of two natural and distinct genders and that gender difference necessarily defines their respective horizons, characteristics, domains of action, and so on. This belief in an innate and fixed natural essence collides head-on with the feminist perspective that gender is a product of social construction and thus mutable. Queer theories go even further and assert that gender, as a discursive category, is a mechanism that constructs sex as a natural essence even prior to discourse.

Scholars began to consider the ways and conditions in which gender categories emerged, cast doubt on their permanence, and ask whether women's place in religious life today is a necessary corollary of these interpretations. They started to inquire whether the gender binary, which modern halakhah sees as inevitable and as the categorical position of classic texts (chiefly in Orthodox interpretations), really is so. For instance, does the prohibition of cross-dressing derive from a concept of gender as an essentialist, binary category? Or does it stem from other halakhic concerns? Does the attention to gender as a category not only generate new ideas about femininity and masculinity but also enlighten us about power relations, make us sensitive to the margins of social discourse, and demonstrate how religious discourse is shaped and regimented?

Genealogy, in Michel Foucault's sense of the investigation of the birth and evolution of beliefs and traditions, aims to uncover the contingent character of the present. In the case of halakhic discourse, it means a diachronic and synchronic study of how a halakhic position was consolidated on the way to achieving its current hegemony. A genealogical presentation of the halakhic literature can demythologize today's prevailing notions by demonstrating that halakhic decisions are not the product of an inevitable trajectory. A genealogical inquiry from the Talmud to the rabbis of today looks not only at the notions of gender that are the conceptual foundation of some laws but also at exegetical decision-making when a decisor faced multiple options and chose one of them, with its gender implications.

Feminist research is willing to cast doubt on the inevitability of the "halakhic story" woven by decisors based on classic texts. For example, the genealogical approach may wonder how family planning based on economic considerations became "problematic" or a sign of "weak faith" when early halakhic texts do not hesitate to mention it or how laws of modesty turned into a problem for women and an obsession about their bodies. A critical genealogy of gender may ask about the inevitability of current halakhic ideas and how they impose values that do not always reflect previous halakhic ideas. One of the main goals of gender-critical genealogy is to identify within the developmental process of halakhah itself other modes of thought and exegesis that have been shunted aside, even when they were not minority positions. The chief advantage of the genealogical method is thus its exposure of the historical and social contingency of halakhic rulings and thus their liberation from a spurious necessity.

Texts do not answer questions they were not asked. Gender studies forces the study of halakhah to confront troubling questions about what had previously been taken to be self-evident. It questions essentialism, probes the emergence and development of ideas, and extends the research horizon to domains that were invisible in Jewish studies before gender theories originated. This expands and deepens the diversity of scholarship and consequently the gender-related and social knowledge that is encoded in it. Gender studies became a catalyst for creating new knowledge in Jewish studies and, perhaps more than that, created more gender freedom and gender justice within the boundaries of Jewish law.

## About the author

**Ronit Irshai** is an associate professor in the gender studies program at Bar Ilan University and a research fellow at the Shalom Hartman Institute in Jerusalem.

## Suggestions for further reading

### In this book
See also chapters 6 (What is Jewish law?) and 62 (What's the connection between Jews and feminism?).

### Elsewhere
Fonrobert, Charlotte E. *Menstrual Purity: Rabbinic and Christian Reconstructions of Biblical Gender.* Stanford, CA: Stanford University Press, 2000.

Irshai, Ronit. "Cross-Dressing in Jewish Law (Halakha), and the Construction of Gender Identity." *Nashim* 38 (2021): 46–68.

Irshai, Ronit. "Feminist Research in Jewish Studies: What's in a Name." In *Re-Making the World: Christianity and Categories*, edited by Taylor G. Petrey, 257–276. Tübingen, Germany: Mohr Siebeck, 2019.

Irshai, Ronit. *Fertility and Jewish Law: Feminist Perspectives on Orthodox Responsa Literature.* Waltham, MA: Brandeis University Press, 2012.

Kessler, Gwynn. "Rabbinic Gender: Beyond Male and Female." In *A Companion to Late Ancient Jews and Judaism: Third Century BCE to Seventh Century CE*, edited by Naomi Koltun-Fromm and Gwynn Kessler, 353–370. Hoboken, NJ: Wiley-Blackwell, 2020.

Strassfeld, Max K. *Trans Talmud: Androgynes and Eunuchs in Rabbinic Literature.* Oakland: University of California Press, 2022.

# 16
# What does it mean to be Hasidic?

## Sam Shuman

It seems that every year brings a new TV series, documentary, or film to Netflix about Hasidic Jews: *Unorthodox, Menashe, Rough Diamonds, One of Us*. These series, to varying degrees, play on a series of tropes. They provide the viewer with the promise of exclusive access to an otherwise insular and inaccessible world, one that is often problematically painted as exotic. We can likely glean that Hasidic Jews hold Jewish law (halakhah) as central, distinguish themselves through dress, divide their lives according to strict gender roles, and often speak Yiddish. But these productions rarely if ever provide us with a clear explanation of how Hasidic Jews are different from *other* "ultra-Orthodox" Jews.

To answer this is no easy task. Historians may respond to the question by focusing on the features of Hasidism as a movement. They will likely tell you that, despite all appearances, Hasidism is not *pre*modern. In fact, Hasidism is very much a product of and a response to modernity. It emerged as a pietistic movement in eighteenth-century Eastern Europe, in the southeastern section of the Polish-Lithuanian Commonwealth. The movement's founding figure is Israel ben Eliezer, the Baal Shem Tov ("the master of the good name") or the BeShT, who lived approximately between 1700 and 1760. Like many in his circle, he was involved with practical magic, Kabbalistic amulets, and various shamanic practices.

Older scholarship frequently romanticized the origins of Hasidism as a populist movement that challenged the authority of rabbinic elites. They argued that Hasidism's focus on the spiritual and ecstatic experiences of everyday Jews radically democratized Jewish life. One did not need to be educated as a Talmud scholar to access the divine.

Yet from its inception, the Hasidic movement organized itself around dynasties led by *tzadikim* (saints) or *rebbes*. These figures act as divine intercessors. They advocate on behalf of and connect their followers, their Hasidim, to God. Early Hasidic courts catered exclusively to men. Moreover, nearly all Hasidic dynasties have been officially led by men. The exception to the rule was the Maiden of Ludmir, Hannah Rachel Vermermacher, who lived from 1805 to 1888.

The spread of Hasidism was not welcomed by all Jews. In the eighteenth century, a movement of rabbinic adversaries called *Misnagdim* (literally, opponents) emerged across Lithuania and sections of Belorussia and Poland. Their descendants are known today as *Litvaks*. Fighting occurred not only between Hasidim and Misnagdim but also *between* and *within* Hasidic dynasties.

Challenging common assumptions about the origins and evolution of Hasidic Judaism is useful not only for historians but also for scholars of contemporary Hasidic life. It allows us to see resonances, for example, between the Maiden of Ludmir and Rebbetzin Sarah Hager, whose charisma rivals that of her husband, who is the official leader of the Belz Hasidic dynasty. With this knowledge, we can also track how Hasidic Judaism is constantly changing. Hasidic Judaism is not a window into the past, nor has it remained unchanged for centuries.

We still need more research about various "conversions" to Hasidism that have occurred over the last century. How are these conversions transforming the very fabric of Hasidic communities? And how are they forcing us to reexamine who Hasidic Jews are today? There are now several generations of Hasidim, for example, who descend from communities in the Middle East and North Africa, far from the Eastern European lands where Hasidism emerged. Included among them are Yemeni Jews who, in the early 1990s, were "rescued" by Satmar Hasidim, the world's largest Hasidic dynasty. It has been alleged that Satmar coerced them to adopt Hasidic practices and abandon their customs. Conversely, other groups of Jews elected to become Hasidic. The Hasidic dynasty of Vien, for example, founded in Vienna in 1941 among traditionalist Jews, only became Hasidic after their migration to Williamsburg in Brooklyn after the Holocaust.

The boundaries of Hasidic belonging are currently shifting in other critical ways. Exiting Hasidic life can lead to protracted custody battles where the community rallies around the parent who stays within the community and raises the money for their legal fees. But recent scholarship suggests that most Hasidim who leave do maintain ties with their families. And not all those who exit do so permanently. Men who return to their communities are frequently valorized, and returning is frequently rendered in miraculous terms. Still others lead double lives within their communities ("double-lifers") and forge secretive bonds across social media platforms, which connect them to other Hasidic "double-lifers" from across the Hasidic diaspora—from Antwerp to Montreal, from Williamsburg to Jerusalem.

## About the author

**Sam Shuman** is an assistant professor of religious studies and core faculty member in the Jewish studies program at the University of Virginia. Shuman is an anthropologist whose research situates Hasidic Judaism within a global context. They are currently writing a book about Reb Shayele (1851–1925), a Hasidic miracle-worker from Hungary, who has witnessed a populist revival in the past decade. Their research has been supported by the Social Science Research Council, the National Science Foundation, and Fulbright. Shuman's work has appeared in the *Jewish Quarterly Review*, *Current Anthropology*, and *Religions* and as chapters in *Critical Jewish Studies Now* and *How Transparency Works*.

## Suggestions for further reading

*In this book*
See also chapter 20 (What are the differences among Reform, Conservative, Reconstructionist, and Orthodox Judaism?).

*Elsewhere*
Dynner, Glenn. *Men of Silk: The Hasidic Conquest of Polish Jewish Society*. Oxford: Oxford University Press, 2006.

Everett, Samuel Sami. "From Les Petites Jérusalems to Jerusalem: North African Postcolonial Racialization and Orthodoxy." *AJS Review* 46(1) (2022): 113–130.

Fader, Ayala. *Hidden Heretics: Jewish Doubt in the Digital Age*. Princeton, NJ: Princeton University Press, 2020.

Newfield, Schneur Zalman. *Degrees of Separation: Identity Formation While Leaving Ultra-Orthodox Judaism*. Philadelphia, PA: Temple University Press, 2020.

Rosman, Moshe. "Introduction: Changing the Narrative of the History of Hasidism." In *Hasidic Studies: Essays in History and Gender*, edited by Ada Rapoport-Albert, 1–20. Liverpool, UK: Liverpool University Press, Littman Library of Jewish Civilization, 2018.

Shuman, Sam. "Of Mice and Hasidic Men: Reb Shayele as Populist Patron Saint." *The Jewish Quarterly Review* 115(1) (2025): 99–135.

# 17
# What do Jews do on the Sabbath?

## Adrienne Krone

Jews do many things on the Sabbath, but to start, it will be helpful to shift our focus toward what Jews don't do on the Sabbath. The Hebrew word for Sabbath, Shabbat, means "to cease, to end, or to rest," and that is what Shabbat is about—resting and refraining from work. In his book *The Sabbath*, Abraham Joshua Heschel, an influential twentieth-century rabbi and Jewish philosopher, described Shabbat as a special, holy period of time that "is not an interlude but the climax of living." He emphasized the restorative nature of Shabbat, which he understood as a gift and a window into a more perfect world that doesn't yet exist. Shabbat is a holiday that occurs fifty-two times each year, at the end of each week. It starts at sundown on Friday nights and ends an hour after sundown on Saturday nights. During this twenty-five-hour period, Jews all over the world observe Shabbat in ways that are meaningful and traditional for them. Some refrain from work and attend worship services, others enjoy a festive meal, and for many Jews, Shabbat is just a regular Saturday. In order to understand how Jews got to this diverse array of Sabbath observance, we have to start at the beginning.

This first Sabbath is described in the book of Genesis, at the beginning of the Hebrew Bible, when the text says that God rested after working for six days to create the world and then "blessed the seventh day and declared it holy" (Gen. 2:3). This declaration of the Sabbath as a holy day is repeated many times throughout the Hebrew Bible. One of the most well-known iterations is the fourth of the Ten Commandments: "Remember the sabbath day and keep it holy" (Ex. 20:8). The text goes on to explain what remembering and keeping the Sabbat day holy means: "Six days you shall labor and do all your work, but the seventh day is a sabbath of your God. You shall not do any work" (Ex. 20:9–10). Though a few activities were used as examples of forbidden work in other parts of the Hebrew Bible, it was the rabbis who determined what counted as labor and work, and their conversations were recorded in Tractate Shabbat in the Mishnah and in the Talmud.

The rabbis came up with a list of thirty-nine categories of work that were forbidden on the Sabbath. The categories of forbidden work include activities related to building and maintaining the Tabernacle (a portable tent where God dwelled before the First Temple was built), growing wheat and baking bread, and making cloth and leather. There are a few particular categories that require ongoing attention in modernity, like burning and extinguishing fires, which were understood to apply to car engines and electrical appliances. Jews who avoid these categories today often prepare their homes before Shabbat by turning on lights they will need, preparing food for the holiday, and turning on the oven to keep food warm. Some Jews have also adapted their observance of Shabbat to the modern world. For example, in the mid-twentieth century, the Conservative movement decided to permit driving to synagogue on Shabbat so people who did not live within walking distance of a synagogue could participate in worship services. For other Jews, observing Shabbat may not be related to refraining from work at all but may instead focus on eating certain foods, gathering with loved ones, and resting.

Shabbat begins on Friday night with a ceremony, often held in the home, that involves saying blessings and lighting candles, drinking wine, and eating challah (a sweet braided bread), followed by a festive meal. Many synagogues offer shorter worship services on Friday night to welcome Shabbat with music and longer services on Saturday morning that include a Torah service, where the weekly Torah portion is read. These services vary widely in their use of professional clergy, the Hebrew language, and music. On Shabbat afternoons, Jews may eat meals with their community, visit friends and family, go for walks, take naps, study Torah, and/or read books, among other things. Shabbat ends with the Havdalah ceremony, which involves more blessings, lighting and extinguishing a multiwicked candle, drinking wine, and smelling spices. Havdalah marks the transition from the holy period of Shabbat into the rest of the week.

## About the author

**Adrienne Krone** is an associate professor of religious studies at Allegheny College in Meadville, Pennsylvania.

## Suggestions for further reading

*In this book*
See also chapters 2 (What is the Torah?), 3 (What is the Talmud?), 7 (What is a rabbi?), and 20 (What are the differences among Reform, Conservative, Reconstructionist, and Orthodox Judaism?).

*Elsewhere*
Heschel, Abraham Joshua. *The Sabbath: Its Meaning for Modern Man*. New York: Farrar, Straus, and Giroux, 1951.

Stein, David E. S., ed. *The Contemporary Torah: A Gender-Sensitive Adaptation of the JPS Translation*. Philadelphia, PA: Jewish Publication Society, 2006.

Wolfson, Ron. *Shabbat: The Family Guide to Preparing for and Celebrating the Sabbath* (2nd edition). Woodstock, VT: Jewish Lights, 2002.

# 18
# Can Jews get tattoos?

## Chaim McNamee

The text of Leviticus 19:28 seems to prohibit Jewish people from getting tattoos. Like much of the Torah, however, the proper translation is variable. Sefaria, a nonprofit website that hosts some three thousand years' worth of Jewish texts, offers the following translation: "You shall not make gashes in your flesh for the dead, or incise any marks on yourselves: I am [The Name of God]." Rashi, a well-known Torah commentator who lived in medieval France, defined such a "mark" as writing engraved or "dug into" the flesh and "which can never be erased because it is pricked in with a needle and remains forever." Possibly because of Rashi's interpretation, the Hebrew phrase that Sefaria renders as "incise," *k'tovet ka'aka*, is sometimes translated as "tattoo."

This passage in Leviticus has served as the grounds for a long-standing taboo on tattooing in Jewish cultures. In the United States, many Jewish authorities representing major streams of contemporary American Judaism—Orthodox, Reform, and Conservative—agree that Leviticus 19:28 is meant to prohibit Jews from getting tattooed. There are, of course, dissenting opinions on this question, especially from scholars, rabbis, and practitioners of the Reform tradition. (This is not to say, however, that the only Jews getting tattooed come from more "liberal" or "progressive" traditions.)

However contested it may be, the Leviticus prohibition has proved forceful in American Jewish culture. Many American Jews today may recall being told by an older family or community member that they couldn't be buried in a Jewish cemetery if they got tattooed, but this is a legend rather than a halakhic prohibition. The text of the Torah certainly does not prohibit it, nor does it prescribe any particular punishment for a Jew who gets tattooed. This means that the consequences of getting a tattoo are largely litigated by individual Jewish communities.

Beyond myths about burial permissions, however, modern Jews may be dissuaded from getting inked by the role tattooing played in marking

Jewish bodies during the Holocaust. Contrary to the popular misconception that all of the Holocaust's Jewish victims were marked with a number, this practice was particular to Auschwitz, where approximately four hundred thousand Jewish prisoners selected for forced labor were marked with identification numbers. The numbered tattoos at once dehumanized the Jewish prisoners who received them and marked them as a resource of the Third Reich's war machine. Italian Holocaust survivor Primo Levi likened the Auschwitz tattoos to the brands put on cattle that are sent to slaughter. The tattoos, he wrote, stripped prisoners of their identities; their number became all they were.

Holocaust tattoos are indelibly a symbol of historical trauma and dehumanization, but they carry other meanings as well. A prisoner named Szlamach Radosynzki took comfort in the fact that the numbers of his Auschwitz tattoo, 128232, added up to 18, the Jewish mystical number of life. Radosynzki was among the tattooed survivors of Auschwitz who would immigrate to the US after the war's end. Today, tattooed Auschwitz survivors and their descendants are part of American Jewish communities. A curious and controversial practice has emerged among these descendants in recent years: Some have chosen to have their relative's Auschwitz numbers tattooed on their own bodies as a memorial of their family's suffering and resilience.

Numerous Jewish publications have documented a rise in Jewish people, especially younger folks, choosing to get inked. While the decline of the Leviticus prohibition's influence (or perhaps the rise of alternate interpretations) marks an interesting moment in US Jewish culture, perhaps more interesting is that many of these individuals choose to get tattoos with distinctively Jewish subject matters. It is not uncommon to see (usually younger) Jewish people with tattoos depicting Hebrew words, Stars of David, pomegranates, olive branches, hamsa, and other quintessentially Jewish symbols. These tattoos serve as markers of Jewish identity; indeed, some tattooed Jews have told me that they sought out tattoos as a way of *feeling Jewish* or *doing Judaism*. Similarly, some Jews (like this humble author) feel drawn to the other side of the tattoo machine and have begun tattooing other Jews as an expression of Jewish religious practice, identity, history, and community.

Whether Jews *can* get tattooed, then, is perhaps not the right question. What is more interesting at this moment in time is why contemporary Jews are drawn to tattoos and what role tattooing might play in future iterations of Judaism and Jewish practice. How Jewish communities will debate, confront, embrace, and litigate the place of tattoos on our bodies and in our traditions remains to be seen.

## About the author

**Chaim McNamee** (he/him, they/them) is a PhD candidate in rhetoric in the Department of English at Indiana University, Bloomington.

## Suggestions for further reading

*In this book*

See also chapters 2 (What is the Torah?), 20 (What are the differences among Reform, Conservative, Reconstructionist, and Orthodox Judaism?), and 50 (What is the Holocaust?).

*Elsewhere*

Bloch, Alice. "Why Descendants of Holocaust Survivors Are Replicating Auschwitz Tattoos." *Smithsonian Magazine*, January 25, 2024. https://www.smithsonianmag.com/history/why-descendants-of-holocaust-survivors-are-replicating-auschwitz-tattoos-180983648/.

My Jewish Learning. "The Tattoo Taboo in Judaism." Accessed November 20, 2024. https://www.myjewishlearning.com/article/the-tattoo-taboo-in-judaism/.

Piatigorsky-Roth, Sivan. "I Love My Tattoos and I Love Halakhah." *Lilith*, February 7, 2022. https://lilith.org/articles/i-love-my-tattoos-and-i-love-halakhah/.

Raviv, Shaun. "For Life." *Moment Magazine*, June 2006. https://momentmag.com/wp-content/uploads/2023/09/markedforlife.pdf.

United States Holocaust Memorial Museum. "Receiving Tattoos at Auschwitz." Holocaust Encyclopedia, accessed November 20, 2024. https://encyclopedia.ushmm.org/content/en/gallery/receiving-tattoos-at-auschwitz.

# 19
# Why is the name of God important?

## James A. Diamond

The Hebrew Bible has many different names for God, including *Elohim, El, Adonai, Shaddai, Zevaot,* and notably, *Yahweh* (YHWH), the four-letter name singled out as the *Tetragrammaton,* or the unpronounceable "articulated name." Each of these has different meanings in Hebrew, yet they are often blurred by their indiscriminate English translations as "God" or "Lord." Those acquainted with the Hebrew Bible solely through translation miss the critical clues that the various names of God offer in determining God's nature.

The name YHWH originates in the seemingly tautological play on the root "to be" of *ehyeh asher ehyeh,* "I will be who I will be" (Ex. 3:14), introduced formally in direct response to Moses's request at the burning bush theophany. It is the sole exposition of YHWH in the Hebrew Bible. Evasively formulated, it has provoked an endless stream of translations, interpretations, and scholarship, from the Septuagint, the ancient Greek translation, to twentieth-century philosophers, including Martin Buber and Franz Rosenzweig. This contentiousness attests to its deliberate ambiguity and irresolvable open-endedness.

Abstract conceptions of God originated with the ancient Greeks, influencing philosophical theology through the Middle Ages to today. The Greek Septuagint version of *ehyeh asher ehyeh* as "I am the One who is" overwhelmingly influenced biblical translation throughout history. It overshadowed much ensuing interpretation with a present tense that is amenable to Greek metaphysics. Jewish theology has consequently been torn between a perfect, immutable, impersonal God that simply *is* and a personal, relational God that *becomes.*

Judaism, importantly distinct from biblical religion, evolved in its rabbinic form since the first centuries of the Common Era. Classical rabbinic thought, midrash, and Kabbalah constructed YHWH as a relational being in a reciprocal partnership with Israel. It connotes a God continually shaped and reshaped by respective partners. Rashi, the medieval Jewish commentator, fleshed out the meaning of *ehyeh asher ehyeh* as "I will be with them during this affliction as I will be with them during their oppression by other kingdoms"; God provides the comfort and empathy expected of any partner in a meaningful relationship.

Midrashic traditions deepen the interdependence required by authentic relationships: A condensed form of the name YHWH as YH (*Yah*) (Ex. 17:16) indicates for the rabbis a God whose imperfect state of brokenness, alienation, and exile, especially in the face of palpable evil in the world, can only be remedied by the restorative acts of human beings. The notion of a broken, fragmented deity in need of repair became a virtual theological staple of Kabbalah.

However, Moses Maimonides, Judaism's pioneering rationalist, held that all divine names except YHWH "derive from actions." Since his fundamental premise is that God is immutable and possesses no attributes, the referent of these names is not God but rather phenomena in the natural world, where, as God's creation, a particular name "corresponds to actions existing in the world." It is then metaphorically projected onto God in His capacity as the remotest prime cause in the long chain of natural causation. The only name that correctly points to a wholly abstract being of pure divine essence without attributes is YHWH, a name that midrashically preexisted the creation.

On the other end of the Jewish theological spectrum is Moses Nahmanides, the pioneering medieval kabbalist, for whom names capture different dimensions of God's dynamic being. The Torah can be read as an elongated thread of divine names through which a deeper narrative pulsating beneath surface narratives and laws charts the life of God. The transition from a solid block of names to an individuated one of discrete words marks a transition from a primordial Torah to a written one. Rabbinic and mystical interpretations of an evolving and impressionable God trend closer to the personal interventionist God of the Hebrew Bible. Conversely, the philosophical abstractions consistent with notions of divine perfection impose a notion of the deity that is foreign to the written text.

Many synagogue congregants in the English-speaking world might be familiar with an existential notion of God via Rabbi J. H. Hertz's commentary, which, until recently, was the standard edition of the Pentateuch used in most modern Orthodox congregations. It advises that the name "must not be understood in the philosophical sense of mere 'being,' but as active manifestation of the Divine existence."

Finally, Abraham Joshua Heschel, one of Judaism's most profound modern theologians, distinguished between the rationalist "notion" of an impersonal God and a "name" associated with traditions endorsing a personal God of history. For him, the two are so different as to be "profoundly incompatible." Addressing Jewish educators, he advocated a named God over and against theoretical conceptions of God and insisted they treat YHWH as evocative rather than descriptive because "the God of Israel is a name, not a notion. . . . Don't teach notions of God, teach the name of God."

## About the author

**James A. Diamond** holds an endowed chair in Jewish studies at the University of Waterloo. His principal areas of research include biblical exegesis, medieval and modern Jewish thought and philosophy, Maimonides, and rabbinics. He has published widely on all areas of Jewish thought in many leading peer-reviewed scholarly journals, such as *Harvard Theological Review* and *Journal of Religion*. His books include, among others, *Maimonides and the Shaping of the Jewish Canon* (Cambridge University Press, 2014) and *Jewish Theology Unbound* (Oxford University Press, 2018).

## Suggestions for further reading

### In this book
See also chapters 4 (What is midrash?) and 5 (What is Kabbalah?).

### Elsewhere
Heschel, Abraham Joshua. "Jewish Theology." In *Moral Grandeur and Spiritual Audacity*, edited by Susannah Heschel, 154–164. New York: Farar, Strauss, Giroux, 1996.

Idel, Moshe. "Defining Kabbalah: The Kabbalah of Divine Names." In *Mystics of the Book: Themes, Topics and Topologies*, edited by Robert A. Herrera, 97–122. New York: Peter Lang, 1993.

Marmorstein, Arthur. *The Old Rabbinic Doctrine of God: The Names and Attributes of God* (volume 1). London: Oxford University Press, 1927.

Rosenzweig, Franz. "The Eternal." In *Scripture and Translation*, by Martin Buber and Franz Rosenzweig, translated by Lawrence Rosenwald and Everett Fox, 99–113. Bloomington: Indiana University Press, 1994.

# Groups and Beliefs

# 20
# What are the differences among Reform, Conservative, Reconstructionist, and Orthodox Judaism?

## Joshua Shanes

Two thousand years ago, Jews were divided between competing sects, all based on Jewish scriptures but with different interpretations. After the Romans destroyed the Jerusalem Temple in 70 CE, one main group, who called themselves "rabbis"—sages or teachers—began to dominate. What we now know as "Judaism" grew out of this group.

There were theological disagreements and regional customs, but Rabbinic Judaism remained a single if diverse religious community until the nineteenth century, when Ashkenazi Jews began to divide themselves into different branches of Judaism. Historically, Judaism had been based in Jewish autonomous communities governed by rabbinic law that took the truth of its beliefs for granted. Political emancipation in Western Europe and political rights in the Americas changed the autonomy of communities, while Enlightenment ideas challenged beliefs. Jews were now free to choose what to believe and how to practice Judaism, if at all.

Competing Jewish denominations emerged in these areas, each one negotiating the relationship between Jewishness and modernity in its own way. Each group claimed that they followed the best or most authentic traditions of Judaism, even as each of them in fact reflected a self-conscious set of choices and particular interpretations of the past. (Judaism evolved differently in the Muslim world, which did not experience this abrupt emancipation. Different "Sephardi" traditions developed instead.)

The first to organize was Reform—first in Germany and soon thereafter in the United States. Reform Judaism is based on the idea that both the Bible and the laws of the Oral Torah are divinely inspired but humanly constructed, meaning they should be adapted based on contemporary moral ideals. Today, for example, this manifests in gender egalitarianism, LGBTQ+ acceptance, and acceptance of intermarriage. Reform congregations tend to emphasize prophetic themes such as social justice more than Talmudic law, though in recent years, many have reclaimed some rituals, such as Hebrew liturgy and stricter observance of Shabbat.

Orthodox Judaism organized in reaction to Reform, rallying to defend the strict observance of Jewish customs and law. Orthodox leaders often blurred the distinction between these categories and put particular emphasis on the sixteenth-century legal code called the *Shulḥan Arukh*. Orthodox Jews are roughly divided between acculturated "Modern Orthodox" iterations and ultra-Orthodox or "Haredi" groups that attempt to segregate themselves from outside society. They all theoretically share a commitment to halakhah and faith in the divinity of the Torah, written and oral. Haredim, however, are more committed to gender separation and the strictest interpretation of halakhah, even when tradition has been more lenient, and also tend to reject Zionism, which most Modern Orthodox have integrated into their religious worldview.

This is especially true of Hasidic Jews, who make up about half of the ultra-Orthodox population worldwide. Hasidism is a mystical movement born in eighteenth-century Ukraine, but today it is mostly concentrated in New York and Israel. Hasidic Jews are divided into smaller communities led by powerful leaders known as "rebbes." They shun secular culture and education, but they remain a mystical movement focused on God's close presence.

Orthodox Judaism sees itself as "traditional." However, it is more accurate to say it is "traditionalist." Not only has Orthodox Judaism innovated many rituals and teachings, but people today are aware that other ways of life are available—creating a firm break with the traditional world Orthodoxy claims to perpetuate.

Conservative Judaism shares many of Reform's views, such as equal roles for men and women. However, Conservative Judaism argues that the Reform movement pulled too far away from Jewish tradition. They insist that Jewish law remains obligatory but that the Orthodox interpretation is too rigid. In practice, most Conservative Jews tend not to be strict about even major rituals, like Sabbath restrictions or kosher food practices, though their synagogues tend to maintain a Hebrew-language liturgy close to the traditional prayerbook.

There are also smaller but still influential Jewish movements. For example, Reconstructionism, created by Rabbi Mordecai Kaplan a century ago, emphasizes community and social responsibility over ritual obligations, which Kaplan said should be observed or discarded based on contemporary moral values. The Jewish Renewal movement, born out of the late 1960s counterculture, seeks to incorporate insights from Jewish mysticism with an egalitarian perspective and without necessarily following the minutiae of Jewish law.

Today in the United States, about 37 percent of Jews identify as Reform, 20 percent as Conservative, and 32 percent as unaffiliated. The percentage of Jews who are Orthodox—especially ultra-Orthodox, whose members tend to have very large families—is growing rapidly. Almost 10 percent of American Jews and nearly 25 percent of Israeli Jews are Orthodox today, although attrition from these communities is also rising.

## About the author

**Joshua Shanes** is the Emanuel Ringelblum Chair of Jewish History at the University of California, Davis. He has published widely on modern Jewish history, religion, politics, and antisemitism in both academic and popular outlets such as *The Washington Post*, *Slate*, and *Haaretz*. He is currently completing a history of Jewish Orthodoxy from its German origins until today for the Key Words in Jewish Studies series with Rutgers University Press.

## Suggestions for further reading

*In this book*
See also chapters 6 (What is Jewish law?), 7 (What is a rabbi?), 10 (What does kosher mean?), 16 (What does it mean to be Hasidic?), and 17 (What do Jews do on the Sabbath?).

*Elsewhere*
Chanes, Jerome A., and Mark Silk, eds. *The Future of Judaism in America*. Cham, Switzerland: Springer, 2023.

Fishman, Sylvia Barack. *The Way into the Varieties of Jewishness*. Woodstock, VT: Jewish Lights, 2007.

Sarna, Jonathan. *American Judaism: A History* (2nd edition). New Haven, CT: Yale University Press, 2019.

# 21
# What are the differences among Ashkenazi, Sephardi, and Mizrahi Jews?

## Max Daniel

Jews differentiate themselves in many ways religiously, nationally, linguistically, politically, and more. Among them are the uniquely Jewish groupings of Ashkenazi, Sephardi, and Mizrahi. These can be loosely defined as cultural, ethnic, or geographic categories, and they can also correspond to particular religious traditions, customs, liturgy, and language. While there are several Jewish communities that do not strictly fall into any of these categories, they encompass the vast majority of Jews today.

*Ashkenaz*, a location originally mentioned in the Torah, eventually came to refer to Central Europe, particularly German lands along the Rhine Valley. The rich Jewish culture that emerged there during the early medieval era gave birth to a distinctive Ashkenazi Jewry. Expulsions, crusades, and discriminatory edicts pushed many of these Jews eastward toward Poland, Russia, and other Slavic lands, where they retained and developed their Ashkenazi Jewish culture. A major part of this was their language, Yiddish (Judeo-German), out of which grew an immense body of literature and cultural production. Much of the food, folklore, music, and clothing of their non-Jewish Eastern European neighbors heavily influenced Ashkenazi culture, such that bagels, klezmer music, and certain surnames have come to be popularly associated with Jews. The vast majority of American Jews are of Ashkenazi background, as are most Jewish communities outside of Israel. Modern religious denominations like Reform, Conservative, or Orthodox and movements like Hasidism emerged in Europe and the Americas primarily among Ashkenazi Jews.

The word *Sepharad* first appears in the biblical book of Obadiah and has commonly been understood to refer to Spain. Jews lived in Spain and Portugal for centuries under Roman, Visigoth, Muslim, and then Christian rule until the 1492 Edict of Expulsion demanded Jews leave or convert to Catholicism. The diaspora of Spanish and Portuguese Jews came to be known as "Sephardim," most of whom settled in North Africa, the Ottoman Empire, Italy, and Western Europe.

Those who settled in places like the Netherlands, England, and the Americas developed a distinctive "Western" Sephardi or "Spanish and Portuguese" Jewish tradition and community apart from those in Muslim-majority lands. The latter branch of this diaspora gave birth to Ladino (Judeo-Spanish) language and culture.

Sephardi Judaism, with its roots in Spanish and Middle Eastern rabbinic thought, has also developed into its own religious philosophy and approach, such that in modern Israel, there are two official rabbinates, Ashkenazi and Sephardi. As a religious system, Sephardi Judaism lacks a history of denominationalism and, in general, signifies an overall philosophy of Judaism that tends toward a more accommodating and flexible orthodoxy.

Unlike Ashkenazi or Sephardi, the label "Mizrahi" is a recent term. The development of modern Zionism and the changing profile of Jewish life in Palestine and later in Israel encouraged an approach to intra-Jewish differences that went beyond national, linguistic, or religious frameworks. One result was the introduction of the label "Mizrahi," meaning "Eastern" or "Oriental" in Hebrew, referring to Jews of Middle Eastern and North African origin. It emerged partly from stereotypes about Jews from Muslim and Arab lands, like Morocco or Iraq, as "backward." Influenced by contemporary Orientalism and racial categories, Mizrahi Jews were seen as needing reeducation and cultural conditioning to be part of a new Israeli nation-state. Having faced discrimination in Israeli society, Mizrahi has come to denote a racialized Jewish underclass in Israeli society and has become a politicized identity for some. Given its origins in Zionist and Israeli circles, "Mizrahi" has not been as ubiquitous among American Jews, who tend to use "Sephardi" instead when referring to Middle Eastern and North African Jews.

Mizrahi Judaism, as a religious system, is thus not homogeneous, and differences largely correspond to national subgroups, like Moroccan, Yemenite, or Iraqi. Due to the wide-ranging influence of Sephardi Judaism in North Africa and the Middle East, many Mizrahi Jews also identify with Sephardi as a religious marker. Appealing to religious traditionalism and shared experiences of class and ethnic inequality, Mizrahi Jews have been drawn to Israel's Shas political party, which is a Hebrew acronym for "Sephardic Guardians [of the Torah]."

While the specific category "Ashkenazi" has yet to be deeply analyzed or deconstructed, understandings of what exactly Sephardi or Mizrahi mean are also far from unanimous. In particular, differences among Israel, the United States, and other places make common definitions of these terms difficult. Nevertheless, the last century of war, migration, and technology have brought Jews into greater contact with one another and have diminished many of the differences among Ashkenazi, Sephardi, and Mizrahi Jews—although many still remain.

## About the author

**Max Daniel** is the public historian and Jewish Heritage Collection coordinator at Special Collections in the Addlestone Library at the College of Charleston.

## Suggestions for further reading

*In this book*

See also chapters 16 (What does it mean to be Hasidic?) and 20 (What are the differences among Reform, Conservative, Reconstructionist, and Orthodox Judaism?).

*Elsewhere*

Benbassa, Esther, and Aron Rodrigue. *Sephardi Jewry: A History of the Judeo-Spanish Community, 14th–20th Centuries*. Berkeley: University of California Press, 1995.

Gerber, Jane S. *The Jews of Spain: A History of the Sephardic Experience*. New York: The Free Press, 1992.

Katz, Dovid. *Words on Fire: The Unfinished Story of Yiddish*. New York: Basic Books, 2004.

Petrovsky-Shtern, Yohanan. *The Golden Age Shtetl: A New History of Jewish Life in East Europe*. Princeton, NJ: Princeton University Press, 2014.

Shohat, Ella. *On the Arab-Jew, Palestine, and Other Displacements: Selected Writings of Ella Shohat*. London: Pluto Press, 2017.

# 22
# What is Karaite Judaism?

## Meira Polliack

The name "Karaites" is derived from the Hebrew root *qara*, which means "to read," "to read out loud," "to exclaim," and also "to preoccupy oneself" (through learning or teaching) with the Hebrew Bible, which is also known as *miqra* in Hebrew. The name is documented in Judeo-Arabic and Hebrew sources from the tenth and eleventh centuries. It designates a scripturalist community within medieval Judaism that rejected the authority of Jewish oral law, as canonized in the major works of rabbinic literature, such as the Mishnah and Babylonian Talmud.

The Karaites hailed from established as well as marginal Jewish communities in Persia and Iraq, including from families of distinguished rabbis who came from important centers of learning in Baghdad and the land of Israel. They were united by their quest to return to an immediate and unhindered study of the biblical text and by their antiestablishment views, which considered rabbinic law as a "tradition learned by rote" rather than a God-given revealed system of Jewish religious belief and practice. The Karaites were also inspired by figures who belonged to the rabbinic establishment but were deeply critical of rabbinic laws, among them the thinker Anan ben David (Iraq, eighth century). While the Karaites generally regard Anan as the founder of their movement, most scholars consider the movement to have been inspired by Anan but to not have fully developed until two centuries later.

By the tenth century, Arabic language and literature permeated Jewish thought in the Near East, and Jews in general embraced a more literate orientation, which gradually decreased their traditional orality in learning. The rise of literacy also enabled Jewish scholars to engage with Islamic literary and scripturalist models. These developments contributed to Karaism maturing into a major stream of medieval Jewish thought.

Karaite scripturalism was also, and naturally, accompanied by a rejection of the diasporic model of Rabbinic Judaism. Instead, its thought is characterized by a strong pull to the land of the Bible as the center for

Jewish life and practice. Hence they began a process of "return," as they called it, to the land of Israel in about 880 CE. Once there, they established thriving communities, especially in the cities of Ramla and Jerusalem. For two centuries, Jerusalem served as the major Karaite center of learning in which most of the classical Karaite works in biblical exegesis, philosophy, linguistics, law, and science were composed. Major Karaite figures such as Salmon ben Yeruham, Yefet be Eli, Yeshua ben Yehuda, Ali be Sulayman, and others also lived in the city.

During the 1099 Crusade, the Karaite communities in the Holy Land were destroyed, and the remaining flock dispersed to Egypt in the south and Byzantium in the north. These centers functioned up to modern times: The Byzantine community gradually spread to the Crimea and Eastern Europe, while the Cairo community remained the closest to its medieval origins. Most of the Egyptian Karaites immigrated to the State of Israel in the 1950s, where they live in established communities in Ashdod, Ramla, and villages in the south of Israel (such as Ranen and Mazliah). While some Israeli Karaites have assimilated to secular life, others keep diligently to their religious practices and unique forms of worship in Karaite synagogues and community centers, some of which exist in North America as well.

As a Jewish school of thought that turned its exclusive attention to the Hebrew Bible, Karaism had a deep and crucial influence on novel directions in Jewish Bible exegesis at large and especially on the Spanish Jewish commentators who shared with the Karaites a wider Arabized background of rational and linguistic biblical interpretation. The prominent Hebrew commentaries of Abraham Ibn Ezra and other Spanish émigrés to Christian Europe (such as the Kimhi family) share many insights with Karaite exegetes, and the authors clearly knew some of their works, whether in the Judeo-Arabic original or through medieval Hebrew renditions and compilations prepared by the Karaites in Byzantium during the twelfth and thirteenth centuries.

The Karaites' intellectual tradition has been unjustifiably cut off in many discussions from the body of "mainstream" Judaism and usually viewed in isolation as irrelevant or secondary. Karaite thought on the Hebrew Bible formed an inseparable part of medieval Jewish history and intellectual tradition, fostering and carrying further its innovative spirit, especially in the realm of biblical interpretation. The unprecedented and unparalleled linguistic and exegetical achievements of the medieval Karaites engendered linguistic-contextual and literary study of the biblical text and were essential to the rise of the Jewish school of *peshat*, or literal interpretation. No less importantly, the Karaites represent a live and continuous artery of Jewish identity and thought, an alternative Judaism, from medieval to current times.

## About the author

**Meira Polliack** is a professor of Bible and the Joseph and Ceil Mazer Chair in Jewish Culture in Muslim Lands and Cairo Genizah Studies at Tel Aviv University. She is coeditor with Michael G. Wechsler of the book series Karaite Texts and Studies (Brill). She researches literary approaches to the Hebrew Bible, its reception and exegesis, medieval Jewish interpretation in the Islamic world, and Karaite and Judeo-Arabic literature.

## Suggestions for further reading

*In this book*
See also chapters 3 (What is the Talmud?), 4 (What is midrash?), and 7 (What is a rabbi?).

*Elsewhere*
Andruss, Jessica Hope. *Jewish Piety in Islamic Jerusalem: The Lamentations Commentary of Salmon Ben Yerūḥīm*. New York: Oxford University Press, 2023.

Erder, Yoram. *The Karaite Mourners of Zion and the Qumran Scrolls: On the History of an Alternative to Rabbinic Judaism*. Turnhout, Belgium: Brepols, 2017.

Polliack, Meira, ed. *Karaite Judaism: A Guide to Its History and Literary Sources*. Boston: Brill, 2003.

Walfish, Barry, and Mikhail Kizilov. *Bibliographia Karaitica: An Annotated Bibliography of Karaites and Karaism*. Boston: Brill, 2011.

Wechsler, Michael G. *The Arabic Translation and Commentary of Yefet Ben 'Eli the Karaite on the Book of Esther*. Boston: Brill, 2008.

# 23
# What languages do Jews speak?

## Sarah Bunin Benor

From Jerusalem to Johannesburg, from Baghdad to Bialystok, Jews have spoken dozens of languages. The Jewish people's linguistic journey began with Biblical Hebrew around the tenth century BCE in the land of Israel. New empires brought new languages to the region, including Aramaic, Persian, and Greek. When Jews migrated for economic reasons or due to persecution or expulsion, they encountered additional languages. In each case, Jews adopted the local language and distinguished it. This led to Jewish languages throughout the Middle East, Europe, parts of Asia and Africa, and eventually the Americas and Oceania. Scholars often refer to these languages as Judeo-X, like Judeo-Greek, Judeo-Arabic, and Judeo-Georgian. More recent languages are sometimes called Jewish X, like Jewish English, Jewish Papiamentu (Curaçao), and Jewish Latin American Spanish.

The two most widely known diaspora Jewish languages—Yiddish and Ladino—are exceptions in this history. Both were maintained for centuries away from their original regions, so Jews and their new neighbors could not understand each other. Ashkenazi Jews started speaking Western Yiddish, or Judeo-German, in Germanic lands around the tenth century. When they moved to places where their neighbors spoke Polish, Hungarian, Lithuanian, and so on, they maintained their Germanic language, which became known as Eastern Yiddish. Judeo-Spanish originated among Sephardi Jews in the Iberian Peninsula. When Jews were expelled from Spain in the late fifteenth century, they scattered to many places. In Morocco and the Balkans (Yugoslavia, Bulgaria, Greece, Turkey), they maintained their Spanish language, which came to be known as Judezmo, Spanyol, or Ladino.

After the seventh-century Islamic conquests, Jews adopted Arabic from Iraq and Yemen in the East to Spain and Morocco in the West. Judeo-Arabic in each of these places was similar to that of local Muslims, distinguished by Hebrew words and other unique features. Throughout the Persian Empire, from Iran to Bukhara, Jews spoke Jewish varieties of Persian and Median languages, like Judeo-Shirazi, Judeo-Hamedani, and Judeo-Tajik (Bukharian). In India, Jews spoke Jewish varieties of Malayalam in the south and Marathi in the center. Jews in Ethiopia spoke Amharic and maintained sacred texts in Geʻez. In Italy, Jews spoke Judeo-Romanesco, Judeo-Piedmontese, and other varieties of Judeo-Italian, and Romaniote Jews in Greece spoke Judeo-Greek.

Throughout these migrations, Jews continued to use ancient Hebrew and Aramaic in their prayers and study of biblical and rabbinic scripture, with some exceptions, like Ethiopia and parts of India. Most Judeo-X and Jewish X languages are influenced by these sacred texts, incorporating Hebrew and Aramaic words and sometimes using Hebrew writing systems. In addition, Jewish languages are influenced by previous Jewish languages, like Yiddish *tsholent* (Sabbath stew) from Judeo-French *chalent* (hot) and Ladino *al had* (Sunday) from Judeo-Arabic, avoiding Spanish *domingo* (Sunday / Lord's Day). Some Jewish languages include displaced regionalisms due to Jews migrating or maintaining contact with other Jewish communities within a language territory. For example, Judeo-Italian in Central and Northern Italy uses a plural article from Southern Italy, and in Neo-Aramaic in Kurdistan, Jews sound more similar to Jews in other towns than to nearby Christians.

Other distinctive features stem not from textual contact or migrations but from Jews sustaining a degree of insularity, imposed both internally and externally. Many Jewish languages maintain fossilized archaisms—words and grammatical features that local non-Jews previously used but no longer do. For example, Judeo-Baghdadi Arabic preserves the [q] sound (like [k] but lower in the throat), while Muslim Baghdadi Arabic switched to [g]. Jewish Malayalam maintains a dative morpheme that local Hindus stopped using centuries ago (e.g., *avan-ikkə*, rather than *avan-ə*, meaning "to him"). Jewish languages also use innovative features. Jews in Kutaisi, Georgia, have distinctive pitch patterns in questions, and in Judeo-Tat (Juhuri), the passive form uses *omore* (to come), while Tat uses *biræn* (to be). Distinctive features like these lead to a continuum—some Jewish languages are only minimally distinct, while others are different enough that Jews must code switch to communicate with their non-Jewish neighbors.

In recent decades, most long-standing Jewish languages have become endangered due to migration, genocide, and restrictive language policies. Families who spoke them have shifted to new Jewish languages, especially revernacularized Modern Hebrew in Israel and Jewish English in the US and elsewhere. Smaller Jewish communities speak Jewish French, Spanish, Portuguese, Hungarian, Swedish, and so on. While these new languages (except Modern Hebrew) are not written in Hebrew letters, they tend to have many of the distinctive features discussed here. They also include influences from Modern Hebrew, which is taught in diaspora Jewish schools, and from Yiddish, Ladino, Judeo-Arabic, Bukharian, and others, continuing the ancient trend of Jewish language shifts.

### About the author

**Sarah Bunin Benor** is a professor of contemporary Jewish studies and director of the Jewish Language Project at Hebrew Union College and an adjunct professor in the University of Southern California Linguistics Department.

### Suggestions for further reading

*In this book*
See also chapters 21 (What are the differences among Ashkenazi, Sephardi, and Mizrahi Jews?), 45 (Are Jews European or Middle Eastern or something else?), and 67 (What's the deal with Jews and comedy?).

*Elsewhere*
Benor, Sarah Bunin, ed. *Jewish Language Website*. Last updated December 7, 2024. www.jewishlanguages.org.

Rubin, Aaron D., and Lily Kahn. *Jewish Languages from A to Z*. London: Routledge, 2021.

Spolsky, Bernard. *The Languages of the Jews: A Sociolinguistic History*. New York: Cambridge University Press, 2014.

# 24
# What does it mean to be a secular Jew?

Jennifer Caplan

There has long been a stereotype about Judaism that it is not about "faith" and is instead about "action." By this, people mean that Jews don't have to *believe* in any particular thing; they just need to perform the right rituals, celebrate the right holidays, or behave in a particular way. This is, of course, both an oversimplification and also fundamentally incorrect in many ways, but as with all stereotypes, there is a kernel of truth. Understanding what it means to be Jewish becomes even more complicated when we add in the fact that, for many people, Judaism is an ethnic identity as much as (or more than) it is a religion. Judaism is, for many people, an identity you are born with because one or both of your parents were Jewish; nothing needs to be done to or by you to make that so.

What does it mean, then, to be Jewish but not identify with any religion at all and not to understand Judaism as your ethnic identity? For many years, these people have been identified as "secular Jews," but that is a problematic label that stems, in part, from an equally problematic notion referred to as "the continuity crisis." This language came to prominence in the 1970s when sociologists and Jewish institutions saw the rising intermarriage rate as an imminent existential threat to the survival of the Jewish people. They argued that the children of intermarried parents were much less likely to be raised with a strong Jewish religious identity and would, at best, become "secular Jews" or, at worst, not identify as Jewish at all.

These "secular Jews" were seen as a problem because no one thought they would have any inclination to marry a Jewish spouse, and as their Jewishness was already seen as "less than," they would almost certainly not convey a strong Jewish identity to their children. Within three generations, this argument went, there would be no Jews left in North America other than the small minority of the most traditional Jews.

These fears have proven to be largely unfounded, as the number of Jews in North America has remained stable, even decades later. What has proven true, however, is that more and more North American Jews experience and engage with their own Jewishness differently than people did before the late twentieth century, and this has come to be labeled by some as "cultural Judaism." Even before the twentieth century, many Jews identified as Jewish but saw that as motivation toward leftist politics, including Socialism, Bundism, Communism, and even anarchism. There was not a specific term for these Jewish-but-secular Jews, and the only fear seemed to be over the association between Jews and leftism branding all Jews as "un-American" during the McCarthy era. Today, being a "cultural" or "secular" Jew seems to mean that you identify as Jewish (even if you also identify as atheist or having no religion), and your engagement with Judaism comes through things like food, music, movies, and literature. The term "cultural Judaism" has usually been used in a negative way to denote a Jewish identity that is not engaging with Judaism correctly.

In recent years, quite a few scholars have begun to produce research that pushes back against most of these earlier assumptions. They argue, for example, that the continuity crisis was misogynistic and put undue pressure on women to "produce the next generation of Jews" and that all evidence points to it not really being a crisis after all. They also argue that the problem is not "secular Jews"; the problem is that Jewish life and culture are always changing, but our ways of measuring Jewish engagement have stayed the same. Younger Jews may be joining synagogues in smaller numbers, but if they see their patronage of a Jewish deli or their love of comedy as a distinctly Jewish act, then we need to think up new ways of surveying Jewish life that capture this engagement not as an inferior or vestigial way of being Jewish but as simply another valid way of being Jewish. Mordecai Kaplan wrote in 1934 that what Jews needed to worry about protecting were the distinct Jewish cultural forms (or what he called "Jewish civilization"). Jewish religious practice, he believed, would always be OK. Now, almost a century later, it looks as though he was correct, and rather than seeing "secular Jews" as those who have rejected Jewish religion, we should see them as protectors of Jewish culture.

## About the author

**Jennifer Caplan** is an associate professor and the Jewish Foundation of Cincinnati Chair in Judaic Studies at the University of Cincinnati. She is the author of *Funny, You Don't Look Funny: Judaism and Humor from the Silent Generation to Millennials* (Wayne State University Press, 2023) and is currently working on a monograph on Jewish characters in the DC and Marvel universes.

## Suggestions for further reading

*In this book*
See also chapters 25 (Do Jews believe in God?) and 47 (Is Judaism a religion or an ethnicity?).

*Elsewhere*
Gross, Rachel B. *Beyond the Synagogue: Jewish Nostalgia as Religious Practice*. New York: New York University Press, 2021.

Kaplan, Mordecai. *Judaism as a Civilization*. Philadelphia, PA: Jewish Publication Society, 2010.

Kellner, Menachem. *Must a Jew Believe Anything?* Portland, OR: Littman Library of Jewish Civilization, 2006.

Thompson, Jennifer A. *Jewish on Their Own Terms: How Intermarried Couples Are Changing American Judaism*. New Brunswick, NJ: Rutgers University Press, 2013.

Wouk, Herman. *This Is My God*. Boston: Back Bay Books, 1992.

# 25
# Do Jews believe in God?

## Elias Sacks

How we answer the question "Do Jews believe in God?" depends on how we understand each of the query's elements: "do Jews," "believe in," and "God."

Beginning with "do Jews," we might understand this as a question about whether individuals who identify as Jewish affirm the existence of something they call "God." According to a 2020 survey, 26 percent of Jewish Americans believe in the "God of the Bible," with another 50 percent believing in some "other higher power/spiritual force"; in 2014–2015, 50 percent of Israeli Jews reported believing in God with absolute certainty, with another 27 percent doing so with less certainty. Recovering earlier Jews' beliefs is more difficult, but it is notable that references to God appear throughout premodern sources, from the Hebrew Bible to Yiddish women's prayers.

Alternately, we might understand our question as being about what Jews *should* do—about whether Jewish sources present belief in God as something Jews should affirm. Texts rarely suggest that believing in God makes someone Jewish, and Judaism has few examples of creeds (statements outlining required beliefs). Nevertheless, many sources cast God as central to Jewish life. Claiming that Judaism's first commandment is a requirement to affirm God's existence, the twelfth-century philosopher Maimonides outlined specific principles that Jews must accept, including that God is one, incorporeal, the cause of the cosmos, and the only proper object of worship. Other figures link Judaism's purpose or survival to belief in the deity. One modern example is a strand of liberal Jewish thought known as ethical monotheism, which claims that a correct understanding of God is crucial to ethics and society and that Judaism's mission is to spread this understanding throughout the world. Similarly, some contemporary thinkers worry that Jewish life will prove unsustainable without God—that commitment to Jewish practice depends on affirming some sort of connection to a deity.

However, many figures disagree and insist that Jews need not, or even should not, believe in God. Some view Jewishness as an ethnic or cultural identity that people can express without any theological commitments—say, by eating certain foods or enjoying certain music. One contemporary denomination, Humanistic Judaism, describes itself as "affirming that people are independent of supernatural authority and responsible for themselves and their behavior." Some thinkers argue that after the Holocaust, positing a deity—at least one sufficiently benevolent and powerful to have prevented such horrors—is not only incoherent but offensive.

How we address our question also depends on the meaning of "believe in." Philosophers often distinguish *belief that* from *belief in*: The former involves affirming specific statements (what we do when we say, "I believe that the earth is round"), whereas the latter involves an attitude or relationship of trust (what we express when we tell a loved one, "I believe in you"). Some Jewish thinkers, such as Maimonides, focus on *belief that*, calling for Jews to affirm specific claims about God. By contrast, the Jewish philosopher Menachem Kellner argues that earlier sources emphasize *belief in*. Although biblical and classical rabbinic texts endorse many claims about God (for example, it is difficult to call for fidelity to a deity without affirming that one exists), these sources focus not on specifying such propositions but on cultivating trust in God and expressing that trust through obedience to divine commands.

Finally, how we answer our question depends on the meaning of "God." In the 2020 survey cited here, this term is linked specifically to the Hebrew Bible. Scripture does not speak with a unified voice, but it often describes God as a being who possesses characteristics associated with persons, such as emotions, and who cares about humans and acts in history.

Yet many Jews use "God" in other ways. Some medieval philosophers understand God as an impersonal cause of the cosmos that feels nothing, is unconcerned with humans, and spends eternity in contemplation. Some medieval mystics ascribe two parts to God: an unknowable core and emanations from that source possessing characteristics such as gender. Some modern thinkers use the word "God" to denote an aspect of existence they see as powerful or important, such as nature, creativity, or human cultural productions. If we take "God" to encompass all such uses, we might answer our question by emphasizing just how frequently Jews invoke this term—sometimes in surprising ways—to express core ideas and values.

## About the author

**Elias Sacks** is an associate professor of religious studies and Jewish studies and Faculty Director for Public Scholarship in the Office of Faculty Affairs at the University of Colorado Boulder. He studies Jewish thought, philosophy of religion, Jewish-Christian relations, religious ethics, and religion and politics. He is the author of *Moses Mendelssohn's Living Script: Philosophy, Practice, History, Judaism* (Indiana University Press, 2017) as well as articles on a wide range of medieval and modern thinkers.

## Suggestions for further reading

*In this book*
See also chapters 1 (Why are texts sacred to Jews?) and 24 (What does it mean to be a secular Jew?).

*Elsewhere*
Berman, Daphna, et al. "A *Moment* Symposium: Can There Be Judaism Without Belief in God?" *Moment* 36(5) (2011): 34–39.

Jacobs, Louis. "God." In *Contemporary Jewish Religious Thought: Original Essays on Critical Concepts, Movements, and Beliefs*, edited by Arthur Cohen and Paul Mendes-Flohr, 291–298. New York: The Free Press, 1987.

Kellner, Menachem. *Must a Jew Believe Anything?* Portland, OR: Littman Library of Jewish Civilization, 1999.

Pew Research Center. "Israel's Religiously Divided Society." March 8, 2016. https://www.pewresearch.org/religion/2016/03/08/israels-religiously-divided-society/.

Pew Research Center. "Jewish Americans in 2020." May 11, 2021. https://www.pewresearch.org/religion/2021/05/11/jewish-americans-in-2020/.

# 26
# Can you convert to Judaism?

## Michal Kravel-Tovi

Yes, you can! But actually, why would you? And why do you think you are worthy of being accepted as a convert? What makes you think you are able to carry the weight of a considerable set of practical and spiritual obligations? If we need to come up with a succinct answer to the ostensibly straightforward question that provides the title of this essay, it seems that "Yes, but . . ." will do it. This ambivalent, caveated response applies across the dramatically different historical, political, and religious circumstances in which Jews have lived, enacted their Judaism, and encountered others who are not Jewish—some of whom have tried to become Jews.

The slightly longer answer, as reflected in the series of questions above, is that Jewish gatekeepers, in their numerous positionings and capacities, and again in the remarkably diverse contexts in which they operate, have customarily returned the question to the candidate, the convert in the making: *Can you* convert to Judaism? The burden of proof—of religious motivation, of a persistent desire to convert despite clear awareness of the historical position of Jews as a marginalized and persecuted people, of evidenced ability and sincerity to conduct life as a Jew, whatever that means—has always rested upon the one who asked, "Can I convert to Judaism, please?"

The term "conversion" does not capture the ethnonational meanings that form an inseparable part of Jewish identity and thus of conversion to Judaism. It was not until the Rabbinic Era that a non-Jew could formally become a Jew. In the Second Temple period (586 BCE to 70 CE), Jewish communities ritualized this formality by creating conversion ceremonies: circumcision for men to physically mark membership in the covenantal community, a declaration of acceptance of the commandments before three Jewish men, and for both sexes, ritual immersion to symbolize the transition from the convert's old identity to their new one as a Jew. Of these three ritualistic components, "acceptance of the commandments" was and remains the least understood and the most volatile. The Talmudic and post-Talmudic literature on this concept is marked by ambivalence and vagueness, inviting interpretation and controversy among rabbis and scholars.

In the Middle Ages, when political prohibitions against Jewish conversion rendered it marginal, controversies stimulated only hypothetical halakhic disputes. But in the modern era, halakhic discussions about the nature of "the acceptance of the commandments" have assumed heightened urgency. From the middle of the eighteenth century, as emancipation in Europe enabled social and romantic connections between Jews and non-Jews, Jewish communities and leaders were forced to confront often divisive issues of Jewish identity, assimilation, intermarriage, and demography. Conversion has been intrinsically linked to these questions ever since.

In contemporary Jewish life, rabbinic, communal, and political attitudes to this question are far from uniform. This reflects the variety of positions toward the shifting circumstances and ensuing challenges of the Jewish experience. Resistance to religious missionizing sentiments is anchored deep in Jewish self-conceptions. These sentiments are increasingly debated on historical, ideological, pragmatic, and even moral grounds; but generally speaking, they determine the point of departure for any discussion, thus setting a quasi-apologetic tone for any alternative stance. In fact, and alongside this antimissionary formal position, some diasporic Jewish communities, Jewish denominations, and the State of Israel not only allow conversion but even embrace a proactive conversion policy, wishing and laboring to render conversion into a friendly and welcoming procedure and to ultimately secure as many converts as possible.

This is the case, for example, in the context of Israel's proconversion and Zionist policy—in response to the mass immigration and naturalization, under Israel's repatriation law, of people with a Jewish background who are not recognized as Jews by Jewish law. In the context of the high intermarriage rates of American Jews and the "continuity crisis" ambience, some communities and leaders have sought to stem the demographic loss and grapple with the "identity crisis" by reaching out to and then converting non-Jewish spouses—encouraging Jewish choices and commitments on the part of the now "in-married" couple.

Even in such contexts in which converts are clearly wanted, Jewish gatekeepers still pose the scrutinizing question "Can you convert to Judaism?" to potential converts. In Israel, adherence to relatively strict halakhic procedures is still required in the Orthodox, state-run Jewish conversion process. Rabbinic judges often interrogate converts-in-the-making of their certainty in their intent to convert: Can they really make it? Can they handle the strict requirement that is full acceptance of the commandments? To make things even more complicated, in non-Orthodox diasporic contexts, one *can* convert but does not necessarily *need* to convert to be a part of Jewish life. In the increasingly democratized, decentralized, and inclusive Jewish life of non-Orthodox American Jewish communities, formal conversion is gradually losing its role as an exclusive or even preeminent ticket to Jewish identity and belonging. One (i.e., a non-Jewish spouse) can just join in the daily communal life and voluntarily become a contributing member of the community, an active citizen. Under such circumstances, the question "Can you convert to Judaism?" perhaps should be rewritten: "Do you *really* need to convert to Judaism?"

## About the author

**Michal Kravel-Tovi** is an associate professor of sociocultural anthropology at Tel Aviv University.

## Suggestions for further reading

*In this book*
See also chapter 27 (Can Jews marry non-Jews?).

*Elsewhere*
HaLevi S"T, Rabbi Yaakov. *Strangers? Defining a Jewish Convert, Their Status, and an Exposition on the Current "Conversion Crisis."* Independently published, 2022.

Hirt, Robert, Adam Mintz, and Marc Stern, eds. *Conversion, Intermarriage, and Jewish Identity.* Jerusalem: Urim Publications, 2015.

Kravel-Tovi, Michal. *When the State Winks: The Performance of Jewish Conversion in Israel.* New York: Columbia University Press, 2017.

Sagi, Avi, and Zvi Zohar. *Transforming Identity: The Ritual Transformation from Gentile to Jew—Structure and Meaning.* New York: Continuum, 2007.

# 27
# Can Jews marry non-Jews?

## Samira K. Mehta

Historically, Jewish tradition discourages marriage outside of the religion. While there are biblical examples of Israelites who "marry out," most notably Boaz, who married Ruth the Moabite, and Moses, who married Zipporah, the daughter of a Midianite priest named Jethro, both women are framed as having converted, Ruth in the biblical text and Zipporah in an early Talmudic text, which describes her converting to monotheism, since Judaism did not yet exist. These examples have often been held up in Jewish texts as the model for marrying out: If you must marry someone from another tradition, they should convert to Judaism.

For much of Jewish history, interfaith marriage rates remained very low, largely for structural reasons: Jews lived primarily in Jewish communities where marriages were arranged. Very few people, Jewish or not, married for love, and therefore the majority of marriages fit within the expected guidelines of their communities.

This story changed slowly over the seventeenth, eighteenth, and nineteenth centuries, both because of Jewish participation in the colonization of the Americas and because of the emancipation of Jews throughout Europe. In the American colonies, Jewish communities were small, and many Jews, especially Jewish men, found themselves outside of a Jewish community and therefore found non-Jewish spouses. One Jewish woman, Abigail Frank, in eighteenth-century New York City, wrote a collection of letters that addressed the challenges of integrating into society while maintaining Jewishness by focusing on her children's marriages. In 1743, Frank wrote about her anguish at her daughter's secret marriage to a Christian, and as far as historians can tell, Frank and her daughter never spoke again. Despite the fact that Frank's husband was a prominent member of a synagogue, all of the Frank children who remained in the Americas married non-Jews, and none of the couple's American grandchildren were Jewish.

This pattern held true for much of the eighteenth and nineteenth centuries: When Jews married out, they were often lost to the Jewish community, though the work of historian Anne Rose suggests that this trend was shaped by gender. When Jewish men married Christian women, their children were usually raised as Christians, but when Christian men married Jewish women, the home often remained largely Jewish. European Jewish communities also had higher rates of interfaith marriage in times and areas where Jews were more assimilated. While we do not have statistics about Jewish interfaith marriage in these time periods, we do know that other than the conversion of spouses, there was not a widespread attempt to integrate interfaith families into Jewish community.

After the peak of Jewish immigration in the early twentieth century, the rate of interfaith marriage was low for the first few decades but rose as Jews became more assimilated and accepted as "American." By the 1990s, about 50 percent of American Jews married non-Jews, most of whom were Christian, had been raised in Christian households, or were from secular families who celebrated Christian holidays.

In the 1970s and 1980s, because of the high rates of interfaith marriage and the fear that the Jewish community would shrink because of assimilation resulting from interfaith marriage, there was a huge controversy over whether rabbis should perform intermarriages. Would it tacitly give support to interfaith marriages and therefore be "bad for the Jews," or would it welcome interfaith couples, who would otherwise be lost to Judaism, into Jewish community and therefore be "good for the Jews"?

Some rabbis in the Reform, Reconstructionist, and Renewal movements—modern Judaism's more liberal branches—decided that they would be willing to perform weddings as long as the couples agreed to keep a Jewish home. That said, this was not an era of high Jewish observance, so having a Jewish home was often less about Jewish practices like lighting candles for Shabbat and more about keeping Christian elements, like holidays, out of the home—at least until children were old enough to go to Hebrew school.

Conventional wisdom agreed, without much support from science, that raising a child in a home with multiple religions would be problematic for the children. That said, by the turn of the twenty-first century, more interfaith couples have found resources for raising children in multiple traditions with no apparent ill effects.

In the contemporary United States, interfaith marriage is increasingly a fact of Jewish life, though it remains controversial. In 2023, the Conservative movement not only reiterated that its rabbis could not perform interfaith marriages; it also forbade them from attending interfaith marriages, including marriages within their families. Meanwhile, in 2024, the

Reform movement, which is the largest movement of American Judaism, joined the Renewal, Reconstructionist, and secular humanist movements in allowing people in interfaith marriages to be ordained as rabbis.

Some pieces of this article were originally published in *The Conversation*.

## About the author

**Samira K. Mehta** is the director of Jewish studies and an associate professor of women's and gender studies and Jewish studies at the University of Colorado Boulder. She is the author of *Beyond Chrismukkah: The Christian-Jewish Interfaith Family in the United States* (UNC Press, 2018) and *The Racism of People Who Love You: Essays on Mixed Race Belonging* (Beacon, 2023) and is currently completing a book called *God Bless the Pill: Contraception and Sexuality in American Religion*.

## Suggestions for further reading

*In this book*
See also chapter 26 (Can you convert to Judaism?).

*Elsewhere*
McGinity, Keren. *Still Jewish: A History of Women and Intermarriage in America*. New York: New York University Press, 2009.

Mehta, Samira K. *Beyond Chrismukkah: The Christian-Jewish Interfaith Family in the United States*. Chapel Hill: University of North Carolina Press, 2018.

Mehta, Samira K. "I Chose Judaism, but Christmas Cookies Chose Me: Food, Identity, and Familial Religious Practice in Christian/Jewish Blended Families." In *Religion, Food, and Eating in North America*, edited by Benjamin E. Zeller, et al., 154–172. New York: Columbia University Press, 2014.

Mehta, Samira K. "Negotiating the Interfaith Marriage Bed: Religious Difference and Sexual Intimacies." *Theology and Sexuality* 18(1) (2012): 19–41.

Mehta, Samira K., and Brett Krutzsch. "The Changing Jewish Family: Jewish Communal Responses to Interfaith and Same-Sex Marriage." *American Jewish History* 104(4) (2020): 553–577.

Rose, Anne C. *Beloved Strangers: Interfaith Families in Nineteenth-Century America*. Cambridge, MA: Harvard University Press, 2001.

Thompson, Jennifer A. *Jewish on Their Own Terms: How Intermarried Couples Are Changing American Judaism*. New Brunswick, NJ: Rutgers University Press, 2013.

# 28
# How do Jews think about non-Jews?

## Ishay Rosen-Zvi

In the Bible, the term *goy* simply means "nation," and Israel is considered one nation among many, albeit a "holy nation" (Ex. 19:5). Biblical law employs two main terms to describe non-Israelites: the *nokhri* and the *ger*. The *nokhri*, or foreigner, stands in contrast to "your brother" in the book of Deuteronomy (see 14:21; 15:3; 17:15; 23:21; and 29:21). However, this does not create a strict binary distinction; different peoples and categories are treated distinctly, such as the Canaanite tribes (e.g., Deut. 7:1; 20:17) and the various nations surrounding Canaan, each addressed with a different attitude (Deut. 23:4–9).

The *ger*, or resident alien, is someone who is not part of the Israelites' genealogy but still lives among them, becoming part of their community. In biblical texts such as Numbers, the *ger* is subject to various prohibitions and commandments, much like the Israelite: "There shall be one law for you and for the *ger*" (9:14; 15:15). In Deuteronomy, however, the *ger* is distinguished from "the holy people" (14:21) and is not bound by all commandments. Yet even there, the *ger* is described as "your *ger*," and thus the Israelites are obligated to care for the resident aliens (14:29), and they are even considered part of the covenant community (29:9–10).

Jewish texts from the Hellenistic and early Roman periods (third century BCE to second century CE) draw a variety of distinctions, but they do not yet merge into a single, all-encompassing binary distinction between Jews and non-Jews. It is worth noting that chauvinism and even hostility toward others can exist without a unified concept of non-Jews (as seen in the second-century BCE book of Jubilees). Nonetheless, the absence of strict binary divisions may help explain the fluidity of the boundaries of the elect group, which could expand (as in eschatological works from Enoch to Paul) or contract (as in sectarian ideologies).

In rabbinic literature (second to fifth centuries CE), attitudes toward non-Jews range from tolerance to hostility. However, beyond this diversity, we observe the crystallization of a stable Jew/non-Jew binary distinction, accompanied by two significant phenomena: (a) the elimination of in-between categories and (b) the emergence of the conversion ceremony.

The rabbinic stabilization of the Jew/non-Jew distinction as a binary system involved a concerted effort to eliminate the hybrid identities seen in earlier texts, placing them within one of these two categories. The biblical *ger* was reinterpreted as "one who converted"; Judaizers who did not convert (the "God-fearers") were categorized as non-Jews, and uncircumcised or assimilated Jews, previously seen as having left the Jewish people (e.g., in 1 and 2 Maccabees, Philo, and Josephus), were now defined as sinful Jews.

As the distinction between Jews and non-Jews became more clearly defined, the conversion process was institutionalized. A sharp, distinct boundary replaced previous ambiguities, diffusion, and ontological gradations, and conversion became a means of instantaneous, ontological transformation. As the Talmud says in reference to the immersion ritual of conversion, "One who immersed and emerged [from the water] is an Israelite in all regards" (*b. Yev.* 47b).

Many new ideas about non-Jews emerged in medieval Judaism, influenced by both Islamic and Christian contexts. Two contrasting developments, both manifesting in twelfth-century Al-Andalus, stand out: On one hand, universalistic ideas inspired by Islamic philosophy emphasized shared humanity beyond ethnic distinctions (most radically in Maimonidean philosophy); on the other, the distinction between Jews and non-Jews took on new physical and metaphysical dimensions (notably in Judah Halevi's philosophy).

In contemporary Jewish life, we witness a growing divide between how the Jew/non-Jew distinction is approached in the two largest Jewish centers: the United States and Israel. In the US, there is an ongoing, lively discussion about intermarriage and the inclusion of non-Jewish partners and children in Jewish communities. According to a 2020 survey, 72 percent of non-Orthodox Jews who married since 2000 chose non-Jewish spouses. As a result, many Jews are adopting a "big tent" approach, where non-Jews become part of the Jewish community even without formal conversion, leading to a nonbinary understanding of Jewish identity (sometimes termed "postethnic Judaism").

In Israel, the Jew/non-Jew distinction is structured very differently, primarily because it is not entirely voluntary but regulated by state laws and records. For instance, non-Jews cannot legally marry Jews, and immigrants without Jewish ancestry can rarely obtain citizenship. Meanwhile, the Law of Return allows a broader range of individuals than Orthodox Jewish law defines as Jewish to claim rights in Israel. This has led to the formation of a category of immigrants connected to the Jewish state but considered non-Jews according to state law. This, in turn, fosters processes of informal assimilation, expanding the borders of Jewishness while simultaneously sparking anxiety, prompting ongoing state-sponsored conversion efforts.

## About the author

**Ishay Rosen-Zvi** teaches rabbinic literature and is the chair of the Department of Jewish Philosophy and Talmud at Tel Aviv University.

## Suggestions for further reading

### In this book
See also chapters 26 (Can you convert to Judaism?), 27 (Can Jews marry non-Jews?), and 58 (What is the role of Judaism in the State of Israel?).

### Elsewhere
Blidstein, Gerald J. "Who Is Not a Jew: The Medieval Discussion." *Israel Law Review* 11 (1976): 369–390.

Cohen, Shaye J. D. *The Beginnings of Jewishness: Boundaries, Varieties, Uncertainties*. Berkeley: University of California Press, 1999.

Kellner, Menachem. *We Are Not Alone: A Maimonidean Theology of the Other*. Brookline, MA: Academic Studies Press, 2021.

Magid, Shaul. *American Post-Judaism: Identity and Renewal in a Postethnic Society*. Bloomington: Indiana University Press, 2013.

Olyan, Saul. *Rites and Rank: Hierarchy in Biblical Representations of Cult*. Princeton, NJ: Princeton University Press, 2000.

Ophir, Adi, and Ishay Rosen-Zvi. *Goy: Israel's Others and the Birth of the Gentile*. Oxford: Oxford University Press, 2018.

Stern, Yedidia Z., and Netanel Fisher, eds. *Conversion in Israel: Vision, Achievements, and Challenges*. Jerusalem: The Israeli Institute for Democracy, 2018.

# 29
# What do Jews think happens after you die?

Matthew J. Suriano

Jewish beliefs vary regarding what happens after you die. Today, different Jewish communities have a wide variety of ideas about what happens after death, from bodily resurrection, heavenly rewards, and hell to a sense that humans cannot know what really happens after we die. The general notion of the afterlife is known as *olam ha-ba* (the world to come), which can be associated with resurrection, as well as the Garden of Eden as a heavenly locale. These associated concepts, however, are often left vague and undefined. This can be explained in various ways, beginning with the uncertainty of death. Some of it is due to Judaism's strong emphasis on life.

But the ambiguity also stems from the ancient texts, where there is little agreement and no systematic treatment of the afterlife. For example, Josephus tells us that the major Jewish groups of the late Second Temple period disagreed about whether the soul was immortal, with the Sadducees denying the concept entirely. In the Torah, we find detailed instructions regarding the ritual impurity of death (Num. 19:11–22), but there are no guidelines for funerals. Heaven and hell are absent from biblical literature. The closest equivalent to the netherworld is *Sheol*, which is often depicted as a dark, shadowy place that everyone goes to after they die (Gen. 37:35; 44:29–31). Postmortem judgment is absent outside of a late reference to resurrection in Daniel 12:2. Yet there is little clarity in this passage as to what the contrasting references to eternal life and everlasting abhorrence might mean. Moreover, resurrection is referenced in only two other passages, Isaiah 26:19 and Ezekiel 37. In the latter, the famous "valley of dry bones," resurrection is used to portray the revival of a people rather than the individual status of the dead. The belief in resurrection became more prominent in later Judaism, as evident in the Mishnah and Talmud.

So what was the concept of the afterlife in ancient Israel and early Judaism? Some insight can be gleaned from idioms for death found in the

Bible. In Genesis, the phrase "gathered to his people" is used to describe the death of a patriarch (Abraham, Isaac, Ishmael, and Jacob). In Kings and the parallel passages in Chronicles, the phrase used for the death of a king is "lay down with his fathers." Both phrases evoke a collective ancestry and reveal a postmortem ideal of being reunited with dead kin. This ideal is consistent with the importance the biblical writers placed on the family tomb. The patriarch Jacob, on his deathbed in Egypt, instructs his sons to bring his body back to the land of Canaan to be reburied in the Cave of Machpelah (Gen. 49:28–33). Abraham purchased this family tomb for the burial of Sarah, and there Jacob wished to be reunited with Abraham, Isaac, and the matriarchs Sarah and Rebecca. The desire to be buried with one's family is also clear in the words of Barzilai, who chose to remain in his village rather than accompany David to Jerusalem because he wanted to be buried in the same tomb as his mother and father (2 Sam. 19:35–38).

The importance of the family tomb can be identified in the archaeological remains of tombs and cemeteries in the southern Levant from the Iron Age (1200 to 500 BCE) through the early Roman period. Iron Age tombs from the Kingdom of Judah reveal practices of collective burial inside caves, which served as family tombs. Collection pits, called repositories, carved alongside burial benches in the walls of a typical rock-cut burial chamber, allowed families to inter multiple generations inside a single tomb. The bones of former interments would be transferred to the repository, allowing the benches to be reused for subsequent burials. This practice resumed after the exile and was prominent during the late Second Temple period, as seen in the elaborate tomb complexes surrounding Jerusalem. During this period, repositories were replaced by ossuaries, small stone boxes used to store bones. Often these ossuaries had epitaphs inscribed in Hebrew, Aramaic, or Greek naming the dead and indicating kinship affiliation.

In ancient Israel and early Judaism, the attitude toward death was concerned less with where you went after you died and more with things related to family and legacy. Where you were buried and how you died were important issues because they could affect the continuation of your memory. It is for these reasons that the words of the ancient proverb "The memory of the righteous is a blessing" (Prov. 10:7) still resonate today.

## About the author

**Matthew J. Suriano** is an associate professor in the Joseph and Rebecca Meyerhoff Center for Jewish Studies at the University of Maryland. He teaches classes on the Hebrew Bible, the archaeology of ancient Israel, and religions of ancient Western Asia.

## Suggestions for further reading

*In this book*
See also chapter 2 (What is the Torah?).

*Elsewhere*
Avery-Peck, Alan, and Jacob Neusner, eds. *Judaism in Late Antiquity 4: Death, Life-After-Death, Resurrection and the World-to-Come in the Judaisms of Antiquity*. New York: Brill, 1999.

Kraemer, David. *The Meanings of Death in Rabbinic Judaism*. London: Routledge, 1999.

Sonia, Kerry M. *Caring for the Dead in Ancient Israel* (volume 27). Atlanta, GA: Society of Biblical Literature Press, 2020.

Stavrakopoulou, Francesca. *Land of Our Fathers: The Roles of Ancestor Veneration in Biblical Land Claims* (volume 473). London: A&C Black, 2010.

Suriano, Matthew. *A History of Death in the Hebrew Bible*. Oxford: Oxford University Press, 2018.

# 30
# What do Jews believe about the messiah?

## Martin Kavka

In the 1990s, I was a church organist. I supplemented my graduate student stipend by substituting at various churches when their main organists were on vacation. One week, as I was heading to the pastor's office to pick up my paycheck, a woman walked up to me after a church service and said, "The pastor tells me you're Jewish. May I ask you a question?" I feared what might be coming but nonetheless replied, "Sure!" And then it happened: "Why did the Jews reject Jesus Christ as the Messiah, as their redeemer?" she asked. Without missing a beat, I replied, "Because Jesus did not defeat the Roman Empire, and most Jews in Jesus's time expected a messiah who would lead them to political independence." Shocked by the quickness of my response, she made her excuses and left.

Our conversation signals that both Jews and Christians frequently see the dividing line between them in terms of who the Messiah is or isn't. The term "messiah" comes from a Hebrew word for "anointed one"; its Greek counterpart is the origin of the word "Christ," which Christians use to describe Jesus of Nazareth. When the kings of ancient Israel began their rule, their coronation ritual involved being anointed with oil as a way of signaling their authority to act on behalf of God. We see this in several biblical texts, especially in Psalm 2, where the king is described as the Lord's anointed/Messiah and whom God describes as "my king" and "my son." There, the anointed king's explicit task is to defeat the enemies of the people of Israel (Ps. 2:8-9). As a result, Jews have good textual evidence for thinking that someone who does not defeat the enemies of the people of Israel—and especially someone who is killed by those enemies, as Jesus was killed by the Romans—cannot have a justifiable claim to being the Messiah, sent by God to redeem the people from political dependence on other nations and engender an era of stability and prosperity.

By the time that Jesus lived, the idea of what messiah-hood involved had begun to take on a greater variety of forms. Perhaps the Messiah was a priestly figure and not necessarily a kingly one, perhaps the Messiah was supernatural and not necessarily human, or perhaps the idea emphasized a messianic era and not a messianic person. But the kingly ideology remained dominant among Jews. For this reason, to the extent that Jews think about the Messiah at all, they believe that the Messiah is still to come.

Some Jews have focused on techniques for achieving messianic arrival in the near future; in the Middle Ages, a variety of texts focus on performing divine commands, perfecting one's intellect, or doing magic. Today, those Jews who do not explicitly care about the Messiah nonetheless incorporate a messianism into a general hope for peace in the distant future. And the subset of the Chabad Lubavitch sect of Orthodoxy, who believe that the late Rabbi Menachem Mendel Schneersohn (1902–1994) was the Messiah and will soon return, remains controversial within Chabad and Judaism more broadly *and still* remains within the Jewish fold.

It is worth thinking about the effects of the belief that the Messiah or a messianic era is still to come. The German Jewish philosopher Hermann Cohen (1842–1918) associated Jewish messianism with Jews' ethical role in the countries where they lived, working to ensure that all were meaningfully integrated into the fabric of the nation-state. For Cohen, this was indeed messianic work; Jews, like the suffering servant in Isaiah 53 (commonly associated with the Messiah), should see it as their divinely ordained task to ensure that those with less would have more.

Nonetheless, it should not be taken for granted that this kind of ethical life, one that dials up the patience of a political wonk to a deep existential intensity, is an easy one. As the Jewish historian Gershom Scholem famously pointed out in the late 1950s, the tension of messianic expectation—waiting, only to be followed by more waiting—can lead people to act out in ways that verify to themselves that the messianic era either has come or is close at hand. This risks producing a "blazing landscape of redemption" that may not end up bringing stability or prosperity. For Scholem, this risk was endemic to the Zionist enterprise to create a Jewish state.

At present, news stories about how the State of Israel and various Jewish citizens relate to Palestinians in the occupied territories provide, at the very least, opportunities to assess the costs and benefits of that risk. So does the prayer that religious Jews commonly utter in their synagogues and temples on behalf of the State of Israel, since it associates the creation of that state with "the first flowerings of our redemption." To ask what Jews think about the Messiah can consequently also be to ask how much Jews and non-Jews need redemption, and when they need it to come (or have already come), in order for their lives to be bearable.

## About the author

**Martin Kavka** is professor and chair of the Department of Religion at Florida State University. Now in the twilight of his career, he is most proud of his editing work, including (with Aline Kalbian) a decade as coeditor of the *Journal of Religious Ethics*, and (with Anne Dailey and Lital Levy) the volume *Unsettling Jewish Knowledge: Text, Contingency, Desire* (University of Pennsylvania Press, 2023).

## Suggestions for further reading

*In this book*
See also chapters 33 (Why don't Jews believe in Jesus?) and 56 (What is Zionism?).

*Elsewhere*
Cohen, Hermann. *Religion of Reason: Out of the Sources of Judaism*. Translated by Simon Kaplan. Atlanta, GA: Scholars Press, 1995.

Reed, Annette Yoshiko. "Messianism Between Judaism and Christianity." In *Rethinking the Messianic Idea in Judaism*, edited by Michael L. Morgan and Steven Weitzman, 23–62. Bloomington: Indiana University Press, 2015.

Scholem, Gershom. "Toward an Understanding of the Messianic Idea in Judaism." In *The Messianic Idea in Judaism and Other Essays on Jewish Spirituality*. Translated by Michael Meyer, 1–36. New York: Schocken, 1995.

Schwartz, Howard. "Myths of the Messiah." In *Tree of Souls: The Mythology of Judaism*, 481–524. New York: Oxford University Press, 2004.

# 31
# Are there angels and demons in Judaism?

## Sara Ronis

Judaism has traditionally been understood as a monotheistic religion, but that doesn't mean that it hasn't had a robust world of intermediary beings who are more powerful than humans but not gods themselves—angels, demons, and more.

The Hebrew Bible contains numerous references to nameless "messengers of the Lord," many of whom appear to be angelic. The latest book in the Hebrew Bible, Daniel, contains an even more developed angelology, with two angels, Gabriel and Michael, each given a name and a persona. Biblical references to demons are more obscure, and it's not often clear whether the Bible is referring to a wild animal, a demon as we might think of it today, or a different religious community's god.

The Second Temple period (roughly the sixth century BCE to 70 CE) saw an exponential growth in Jewish texts about intermediary beings. Second Temple narratives like the book of Tobit tell stories in which angels and demons affect human lives. Biblical retellings such as the book of Jubilees and 1 Enoch recount how angels taught humankind esoteric knowledge and how angelic misbehavior led to the creation of demons. The Second Temple historian Josephus describes exorcisms, and the Dead Sea Scrolls testify to a large body of incantations that are intended to protect their users from demonic harm. It is clear that the Jewish belief in angels and demons became widespread during this period.

While some scholars point to the cultural interactions between Jews and the Persian Empire during this period as spurring the growth of Jewish interest in intermediary beings, it is important to note that ancient Jews did not simply adopt foreign entities. When ancient Jews thought about angels and demons, they did so *as Jews*, integrating these beings into their own theological understandings of a world created by a single God who had ultimate control over their lives. And because ancient Jews had diverse theological understandings of their place in that world, they also developed diverse understandings of angels and demons, with some seeing angels and demons as two sides in an epic cosmological battle between good and evil and others seeing them as relating to human beings in smaller-scale ways.

After the Second Temple was destroyed and a new Jewish elite known as the rabbis emerged, angels and demons became more holistically integrated into Jewish law and legal discourse. The Babylonian Talmud describes angels and demons studying Torah, enforcing rabbinic law, and offering extraordinary insights to the followers of the rabbis. Jewish liturgy and mystical texts evoke angels and offer pictures of heavenly realms populated by numerous classes of angels. Ritual texts mention angels and demons in terms of both potential dangers and available modes of protection.

In the medieval period, two distinct Jewish positions on angels and demons emerged: Some, most famously the Jewish philosopher and legal codifier Maimonides, rejected the existence of demons and downplayed the theological importance of angels. Others, including Rabbi Judah Halevi, insisted that both angels and demons were important parts of Judaism. And while Jewish philosophers debated the existence and function of intermediary beings, Jewish mystics and kabbalists were developing their own rich understanding of these beings and how they functioned in the human and heavenly realms.

With the rise of the European Enlightenment and its emphasis on rationalism, Jewish beliefs in angels and demons began to diminish among some Ashkenazi Jewish communities, dismissed as superstition or as foreign to an original spirit of Judaism. The founders of the German Reform movement, for example, removed references to angels from the Reform prayerbook. Jewish belief in demons was downplayed across a wider swath of the Jewish world in light of a historical Christian antisemitic association of Jews and demons. However, Sephardi communities, Hasidic communities, and many traditional Ashkenazi orthodox communities continued, and indeed continue, to retain a much more active sense of the presence and activity of these intermediary beings in their lives.

While talk of angels and demons may have diminished in some Ashkenazi public contexts, even there it often survived in more domestic spheres, emerging as folktales and rituals centered on major life cycle events like marriage and pregnancy. And as the modern world has become more comfortable with the mystical and mythical, in recent years, modern Reform prayerbooks have reintegrated some of the traditional references to angels into their liturgies.

Today, while many Jews have an active belief in angels (and to a lesser extent demons), others do not believe that such beings exist at all, and still others remain agnostic. Ultimately, the answers to the question "Do Jews believe in angels and demons?" are as diverse as Jews themselves.

## About the author

**Sara Ronis** is an associate professor of theology at St. Mary's University, Texas. She holds a PhD in ancient Judaism specializing in the Talmud from Yale University and a BA in Near Eastern and Judaic studies from Brandeis University. Her research interests include rabbinic subjectivity and definitions of personhood, constructions of gender and authority in rabbinic literature, and rabbinic imaginings of and encounters with the other in late antiquity. She is the author of *Demons in the Details: Demonic Discourse and Rabbinic Culture in Late Antique Babylonia* (University of California Press, 2022).

## Suggestions for further reading

*In this book*
See also chapters 3 (What is the Talmud?), 7 (What is a rabbi?), 20 (What are the differences among Reform, Conservative, Reconstructionist, and Orthodox Judaism?), and 21 (What are the differences among Ashkenazi, Sephardi, and Mizrahi Jews?).

*Elsewhere*
Ahuvia, Mika. *On My Right Michael, on My Left Gabriel: Angels in Ancient Jewish Culture.* Oakland: University of California Press, 2021.

Ronis, Sara. *Demons in the Details: Demonic Discourse and Rabbinic Culture in Late Antique Babylonia.* Oakland: University of California Press, 2022.

Schwartz, Howard, and Stephen Fieser. *Invisible Kingdoms: Jewish Tales of Angels, Spirits, and Demons.* New York: HarperCollins Publishers, 2002.

Trachtenberg, Joshua, and Moshe Idel. *Jewish Magic and Superstition: A Study in Folk Religion.* Philadelphia: University of Pennsylvania Press, 2004.

# 32
# Who are crypto-Jews?

Sasha M. Ward

Crypto-Judaism refers to the clandestine observance of Judaism while outwardly claiming to be part of another religious faith, and crypto-Jews are its practitioners. The classical origins of crypto-Judaism can be found in the medieval Iberian Peninsula under Byzantine emperor Heraclius (r. 610–641 CE), who facilitated the first major conversion of Jews (approximately ninety-thousand individuals) to Christianity. Following the antisemitic campaign led by Spanish cleric Ferrant Martínez in 1378 that resulted in the deaths of one-third of Spanish Jewry, thousands of Jews converted to Catholicism. Otherwise known as *conversos* or *Marranos*, many of these Spanish Jewish converts to Catholicism remained attached to Judaism by practicing religious traditions in secret (such as keeping Shabbat and abstaining from the consumption of pork) and keeping close familial and social ties to normative Jewish communities. As religious observance became increasingly centered around the home, *conversa* women were involved more intimately in Judaizing practices. While some *conversos* accepted baptism under threat of death, others did so to unburden themselves of exorbitant taxation and gain the economic, social, and political advantages of Christian status.

As a result of *conversos*' increased prominence in social and commercial spheres, the first statute of blood purity (*limpieza de sangre*) was enacted in Toledo in 1449, which effectively barred all *conversos* (or descendants thereof) from holding public or private office on the basis of their perceived Jewish heritage. Continued anxieties surrounding crypto-Judaism and the insincerity of Jewish converts to Christianity led the Catholic monarchs Queen Isabella I of Castile (r. 1474–1504) and King Ferdinand II of Aragon (r. 1479–1516) to establish the Tribunal of the Holy Office of the Inquisition in 1478, with the purpose of eliminating crypto-Judaism from the Iberian Peninsula by separating out Judaizers from sincere converts through persecution. While on the surface this judicial institution sought to prevent heresy, the Inquisition functioned to centralize state power and enforce religious homogeneity through the widespread investigation, persecution, and torture of allegedly Judaizing *conversos*. Those deemed to be crypto-Jews were publicly condemned in *autos-de-fé*, public ceremonies in which the Inquisition tortured, killed, or burned alive those it found guilty of Judaizing acts. When the initial attempts to distinguish those remaining Spanish Jews from normative Christians proved insufficient, the Catholic monarchs enacted the Edict of Expulsion on March 31, 1492, which demanded Spanish Jewry to accept baptism or face expulsion. As many as two hundred thousand Jews converted to Christianity, thereby bolstering the existing crypto-Jewish community with new members.

Jews who did not convert to Catholicism went into exile in Portugal, North Africa, and Italy, where a series of political developments led to additional crypto-Jewish communities. In 1497, King Manuel I of Portugal (r. 1495–1521) ordered the forced conversions of all Portuguese Jewry, which led to the creation of a large crypto-Jewish community who thereafter referred to themselves as the *Nação* (Nation). As the Spanish Inquisition did not establish branches in Portugal until 1536, crypto-Judaism in Portugal developed more robustly, permitting *conversos* to obtain positions in Portuguese commerce and finance and create viable social and mercantile networks. With the unification of Spain and Portugal in 1580, the Spanish Inquisition began to increase its persecution of Portuguese *conversos* for Judaizing. As a result, thousands of *conversos* left the Iberian Peninsula, reverted to Judaism, and established normative communities in Amsterdam, Hamburg, Bordeaux, and Leghorn.

Crypto-Judaism and crypto-Jews are not only confined to Christian Europe but also found in the seventeenth-century Ottoman Empire with the Salonican Dönme (Ottoman Turkish for "those who turn"), the descendants of the followers of Smyrna (Izmir) pseudomessiah Shabbatai Tzvi (1626–1676), who joined Tzvi's apostasy into Islam in 1666. The Dönme of Salonica followed a hybrid religious tradition of Lurianic Kabbalah (Isaac Luria, 1534–1572) and Tzvi's own messianic doctrines (known as the "Eighteen Commandments"), practiced endogamy, and established their own religious, social, legal, and educational institutions. By the nineteenth century, this original group of some three hundred families grew to between three thousand and five thousand individuals. Due to their official status as Muslims, Salonican Dönme secured high positions in the Ottoman bureaucracy and monopolized trade in important sectors like textiles and manufacturing.

Dönme had regular contact with Sephardi Jews in Salonican Masonic lodges and through participation in the Committee of Union and Progress (CUP). Following the Greek-Turkish population exchange in 1923,

Salonican Dönme resettled in Turkish metropolitan centers such as Istanbul and Izmir, where they increasingly assimilated to secular Turkish culture. In contemporary Turkey, there is a small number of practicing Dönme, particularly the Karakaş sect, that remain largely insular, and a larger diaspora of Yakubi Dönme, who are coming forward to educate the scholarly community about their religious traditions, which have largely been obscured from historical view.

The convergence of Sabbatianism and crypto-Judaism continued throughout the modern Polish-Lithuanian Commonwealth with the emergence of Jakob (Jakub) ben Jehuda Leib Frank (1726–1791), a follower of Tzvi who claimed to be the final incarnation of the messiah and led a mass voluntary conversion to Roman Catholicism in 1759. Frankists practiced a distinctive confluence of Jewish, Christian, and Islamic religious rites and formed sizable communities in cities like Lwów (Lviv), where this strand of crypto-Judaism was practiced openly. (Some estimate there to have been some twenty-four thousand Frankists in Poland toward the end of the eighteenth century). Today, there are no longer any communities of practicing Frankists.

Throughout history and across geographies, crypto-Judaism has been practiced by a diverse array of Jewish communities in the face of religious persecution and against the grain of orthodox religious observance and halakhic traditions.

### About the author

**Sasha M. Ward** is a PhD candidate in Near and Middle Eastern studies at the University of Washington. Her research focuses on Sephardi Jewish life in the Eastern Mediterranean, with an emphasis on the late Ottoman and early Turkish Republican periods. Her dissertation explores the political weaponization of antisemitic conspiratorial rhetoric by the Turkish government throughout the twentieth century. Specifically, Sasha is interested in the quotidian history of the real descendants of those crypto-Jews who followed the "mystical messiah" Shabbatai Sevi (seventeenth century) into Islam (known broadly as Dönme), and their imagined political, social, and economic influence.

### Suggestions for further reading

*In this book*
See also chapters 10 (What does kosher mean?), 17 (What do Jews do on the Sabbath?), and 30 (What do Jews believe about the messiah?).

*Elsewhere*

Ingram, Kevin, ed. *Conversos and Moriscos in Late Medieval Spain and Beyond. Volume 1: Departures and Change.* Boston: Brill, 2009.

Leibman, Laura. *Messianism, Secrecy, and Mysticism: A New Interpretation of Early American Jewish Life.* Portland, OR: Vallentine Mitchell, 2013.

Maciejko, Pawel. *The Mixed Multitude: Jacob Frank and the Frankist Movement, 1755–1816.* Philadelphia: University of Pennsylvania Press, 2015.

Ray, Jonathan. *Jewish Life in Medieval Spain: A New History.* Philadelphia: University of Pennsylvania Press, 2023.

Şişman, Cengiz. *The Burden of Silence: Sabbatai Sevi and the Evolution of the Ottoman-Turkish Dönmes.* Oxford: Oxford University Press, 2015.

# Judaism and Other Religions

# 33
# Why don't Jews believe in Jesus?

## Adam Gregerman

In his lifetime, Jesus was viewed by Jews he met just as they viewed other first-century Jewish preachers and miracle-workers. Some were impressed by his words and deeds, and some even followed him, while others were indifferent or skeptical. Only after his death, when his followers began to make increasingly bold and unprecedented claims about his resurrection and even divine status, did the idea of "belief" (and "unbelief") emerge. The message these Jewish followers preached about a man tragically executed by Roman rulers who later transcendently appeared to his followers was apparently met with disbelief or derision from most fellow Jews. Our evidence for this is found only in the New Testament (there are no contemporaneous Jewish sources), which contains not eyewitness accounts but collections of sources in letters and narratives gathered together by editors a few generations after Jesus. Though they tell the story of Jesus and his times, they simultaneously incorporate the sorts of theological claims made about Jesus at the end of the first century as well as the largely negative responses they received from other Jews.

What did his later followers (including the Gospels' authors) preach, and why did few Jews believe them? The sources highlight a theological clash. Jesus in the Gospel of John says, "The Father and I are one," claiming at least a semidivine status (John 10:30). Most of "the Jews," John angrily admits, found this unacceptable because they thought it compromised monotheism. They likely saw other claims about his status as unacceptable or false. He is often called "Lord," recalling the title used for God in the Hebrew Bible, and people are told that "every knee should bend" when his name is heard during worship. Likewise, Jesus (or his followers) proclaimed he was Israel's messiah and had "conquered the world," but then he faced a brutal and ignominious execution. While messianic expectations were not uniform in this period, Jews widely believed that a messiah would inaugurate an epochal change in the world. However, injustice and oppression under Roman rule continued after Jesus as before; the Romans destroyed Jerusalem and its temple, for example.

Importantly, Jesus was not unusual in this regard. The Jewish historian Josephus writes of more than a dozen other Jewish messiahs in this period. Most yearned for an imminent end to Israel's present low status, and most were tragically and violently repressed by Rome. The Jesus movement surely appeared to most Jews who knew of it to fit this relatively common model. Thus, assigning Jesus the title "messiah" (Greek: *Christos*) required a profound reinterpretation by his followers, since there was no precedent for a messiah who died and was resurrected. In light of the seeming disconfirmation of expected visible changes because of Jesus's death, his followers' promise that if one believed their claims, one would have one's sins forgiven, receive the Holy Spirit, or have eternal life appears not to have persuaded many Jews.

Throughout the New Testament, unsuccessful preaching to Jews prompts anger and a painful sense of betrayal by Jesus's Jewish followers, apparent in sometimes vicious invective. In some cases, unbelieving Jews are said to be sons of the devil and murderers, accusations that came not from Jesus but from the times of the Gospel writers, when a Jewish mission seems to have failed. In particular, accusations that (sometimes all) Jews are responsible for Jesus's death on a Roman cross were surely a redirection of culpability for his death against fellow Jews for their failure to accept claims made by Jesus's followers. Concomitantly, the unexpected influx into a previously Jewish movement of non-Jews, who were invited to believe in a dying-and-rising cosmic savior and to reject observance of Torah law, dramatically changed the nature and demography of the movement. This presumably helps explain why Jews, and even Jewish believers, were increasingly not welcomed in churches and not interested in joining.

For centuries, the small number of Jews who knew of these claims about Jesus seldom actually engaged theologically with what became an almost-exclusively non-Jewish religion called Christianity. Our sources are sparse, but for many centuries, almost none seem to have even thought of it as related to Judaism. As much as anything, indifference and ignorance explain why Jews did not believe in Jesus (except for a small number who converted for genuine spiritual or—in modern times—social reasons). Finally, Christians' hostile views of Jews as Christ-killers and as blind to their own scriptures, expressed with increasing vehemence over time, were almost never conducive to conversion. More positively, in the last few decades, Jews and Christians have engaged in constructive dialogues about Jesus and his Jewishness. Without polemical or missionary motives, they have sought to better understand him in his Jewish context and to explore the theological implications of his Jewish identity.

## About the author

**Adam Gregerman**, PhD, is a professor of Jewish studies in the Department of Theology and Religious Studies and associate director of the Institute for Jewish-Catholic Relations at Saint Joseph's University in Philadelphia, Pennsylvania. He is the author of *Building on the Ruins of the Temple: Apologetics and Polemics in Early Christianity and Rabbinic Judaism* (Mohr Siebeck, 2016) and numerous book chapters and articles in journals such as *Theology Today*, *Journal of Ecumenical Studies*, *Modern Theology*, *Studies in Christian-Jewish Relations*, and *Interpretation*.

## Suggestions for further reading

*In this book*
See also chapter 30 (What do Jews believe about the messiah?).

*Elsewhere*
Levine, Amy-Jill, and Marc Zvi Brettler, eds. *The Jewish Annotated New Testament* (2nd edition). New York: Oxford University Press, 2017.

Sandmel, Samuel. *We Jews and Jesus: Exploring Theological Differences for Mutual Understanding*. Woodstock, VT: Jewish Lights, 2006.

Setzer, Claudia J. *Jewish Responses to Early Christians: History and Polemics, 30–150 C.E.* Minneapolis, MN: Fortress, 1994.

# 34
# Was Jesus Jewish?

## Meira Z. Kensky

The short answer is yes, Jesus was Jewish. The longer answer is that all of our extant sources say that Jesus was Jewish. The even longer answer involves thinking about what kind of sources we have, whether they are historically accurate, and in what way they present Jesus's Jewishness. Our main source for information about the historical figure of Jesus of Nazareth is the New Testament, particularly the letters of Paul and the Synoptic Gospels (Mark, Matthew, and Luke).

Jesus is not mentioned in a pagan source until at least 112 CE, and then only in Tacitus's recounting of how Nero blamed Christians for the fire at Rome. The "Testimony of Josephus" is likely heavily redacted by Christian scribes and thus of limited historical value. The New Testament texts, our best sources, are all written at least in part as invitations to faith from people inside of a believing community, so any historical information presented must be heavily scrutinized. Nevertheless, all New Testament sources expect readers to know that Jesus was a Jewish man and present him accordingly.

The letters of Paul are the earliest sources, written around 50–62 CE. Paul, however, is much less interested in Jesus the historical person than what he sees as the effects of Jesus's death and resurrection on humanity, so he does not give us much information about Jesus's life. The earliest definition of the gospel message, found in 1 Corinthians 15:3, is that "Christ died for our sins according to the Scriptures." For Paul, the good news begins with Jesus's death, and his actual life is less important. Nevertheless, Paul does relay some important information: Jesus was born a Jew (Gal. 4:4), had brothers (1 Cor. 9:5), ministered among the Jews (Rom. 15:7), instituted the ritual of the Lord's Supper (1 Cor. 11:23–25), and was crucified (1 Cor. 2:2).

Mark, the earliest "Gospel," presents Jesus as a Jewish apocalyptic teacher and prophet, similar to the first-century figures in Judea whom Josephus tells us about in the *Jewish Antiquities* and the *Jewish War*, many of whom met violent fates at the hands of Roman procurators. In Mark, Jesus's public ministry begins with Jesus teaching in Galilee that "the time is fulfilled, and the kingdom of God is come near" (1:15), a message consistent with Jewish apocalyptic teaching, and Jesus gives an apocalyptic address in Mark 13. Likewise in Mark, Jesus teaches primarily in parables, a genre that appears throughout later rabbinic literature. Mark relays several stories in which the Pharisees confront Jesus and his disciples about picking grain or performing miracles on the Sabbath (Mark 2:22–3:6), which only make sense if all of the figures involved are expected to be following Jewish law.

Both Matthew and Luke build on Mark's presentation of Jesus as a Jewish apocalyptic figure. One of Matthew's goals is to demonstrate that Jesus fulfills all the Jewish prophecies of a Davidic messiah. Matthew begins with a genealogy linking Jesus back to David and even Abraham in a carefully orchestrated series of generations (Matt. 1:1–17). He peppers his Gospel with eleven "fulfillment citations," strategically placed quotations from the Hebrew Bible that demonstrate that Jesus is the long-awaited Davidic messiah or that key moments in the Hebrew Bible foreshadow specific events in Jesus's life. Matthew also presents Jesus as a "new Moses," the best and most accurate interpreter of Jewish law. In the Sermon on the Mount, Jesus tells his disciples that in order to enter the kingdom of heaven, their righteousness has to *exceed* that of the Pharisees and teachers of the law (Matt. 5:20); the antitheses that follow educate followers as to what it really means to follow the law (Matt. 5:21–48).

While Matthew is concerned with the identity of Jesus as the long-awaited Jewish Messiah, one of Luke's goals is to demonstrate why the good news spread away from Jews to Gentiles, a two-volume story that continues in the Acts of the Apostles. Luke thus paints a deeply pious picture of Jesus's background. Beginning and ending in the Jerusalem Temple, Luke's Gospel is filled with allusions to and quotations from Jewish scripture. Jesus's family makes a pilgrimage to the Temple when he is a boy (Luke 2:22–40), he teaches publicly in synagogues (Luke 4:14–37), and his parables draw heavily on Jewish values and traditions, particularly treating your neighbor as yourself and demonstrating true hospitality (e.g., Luke 10:25–37). Luke presents Jesus as the absolute heir to Jewish history, prophecy, and tradition, the fulfillment of Isaianic prophecy in particular (e.g., Luke 4:18–19; 22:37), and one whose death and resurrection are only understandable through Jewish scripture. God's plan, though, according to Luke, is to spread the good news to all nations, a story woven through both books by narrating the effects of the Jewish rejection of Jesus.

## About the author

**Meira Z. Kensky** is the senior assistant dean and director of Undergraduate Advising for the University of Virginia College of Arts & Sciences. Previously she was Joseph E. McCabe Professor of Religion and director of advising at Coe College. Kensky is the author of *Trying Man, Trying God: The Divine Courtroom in Early Jewish and Christian Literature* (Mohr Siebeck, 2010) and is working on a book for Eerdmans on the Apocalypses of Peter and Paul and Early Christian tours of Hell.

## Suggestions for further reading

*In this book*
See also chapters 33 (Why don't Jews believe in Jesus?) and 36 (Was Paul Jewish?).

*Elsewhere*
Ehrman, Bart. *Jesus: Apocalyptic Prophet of the New Millennium*. New York: Oxford, 1999.

Kensky, Meira Z. "The Gospel of Luke." In *Judeophobia and the New Testament*, edited by Sarah Rollens, Eric Vanden Eykel, and Meredith Warren. Grand Rapids, MI: Eerdmans, 2024.

Levine, Amy-Jill. *Short Stories by Jesus*. New York: HarperOne, 2015.

# 35
# Did Jews kill Jesus?

## Eric Vanden Eykel

Who killed Jesus? Was it the Romans? Or was it "the Jews"? Questions like these have persisted for centuries, which may give the impression that the matter is complicated or that historians don't have enough information to answer confidently. This is not the case, however. Such questions persist because what is known about Roman crucifixion in the first century doesn't always match what New Testament authors claim about the death of Jesus. The following discussion addresses crucifixion in the ancient world and the political situation in first-century Judea to establish that the Romans should be held responsible for the death of Jesus. It then examines certain passages in the New Testament that may appear to contradict this claim and provides explanations for why these contradictions exist.

Crucifixion was a brutal form of execution in which a condemned person was fastened to a cross with either nails or rope and then left to die from exposure, infection, or suffocation. In the first century, it was also a uniquely Roman form of execution. Jesus lived during a time when Judea was under Roman rule, which means that the Judeans paid taxes to the Roman government and were subject to Roman laws as well as the Roman consequences for breaking these laws. Crucifixion was reserved for the most serious crimes, but that does not mean that it was a rare occurrence. The Jewish historian Josephus, for example, writes that the Romans crucified two thousand people in Jerusalem for rebelling against Rome (*War* 2.75).

At the time of Jesus's execution, Pontius Pilate was the Roman governor of Judea. The Jewish philosopher Philo describes him as having a reputation for being easily angered, inflexible, and relentless (*Embassy* 38). In his position, Pilate had ultimate authority when it came to preserving law and order in his territory. He also had ultimate authority when it came to executing persons that he saw as a threat to that order. The New Testament Gospels all indicate that Pilate is the one who sentenced Jesus to die (Matt. 27:24; Mark 15:15; Luke 23:25; John 19:6). But the story that they tell is also more complex because it implicates not only Pilate but also the Jews living in Jerusalem at the time.

In all four Gospels, the party that comes to arrest Jesus is led by Judas, one of Jesus's Jewish followers. Jewish authorities—namely, the "chief priests" and "elders"—are also mentioned (Matt. 26:47; Mark 14:43; Luke 22:52; John 18:3). After they arrest Jesus, the mob takes him not to Pilate but to the Jewish council known as the Sanhedrin. According to Matthew, Mark, and Luke, this council finds Jesus guilty of blasphemy (Matt. 26:63–66; Mark 14:61–64; Luke 22:67–71) before they take him to Pilate and request his execution. The Gospels depict Pilate not as a relentless leader with ultimate authority but as someone who was easily manipulated and also thoroughly conflicted about whether he should execute Jesus. As a non-Jewish Roman, Pilate would have little reason to care about the Sanhedrin's charge of blasphemy; his primary concern would have been whether Jesus posed a threat to Rome. This is why he asks Jesus the question, "Are you the king of the Judeans?" Jesus dodges this question (Matt. 27:11; Mark 15:2; Luke 23:3; John 18:33–34), and in the end, Pilate gives in to the demands of the crowd and reluctantly orders him to be crucified.

This portrayal of Jewish leaders manipulating Pilate does not align with other historical evidence. As governor, Pilate had the final say on matters of execution and had reason to view Jesus as a potential political threat, not as someone guilty of blasphemy. The Gospels were written decades after Jesus's death, and their depiction of "the Jews" as a group bearing responsibility for Jesus's death reflects the fraught relationship between early Christian and Jewish communities that developed during those decades. Christianity began as a movement within Judaism, but by the end of the first century, they no longer enjoyed that close proximity. The precise reasons behind the "split," as well as the timing of it, are debated by scholars of early Christianity and ancient Judaism.

The misrepresentation of Jewish involvement in Jesus's crucifixion has contributed to centuries of misunderstanding and Christian hostility toward Jews. Early Christian writers, seeking to articulate their identity as distinct from Judaism, often portrayed Jewish leaders in a negative light, which later fueled anti-Judaism. Over time, these distortions shaped how Jews were perceived, leading to harmful stereotypes and persecution. By recognizing the complexities and historical realities behind these narratives, we can better understand the roots of anti-Judaism and work to dismantle the harmful legacies that have followed.

## About the author

**Eric Vanden Eykel** is an associate professor of religious studies at Ferrum College in Virginia. His research focuses on Christian apocryphal literature, with a special emphasis on texts and traditions about the infancies and childhoods of Jesus and Mary. He is the author of *"But Their Faces Were All Looking Up": Author and Reader in the Protevangelium of James* (T&T Clark, 2016), coeditor of *Sex, Violence, and Early Christian Texts* (Lexington, 2022), and author of *The Magi: Who They Were, How They've Been Remembered, and Why They Still Fascinate* (Fortress, 2022).

## Suggestions for further reading

*In this book*
See also chapter 43 (What is antisemitism?).

*Elsewhere*
Bond, Helen K. *Pontius Pilate in History and Interpretation*. New York: Cambridge University Press, 1998.

Edwards, J. Christopher. *Crucified: The Christian Invention of the Jewish Executioners of Jesus*. Minneapolis, MN: Fortress Press, 2023.

Reinhartz, Adele. *Cast Out of the Covenant: Jews and Anti-Judaism in the Gospel of John*. Lanham, MD: Lexington Books / Fortress Academic, 2018.

# 36
# Was Paul Jewish?

## Elias Sacks

How we answer the question "Was Paul Jewish?" depends on how we understand "Paul" and "Jewish."

Paul was a key figure among first-century followers of a recently executed Jewish teacher named Jesus (a group that scholars often describe as "the Jesus movement" rather than "Christianity," since many adherents did not claim to break with Judaism). It is generally accepted that Paul was born Jewish and—after initially opposing the Jesus movement—had a revelatory experience and renounced that opposition; by the mid-40s CE, he was traveling around the Mediterranean, establishing and sending letters to communities of fellow Jesus-followers.

Later readers, however, have reconstructed the details of his life and thought in diverse ways. He appears in the New Testament book the Acts of the Apostles and is traditionally seen as the author of thirteen or fourteen letters that became part of Christianity's Bible; some individuals thus see "Paul" as someone who experienced events, and held views, described across all these sources. However, many scholars see Acts as historically unreliable and hold that only seven New Testament letters were actually written by Paul; some readers (including some Christians) therefore view "Paul" as someone whose life story and teachings should be derived only from those seven epistles.

Turning to "Jewish," we might understand this word *biographically*—as asking whether Paul came from a Jewish background. The answer is yes. Most readers accept his insistence, echoed throughout his letters, that "I myself am an Israelite" (Rom. 11:1) who "advanced in Judaism beyond many among my people" (Gal. 1:14; Romans and Galatians are Paul's letters, included in the New Testament, to Jesus-followers in Rome and a region called Galatia). Paul cast himself as born Jewish and immersed in Judaism.

Alternately, we might understand "Jewish" *canonically*—as asking whether Paul's letters are part of the traditional Jewish canon, texts traditionally deemed worthy of study and even obedience by Jews. The answer is no. For centuries, he attracted little attention from Jews (with some exceptions, such as a medieval source in which he secretly works for the Jewish people). More recently, Paul has frequently been portrayed by Jewish readers as an archvillain who abandoned Judaism, attacked Jews for rejecting Jesus, and helped found Christianity by disseminating anti-Jewish teachings—for instance, that a relationship with God requires faith in Jesus rather than adherence to Judaism's laws. Indeed, Paul seems to speak harshly of Judaism's laws and adherents, declaring that "Christ redeemed us from the curse of the law" (Gal. 3:13) and that Jews are "enemies of God" (Rom. 11:28).

Finally, we might understand "Jewish" *contentfully*—as asking whether Paul's views are consistent with the content of other Jewish teachings and even whether he claimed to practice, and ascribed value to, Judaism. The answer is mixed. Most Jews find Paul's teachings alien to Judaism, and most Christians agree that he left his ancestral religion. Yet others disagree. One alternative appears among non-Jewish historians such as John Gager. For these scholars, standard interpretations forget that Paul's letters were precisely that—letters he sent to specific communities of Jesus-followers. In particular, Paul wrote letters as an "apostle to the Gentiles" (Rom. 11:13)—as someone charged with proclaiming Jesus to non-Jews. Rather than criticizing *all* observance of Judaism's laws, Paul was insisting that his *non-Jewish addressees* did not need to follow these laws. While some of his contemporaries urged non-Jews to adopt certain Jewish practices or even convert to Judaism, Paul vehemently disagreed, arguing that what was required of non-Jews was allegiance to Jesus. By contrast, Paul held, Jews should continue obeying Judaism's laws, since this had long been the way such individuals expressed and maintained their relationship with God. Paul thus proposed two paths: Jesus for non-Jews and the law for Jews.

While some Jewish readers adopt this new interpretation of Paul, other Jewish thinkers locate Paul within Judaism on different grounds. Some conclude that he rejected or left aside Judaism's laws but discover Jewish precedents for this posture: Having come to the conclusion that Jesus was the Messiah, Paul then took up a strand in Jewish thought that holds that Judaism's laws will be transcended in the messianic age. Some take Paul to echo Jewish views on universalism, gender, and other topics. Perhaps Paul's most controversial Jewish reader is the twentieth-century rabbi Jacob Taubes. Notorious for his feuds with contemporaries and problematic treatment of women, Taubes identified Jewish dimensions of Paul's views on messianism and atonement and portrayed Paul as a political thinker: For Taubes, Paul argued that the authority of God and the Messiah undermines all earthly states.

New Testament translations are from the New Revised Standard Version.

## About the author

**Elias Sacks** is an associate professor of religious studies and Jewish studies and Faculty Director for Public Scholarship in the Office of Faculty Affairs at the University of Colorado Boulder. He studies Jewish thought, philosophy of religion, Jewish-Christian relations, religious ethics, and religion and politics. He is the author of *Moses Mendelssohn's Living Script: Philosophy, Practice, History, Judaism* (Indiana University Press, 2017) as well as articles on a wide range of medieval and modern thinkers.

## Suggestions for further reading

*In this book*
See also chapter 30 (What do Jews believe about the messiah?).

*Elsewhere*
Eisenbaum, Pamela. *Paul Was Not a Christian: The Original Message of a Misunderstood Apostle*. New York: HarperOne, 2009.

Gager, John. *Reinventing Paul*. New York: Oxford University Press, 2000.

Gager, John. *Who Made Early Christianity? The Jewish Lives of the Apostle Paul*. New York: Columbia University Press, 2015.

Langton, Daniel. *The Apostle Paul in the Jewish Imagination: A Study in Modern Jewish-Christian Relations*. New York: Cambridge University Press, 2010.

Nanos, Mark. "Paul and Judaism." In *The Jewish Annotated New Testament*, edited by Amy-Jill Levine and Marc Zvi Brettler, 551–554. New York: Oxford University Press, 2011.

# 37
# Why do Jews and Christians disagree if they read a lot of the same Bible?

## Benjamin E. Sax

Before we can answer this question, we need to know something important: There is no one book called "the Bible." Jews and Christians have different Bibles, which consist of different books in different orders and, most importantly, were composed in different languages and at different times. What Jews call the Hebrew Bible or TaNaKh—an anagram for Torah, Prophets, and Writings—is very similar to what Christians call "the Old Testament." Yet the Tanakh and the Old Testament are not the same. For example, some Christian Bibles include books like Judith and the book of Maccabees, which are not included in the Tanakh. Also, the orders of the books are different, which can change the meaning of narratives. Christian Bibles always include "the New Testament," which is understood to have changed the meanings of the Old Testament through the death and resurrection of Jesus Christ. Once we learn that each community is interpreting different books, it becomes a little easier to understand why they disagree.

To start, each community may translate and interpret biblical passages differently. The biblical text itself acknowledges the possibility of multiple interpretations: In Psalm 63:12 in the Tanakh (or Ps. 63:11 in the Christian Bible) we read, "One thing God has spoken; two things have I heard." For example, in the book of Isaiah, Ahaz asks God for a sign: "Assuredly, my Lord will give you a sign of His own accord! Look, the *'almah* is with child and about to give birth to a son. Let her name him Immanuel" (7:14). The word *'almah* in Hebrew means "young woman." In the Septuagint, the earliest Greek translation of the Hebrew Bible, *'almah* is translated into Greek as *parthenos*, or "virgin." One variation in the meaning of the word can create enormous, even irreconcilable theological differences. Christians argue that Mary and the virgin birth of Jesus were prophesied in this verse. Jews disagree, but their disagreement is not just theological; it is exegetical. For them, the text does not say *betulah* (virgin). While this example clarifies how Christians and Jews interpret verses differently, it's also important to understand why they do so.

Christians believe that Jesus Christ was prefigured in the Old Testament. This type of interpretation is called "typology." Christians read their Bibles already knowing that Jesus is the Messiah. One goal of biblical interpretation is to bring believers closer to Jesus. The Old Testament is a preamble to the New Testament, and in some Christian communities, it was replaced by the New Testament in a theological process called "supersessionism." Jewish biblical interpretation does not share this goal. According to Jewish tradition, the Messiah has not come, and Jews are forbidden to interpret their Bible with the goal of predicting "his" arrival. Classical rabbinic interpretation is focused on language: Even the most minute variations in grammar or spelling possess endless theological possibilities.

Jews and Christians also disagree about the theology in biblical stories. Both Bibles begin with the book of Genesis. They agree that Adam and Eve are the first people. They also agree that the snake in this account is an important character. For Christians, the snake was the devil—or Satan—who manipulated Eve and brought sin into the world. Jews believe the snake was a snake. This is an important disagreement. In general, Christians believe in a doctrine of original sin, which means as a result of Adam and Eve's conduct in the Garden of Eden and their expulsion, all people are born sinful and possess some orientation to sin. Faith in Jesus can restore humanity to a nonsinful state in the afterlife. Jews, however, do not believe in original sin. Adam and Eve's conduct in the Garden of Eden may have resulted in the loss of immortality and the gaining of the knowledge of sexual desire, but generations of Jewish exegetes have debated the meaning of this encounter, including one commentary that suggested the primordial couple kicked God out of the garden. Regardless, Adam and Eve's sin, according to Jewish interpreters, was their own. As a result, Jews and Christians have developed vastly different understandings of human nature.

Because of these different views of human nature, Jews and Christians disagree on how God will redeem or save the world. Take, for example, the poetry in Isaiah 40–55, what is known as the "suffering servant" passage. Even though many Christian readers of their Bibles know the phrase "suffering servant" as an essential part of the biblical tradition, the phrase itself is not in the original text. Very often Jews do not know it. In fact, it is a recent addition attributed to the German Lutheran scholar Bernhard L. Duhm

(1847–1928), who connected the Hebrew word *'eved* (slave or servant) to faith and suffering. For Christians, this *'eved* who suffers will be Jesus. For Jews, these passages refer to the triumph of monotheism.

## About the author

**Benjamin E. Sax** serves as the head of Scholarship and the Jewish Scholar at the Institute for Islamic, Christian, and Jewish Studies in Baltimore.

## Suggestions for further reading

*In this book*
See also chapters 2 (What is the Torah?) and 30 (What do Jews believe about the messiah?).

*Elsewhere*
Boyarin, Daniel. *Border Lines: The Partition of Judaeo-Christianity*. Philadelphia, PA: University of Pennsylvania Press, 2004.

Boys, Mary C. *Redeeming Our Sacred Story: The Death of Jesus and Relations Between Jews and Christians*. Mahwah, NJ: Paulist Press, 2014.

Levine, Amy-Jill, and Marc Zvi Brettler. *The Bible With and Without Jesus: How Jews and Christians Read the Same Stories Differently*. New York: HarperCollins Publishers, 2020.

Levine, Amy-Jill, and Marc Zvi Brettler, eds. *The Jewish Annotated New Testament: New Revised Standard Version Bible Translation*. Oxford: Oxford University Press, 2011.

# 38
# What are Jewish-Christian relations?

Jessica Cooperman

This fall I was at a *Selichot* service, part of the spiritual preparation undertaken by Jews prior to Yom Kippur, the Day of Atonement. In addition to the traditional prayers, the service featured a talk by a Christian minister about a new book exploring how young people found belonging and fulfillment outside of organized religion. He came to the synagogue to talk about what Christians could learn from Judaism and Jewish ritual to make the church more relevant to this new generation. He displayed deep familiarity with Jewish holidays and correctly used and pronounced Hebrew phrases as he stressed the value of Jews and Christians working together to build community and meaning.

Events like this one, in which a rabbi or a minister visit each other's congregations to make common cause around religion, share a holiday, or express appreciation of each other's traditions have, since the mid-twentieth century, become quite common in the United States. The ease with which some Jews and Christians engage in shared study, advocacy, and communal work may make it easy to miss the remarkable nature of these exchanges, which represent a profound break with a history of Jewish-Christian tensions, suspicion, and even violence.

For centuries, Catholic and Protestant doctrine maintained that the Jewish covenant with God had been superseded by the revelation of Christ. Even when individual Christians and Jews maintained friendly relations, Jews as a group were seen as willfully, and perhaps dangerously, blind to the truth of Christianity. In the best cases, Christians saw Jews as targets for evangelism and conversion. In the worst ones, Jews were suspected of heinous crimes against Christians and Christianity. Accusations that Jews desecrated communion wafers as a sign of their ongoing hostility to Jesus or that they murdered Christian children to use their blood in religious rituals echoed throughout Europe from the twelfth century onward. These claims of "blood libel" grew less common throughout the nineteenth century, but the legacies of these long-standing fears persisted and even shaped Nazi antisemitic propaganda in the twentieth century.

In the 1920s, however, Christians, particularly in England and the United States, began to reevaluate their relationship to Jews and Judaism. In part, this development reflected World War I policies that brought Jewish chaplains into American and British fighting forces and integrated Judaism into the religious services offered to the millions of men called up to fight. As racial tensions in the US and Europe grew during the interwar period, some of the leaders of these World War I military programs began to see Judeo-Christian understanding as an antidote to civic and social tension. In 1928, for example, Newton D. Baker, former US Secretary of War, became the first Protestant co-chair of the newly formed National Conference of Christians and Jews, an organization that worked to promote the sorts of pulpit exchanges that would become normalized in the US later in the twentieth century.

In the 1930s and 1940s, the rise of Nazism and anti-Jewish violence spurred Christian clergy like Rev. James Parkes in England and A. Roy Eckardt in the US to reassess the role of Christianity in promoting antisemitic ideologies, while World War II again brought Jews and Christians together in military service. During the Cold War, opposition to "godless Communism" transformed Jews and Christians into allies in the fight to promote Judeo-Christian values as the basis for Western liberal democracy. And as awareness of the Holocaust grew, increasing numbers of Catholic and Protestant clergy pressed for Jewish-Christian reconciliation and the difficult process of ridding Christianity of its anti-Jewish biases and doctrines.

The advocacy of Christians like Monsignor John Oesterreicher propelled a wave of church statements promoting a new relationship between Christians and Jews. The most significant was perhaps *Nostra Aetate*, or *In Our Time*, issued by the Second Vatican Council in 1965. In this statement, the Catholic Church reaffirmed the status of Christians as "the new people of God" but also stressed the shared "spiritual patrimony" of Judaism and Christianity and emphasized the benefit of mutual understanding, dialogue, and shared theological study.

Jewish leaders met these overtures with some apprehension but also a recognition that as a small minority, they benefited from Catholic and Protestant partners willing to fight antisemitism and advocate for shared causes like civil rights or the liberation of Soviet Jewry. In recent years, support for Israel has upended many Jewish-Christian alliances and brought some Jewish organizations into partnership with evangelical groups who had not initially embraced postwar Jewish-Christian reconciliation. Today, both Jews and Christians sometimes find utility and benefit in working together.

## About the author

**Jessica Cooperman** is the Doris and Simon Konover Chair of Hebrew and Judaic Studies and director of the Center for Judaic Studies at the University of Connecticut. Her book *Making Judaism Safe for America: World War I and the Origins of Religious Pluralism* (New York University Press, 2018) received an honorable mention for the Saul Viener Prize in American Jewish History. Her current project explores Passover celebrations as sites for defining Jewish identity and relationships between Jews and Christians. Her next project will examine projects for promoting interfaith relations after World War II. Cooperman is coeditor of the journal *American Jewish History*.

## Suggestions for further reading

*In this book*

See also chapters 43 (What is antisemitism?), 50 (What is the Holocaust?), 51 (What role did race play in the Holocaust?), and 56 (What is Zionism?).

*Elsewhere*

Ariel, Yaakov. *An Unusual Relationship: Evangelical Christians and Jews.* New York: New York University Press, 2013.

Connelly, John. *From Enemy to Brother: The Revolution in Catholic Teaching on the Jews, 1933–1965.* Cambridge, MA: Harvard University Press, 2012.

Gaston, K. Healon. *Imagining Judeo-Christian America: Religion, Secularism, and the Redefinition of Democracy.* Chicago: University of Chicago Press, 2019.

Teter, Magda. *Blood Libel: On the Trail of an Antisemitic Myth.* Cambridge, MA: Harvard University Press, 2020.

# 39
# Who are Messianic Jews?

## Yaakov Ariel

The term "Messianic Jews" originated at the turn of the twentieth century to designate Jews who had embraced Protestant Christianity and wished to maintain some Jewish customs and rites, such as conducting Sabbath prayers on Friday nights or Saturday mornings and celebrating Jewish holidays. Most Jewish converts at that time had joined Christian communities, and even those few who organized into separate "Hebrew Christian" congregations retained some Jewish symbols but did not actively pursue Jewish practices and customs.

When a vigorous movement of Jewish believers in Jesus emerged in the 1970s, its members called themselves Messianic Jews to designate their independent spirit and determination to identify as Jews. Mostly baby boomers who asserted their right to transcend old boundaries, members viewed the combination of the two traditions as healing old wounds. They noted that for Israeli Jews, the term *nozrim* (Christians) meant members of an alien religion, so they chose the term *meshichiyim* (messianists) instead.

Messianic Jews promote some Jewish cultural attributes and rituals at the same time that they embrace the theology and morality associated with evangelical Christianity. Messianic congregations expect their members to abstain from drugs, alcohol, and premarital sex, and they value thrift and respect for law and order. At the same time, Messianic congregations have been influenced by the Jesus generation and the countercultural movements of the 1960s. Attire in Messianic prayer meetings is informal, and Messianic bands perform contemporary Christian music, often composed by Messianic musicians.

The appearance of a movement that combines Jewish and Christian elements stirred mixed reactions. Many Jews believe that one cannot embrace Jesus as Lord and Savior and remain Jewish. However, at the turn of the twenty-first century, attitudes in liberal Jewish circles have become more accepting. Evangelical Christians have been more welcoming: Most do not object to communities that embrace ethnic symbols and customs as long as they see Jesus as Savior and adopt evangelical codes of morality. Following one strand of evangelical theology, Messianic Jews are nonsupersessionist and believe that the Jewish people have a special role in history. Within the larger conservative evangelical community, Messianic Jews advocate goodwill toward Jewish people. They also see special merit in sharing the gospel with Jews and instructing them in what they consider to be the correct manner of reading the Bible, as historically accurate and prophetically revealing. Messianic congregations serve as centers of evangelism for Jews as well as for non-Jews. For the non-Jews, the spiritual journey has been toward Judaism, or toward Judaism and Christianity at the same time.

Many confuse Jews for Jesus with Messianic Judaism. However, Jews for Jesus is an organization that aims to evangelize individual Jews. The founder of Jews for Jesus, Moishe Rosen, related skeptically to the Messianic Jewish movement and asked members of the group to join regular Protestant churches rather than forming their own congregations.

While struggling to be accepted as both genuinely Jewish and Christian, Messianic Jews built their own subculture, complete with national organizations, youth movements, conferences, retreats, prayer books, hymnals, publications, and periodicals, including theological, apologetic, and evangelistic treatises. David Stern edited a Messianic Jewish New Testament, in which he changed the *Epistle to the Hebrews* to *Letter to the Messianic Jews*. In his *Messianic Jewish Manifesto*, Stern asserted that Messianic Jews were 100 percent Jewish and 100 percent Christian.

Still, the movement is neither united nor uniform. One of the major divisions is between noncharismatics and charismatics, who advocate a direct personal encounter with the divine and practice more expressive modes of worship. In addition, different Messianic congregations have different amalgams of Jewish and Christian liturgical elements. Messianic Haggadot (Passover texts) and *siddurim* (prayer books) include elements of the traditional Jewish liturgy alongside prayers that express faith in Jesus as the Redeemer. Messianic congregations conduct prayer meetings on Friday nights or Saturday mornings, and they often ask men to wear yarmulkes during the services. More and more congregations have arks with Torah scrolls, and some read a passage from the Jewish lectionary each week. Messianic Jews have also incorporated Israeli motifs into their communities, including songs and Modern Hebrew.

By the turn of the twenty-first century, the movement had more than four hundred communities in North America, over one hundred in Israel, and dozens in Europe, Latin America, Africa, and Australia. The early twenty-first century is seeing a new generation of Messianic Jewish leaders and thinkers who have developed a more daring theology. In a group called Post-Missionary Messianic Judaism, Mark Kinzer advocates cutting the cord that has tied Messianic Judaism to the missionary community and moving from Protestant theology to Jewish postbiblical sources. While committed to the basic elements of evangelical theology and devoted to Jewish identity and heritage, Messianic Jews are now creating theological and communal spaces of their own.

## About the author

**Yaakov Ariel** is a professor of religious studies at the University of North Carolina at Chapel Hill.

## Suggestions for further reading

*In this book*
See also chapters 33 (Why don't Jews believe in Jesus?) and 38 (What are Jewish-Christian relations?).

*Elsewhere*
Ariel, Yaakov. "Judaism and Christianity Unite! The Unique Culture of Messianic Judaism." In *Introduction to New and Alternative Religions in America* (volume 2), edited by Eugene V. Gallagher and W. Michael Ashcraft, 191–222. Westport, CT: Greenwood Press, 2006.

Ariel, Yaakov. "Theological and Liturgical Coming of Age: New Developments in the Relationship between Messianic Judaism and Evangelical Christianity." *Hebrew Studies* 57 (2016): 381–391.

Rudolph, David J., and Joel Willitts. *Introduction to Messianic Judaism: Its Ecclesial Context and Biblical Foundations*. Grand Rapids, MI: Zondervan, 2013.

# 40
# What is the relationship between the Bible and the Qur'an?

## Shari L. Lowin

The Qur'an is not considered the word of God in the Jewish tradition and is not mentioned in the Bible. But the reverse is not true regarding the Bible in the Qur'anic and Islamic tradition: Qur'anic verses teach that the Bible *is* God's word, revealed to the children of Israel through the prophet Moses. As Q 6:154 relates, "Then We gave Moses the Scripture, complete for him who had done good, an exposition of everything and a guidance and a mercy, so that they might believe in their meeting with their Lord" (cf., e.g., 5:44; 32:23; 40:53). What's more, the Qur'an presents the Bible as relevant to Muslims, though it does not form part of the Islamic scriptural or legal canon. The Muslim scripture repeatedly teaches that the Qur'an comes not to refute but to confirm the earlier divine revelations of both the Torah (al-*TawrŒh*) and the Gospels (al-*Injīl*; e.g., Q 3:3–4). And in Q 10:94, God instructs Muhammad and his followers, "If you are in doubt as to the nature of what We have sent down to you, then ask those who have been reading the Scripture before you."

At the same time, the Qur'an and Islamic tradition note that the divine revelations collected into the Bible have been distorted or corrupted. The clearest accusation appears in Q 2:79, where the Qur'an fulminates against those (understood to be Jews) who "write the Book with their hands and then say, 'This is from God.'" Other verses accuse Jews of altering the word of God, often in rejection of Muhammad's prophethood, though whether this alteration results in a falsified scripture or falsified interpretation of scripture is less clear (see, e.g., Q 2:75; 3:78).

Perhaps the most famous charge of Jewish (and Christian) alteration of the Bible concerns the Qur'an's claim in 7:157 that Muhammad appears in both the Torah and the New Testament. According to various later Islamic exegetical and polemical texts, Jews and Christians removed all explicit mentions of Muhammad; however, traces of biblical prophecies about him can still be detected, such as in Deuteronomy 18:18 and Isaiah 42:1–4.

This simultaneous confirmation and rejection of the Bible's accuracy manifests in other areas as well. Most obviously, many of the biblical narratives also appear in the Qur'an, though the two versions do not always align completely. For example, in one Qur'anic telling of the story of Noah and the flood, an unnamed son of Noah's refuses to enter the ark and is drowned (Q 11:25–49, esp. 42–43)—an element not present in the Bible. While many have presumed such differences to be "mistakes" or misreadings of the Bible, that is often inaccurate. In some cases, divergences can be attributed to the Qur'an's reaction to midrashic or Christian sources rather than to the Bible. Others are the result of the Qur'an's original theological teachings and differing values and messages.

Some biblical laws are also mentioned in the Qur'an, frequently with differences. Q 5:45 references the laws of an eye for an eye (Ex. 21:22ff.; Lev. 24:17–22), though it encourages remission as almsgiving over retaliation (cf. 2:178). In 2:65, those who violated God's covenant by violating the Sabbath are turned into apes (cf. 7:163–167). Q 3:93–94 seems to refer to the prohibition against consuming the sciatic nerve (Gen. 32:33; cf. Q 5:5), though this is said to be a man-made restriction. Q 4:161 notes that some Jews have violated divine laws against usury.

The connections between the Bible and the Qur'an are not limited to content alone. Rather, Islam and Judaism share similar attitudes toward the very nature of their holy texts. Both are understood as the written word of God orally revealed to His chosen prophet(s), though Jewish tradition and the Bible itself allow for human authorship of portions of the sacred text—a stance the Qur'an and the Islamic tradition reject about the Qur'an. Judaism and Islam use similar terminology for their holy texts: in Judaism, *miqra* (that which is read) and *ha-katuv* (that which is written), and in Islam, *al-qur'ān* (that which is read aloud/recited) and *al-kitāb* (scripture). At the same time, both traditions developed schools of thought that regarded scripture as "uncreated," predating the existence of the world. The language of the divine revelation is of sacred significance for both Judaism (Hebrew) and Islam (Arabic). Both the Bible and the Qur'an form part of the liturgies of their respective traditions. Extensive exegetical traditions have developed around each text. So too each forms the basis of the orthopractic legal systems that subsequently evolved.

## About the author

**Shari L. Lowin** is a professor of religious studies and theology at Stonehill College, where she teaches courses on Islam and Judaism. Her research focuses on intertextual conversations between the Qur'an and the Jewish textual tradition.

## Suggestions for further reading

*In this book*
See also chapters 1 (Why are texts sacred to Jews?), 2 (What is the Torah?), 4 (What is midrash?), 6 (What is Jewish law?), 41 (What is Judeo-Islamic civilization?), and 42 (Who was Moses Maimonides?).

*Elsewhere*
Dost, Suleyman. "Once Again on Noah's Lost Son in the Qur'ān: The Enochic Connection." *Asiatische Studien—Études Asiatiques* 76(2) (2022): 371–388.

Lowin, Shari L., and Nevin Reda. "Scripture and Exegesis: Torah and Qur'an in Historical Retrospective." In *The Routledge Handbook of Muslim-Jewish Relations*, edited by Joseph Meri, 57–75. New York: Routledge, 2016.

Reynolds, Gabriel Said. "Exploring the Qur'an and the Bible." YouTube channel. https://www.youtube.com/c/ExploringtheQuranandtheBible.

Reynolds, Gabriel Said. *The Qur'an and the Bible: Text and Commentary*. New Haven, CT: Yale University Press, 2018.

Saeed, Abdullah. "The Charge of Distortion of Jewish and Christian Scriptures." *The Muslim World* 92(3–4) (Fall 2002): 419–436.

# 41
# What is Judeo-Islamic civilization?

Liran Yadgar

Jews have lived under Islamic rule since the earliest times of Islam. They came into contact in vast territories that encompass the Middle East and North Africa (and during the medieval period, the Iberian Peninsula) and continued to live there as the Muslim population became the majority in these territories in the centuries after the foundation of Islam.

The concept of "Judeo-Islamic civilization" or "Judeo-Islamic tradition" became popular in Western scholarship following the 1984 publication of Bernard Lewis's *The Jews of Islam*. This concept describes the relationships between Judaism and Islam with respect to religious texts, language, literature, law, ritual, sacred spaces, theology, philosophy, mysticism, arts, and sciences from the days of the Prophet Muhammad (570–632 CE) to today. Beginning in the early nineteenth century and spanning more than two hundred years, Jewish-Islamic relations have captivated the attention of Western scholars, many of them Jewish, from Europe, North America, and Palestine/Israel. The terminology these scholars use to describe the relations between Judaism and Islam is somewhat ambiguous, with expressions such as "influence," "borrowing," "creative coexistence," and "cultural symbiosis." Key players in the field of Jewish-Islamic relations include Abraham Geiger, Ignác Goldziher, Bernard Lewis, S. D. Goitein, and Mark R. Cohen, all of whose scholarship mostly portrays Islam in positive terms to Western audiences.

In particular, a number of the scholars mentioned—and many others—have examined the period between the rise of Islam in the early seventh century and the mid-thirteenth century, an era that is characterized in Western scholarship as "classical Islam." Judeo-Islamic tradition, according to this periodization, reached its zenith in the Islamic Early and High Middle Ages, and except for shorter periods of mutual interaction in later times, this tradition has been mostly in decline, which makes the classical age of Islam the most celebrated one for the Jewish-Islamic encounter.

The Judeo-Islamic tradition is usually described as one-directional in the formative Islamic period (seventh to eighth centuries CE): from Judaism, the older or "mother" religion, to Islam, the nascent or "daughter" religion. In this model, terms like "influence," "borrowing," or even "plagiarism" are used to explain the biblical and Jewish materials in the Qur'an, Islam's holy scripture, along with the development of certain aspects of law and ritual in the early Muslim community.

This influence paradigm has been under scrutiny among experts in Islamic studies over the past few decades. Examples of the "Judaism over Islam" trope include the accounts of biblical figures in the Qur'an; references to Jews, the children of Israel, and the Torah within the same text; Jewish vestiges in the early Islamic sources, including "borrowings" from the Hebrew Bible, the Mishnah, and the Talmud; and Muhammad's adoption of monotheism in the pagan milieu of his times and encounters, as well as conflicts with the Jews of Arabia as described in classical Islamic literature. According to this paradigm, the Judeo-Islamic tradition moved from one-directional influence to mutual interactions among members of the two religions by the ninth century CE. Typically, the most notable example of mutual interaction is the renowned theologian, philosopher, and physician Moses Maimonides (d. 1204), whose writings in both Arabic and Hebrew are considered to represent the pinnacle of Judeo-Islamic civilization.

Discussions about Judeo-Islamic civilization often include references to Jewish-Islamic relations during the Islamic medieval period or to relations in the Middle East and North Africa prior to the establishment of Israel in 1948. These depictions, and possibly the entire concept of a Judeo-Islamic civilization, should be understood as a modern myth, a nostalgic portrayal of harmonic relations and exchanges between Jews and Muslims in history. As relayed by the Israeli poet Ronny Someck (b. 1951), who was born to an Iraqi-Jewish family, his mother found consolation for the demise of the Jewish community in Iraq and for the Baghdadi Meir Elias Synagogue, where she wed his father, a building that was transformed into a mosque. She noted that "it doesn't matter who [attends it nowadays], as long as they pray to the same God." Someck's poem might be echoing the words of the famous Spanish poet Judah Halevi (d. 1141) about the Islamic call for prayer coming from the mosque: "Lazy Levite! Aren't you ashamed / to be asleep and silent, though it's morning? / Listen to the Gentiles calling, / worshiping the Lord with all their hearts" (trans. Raymond Scheindlin) or Maimonides's statement that stresses the monotheism of Muslims, saying that they "are not idolaters in any way. They have struck idolatry from their mouths and hearts, and profess the unity of God."

Someck thus expresses an understanding of the common elements within Judaism and Islam that might go unnoticed during times of conflict and war in the twenty-first century.

## About the author
**Liran Yadgar** (PhD, University of Chicago) is the Hebrew language lecturer and coordinator at the University of Oklahoma. His area of expertise is the history of Jews in the premodern Middle East. Prior to the University of Oklahoma, he served as a postdoctoral scholar at Yale University, UCLA, and Oklahoma State University.

## Suggestions for further reading
*In this book*
See also chapters 40 (What is the relationship between the Bible and the Qur'an?) and 42 (Who was Moses Maimonides?).

*Elsewhere*
Lewis, Bernard. *The Jews of Islam*. Princeton, NJ: Princeton University Press, 1984.

Meddeb, Abdelwahab, and Benjamin Stora, eds. *A History of Jewish-Muslim Relations: From the Origins to the Present Day*. Princeton, NJ: Princeton University Press, 2013.

Meri, Josef, ed. *The Routledge Handbook of Muslim-Jewish Relations*. New York: Routledge, 2016.

# 42
# Who was Moses Maimonides?

## Alan Verskin

Moses Maimonides (d. 1204), perhaps the most widely recognized Jewish leader of all time, was born in Cordoba in 1138. When the North African Almohad dynasty conquered the region and began to persecute Jews, Maimonides's family fled and wandered for some twelve years before settling in Fez. In 1165, after conditions for Jews in Fez declined, Maimonides again departed, residing briefly in Palestine before making his permanent home in Egypt. The first historical reference to Maimonides in Egypt is to him as a fundraiser desperately campaigning to liberate enslaved Jews who were being held for ransom by crusaders at an Egyptian port. His talents as a community organizer and his towering status as a scholar eventually led to his appointment as the head of Egyptian Jews, an office that remained in his family for generations afterward.

Maimonides explained that his experiences as a refugee and the erasure of Iberian Jewish culture in his lifetime drove him to become a prolific writer. He saw his writings, some written in rabbinic Hebrew and others in Judeo-Arabic, the mother tongue of his community, as a means of preserving cultural memory and safeguarding Jewish culture from future political disruptions. Maimonides's works fall into three main categories: medicine, law, and philosophical theology.

His early life had been mainly devoted to rabbinic scholarship, a lifestyle that was made possible by his brother, who was a successful merchant. When his brother drowned at sea, Maimonides began a career in medicine in order to support himself, served as a doctor to the sultan, and became well known among both Jewish and Muslim physicians. He wrote many medical works on topics including healthy living, asthma, poisons and their antidotes, and sexual health and commentaries on works of classical medicine.

Maimonides wrote most voluminously in the field of Jewish law. He authored the first comprehensive Jewish legal code, the *Mishneh Torah* (which can be translated as either *Second to the Torah* or a *Repetition of the*

*Torah*). In its fourteen volumes, the code attempted to resolve all the legal debates that appeared in the Talmud. Maimonides made the claim, considered scandalous by many of his early readers, that the *Mishneh Torah* would effectively render consultation of the Talmud superfluous. While there was some initial opposition to the book, and most Jews never treated its pronouncements as legally binding, it did become a cornerstone of Jewish education and is still widely studied in traditional Jewish settings.

Maimonides wrote numerous responses to religious questions during his lifetime that were later collected and distributed after his death. These responses embraced a wide range of topics, including crises of forced conversion and false messiahs, the status of astrology, theological disputes, and questions concerning marital and business law. His positions in these works sometimes differed from those in his legal code, reflecting his striving as a community leader to shape divine law in such a way that it met the needs of the individuals who sought his help.

*The Guide of the Perplexed* was Maimonides's contribution to the field of philosophical theology. It was written as a letter to a particular student "and for all of those like him" who were troubled by the apparent clashes between Aristotelian philosophical truths and those of the Bible and rabbinic literature. As a solution, Maimonides proposed an interpretive strategy that allowed for reading the Bible as a philosophical allegory. He argued that the biblical prophets were philosophers with highly developed imaginations that allowed them to creatively convey abstract ideas to a less rationally developed audience. Key among the truths that they conveyed was God's radical unity, a oneness that precluded God from sharing any of the same characteristics as His creatures. That means that Maimonides did not believe that God had a body, emotions, changing perceptions, or new realizations. Maimonides saw human society as journeying toward an ever more perfect understanding of monotheism with an ever larger community of philosophically sophisticated worshippers.

Maimonides's *The Guide of the Perplexed* is one of those rare texts that has generated a sense of intimacy among its readers. Because it is written as if it is the privileged correspondence between the author and a particularly gifted student, generations of readers have come to see themselves as in a direct relationship with Maimonides. And because the *Guide* is so evocative and multidimensional, Maimonides's self-proclaimed disciples often have vastly differing interpretations of his views. Philosophers and mystics, and secular, Reform, Conservative, and Orthodox Jews have all claimed Maimonides as their own. It is perhaps for this reason that Maimonides's name graces so many diverse research and educational institutions, hospitals, and synagogues, each of which finds inspiration in him.

## About the author

**Alan Verskin** is the Samuel J. Zacks Chair of Jewish History at the University of Toronto. His most recent book is *Diary of a Black Jewish Messiah: The Sixteenth-Century Journey of David Reubeni Through Africa, the Middle East, and Europe* (Stanford University Press, 2023).

## Suggestions for further reading

*In this book*
See also chapters 3 (What is the Talmud?), 6 (What is Jewish law?), 20 (What are the differences among Reform, Conservative, Reconstructionist, and Orthodox Judaism?), and 25 (Do Jews believe in God?).

*Elsewhere*
Halbertal, Moshe. *Maimonides: Life and Thought.* Translated by Joel A. Linsider. Princeton, NJ: Princeton University Press, 2013.

Maimonides, Moses, Abraham S. Halkin, and David Hartman. *Crisis and Leadership: Epistles of Maimonides.* Philadelphia, PA: Jewish Publication Society of America, 1985.

Maimonides, Moses, and Isadore Twersky. *A Maimonides Reader.* New York: Behrman House, 1972.

Melammed, Reneé Levine. "He Said, She Said: A Woman Teacher in Twelfth-Century Cairo." *AJS Review* 22(1) (1997): 19–35.

Verskin, Alan. "Admiration, Discrimination, and Forced Integration: Maimonides's Embrace of Converts to Judaism and His Responsum to Obadiah the Convert." *Journal of Jewish Identities* 14(1) (2021): 31–51.

# Jewish Difference

# 43
# What is antisemitism?

Jeffrey I. Israel

Antisemitism is a term used to identify hostility toward Jews, Judaism, or Jewishness or their subordination. It is used by institutions and activists across the globe to protect Jews from discrimination and violence wherever they remain a vulnerable minority population. But it is a strange word. What, after all, is "semitism"? Thinking carefully about antisemitism involves confronting the history of this strange word. It also means *not* allowing the strangeness and historical contingency of the word to distract attention from the dark truth that it has come to evoke: that for thousands of years, human beings have used Jewishness as a source of negative meaning-making.

The term "anti-Semitic" first appeared in English in a *New York Times* article in 1879, reporting on a new club for reactionaries in Berlin who hoped to reverse the legal emancipation of Jews. The *Times* added a hyphen when translating the German term *antisemitisch*, which had only recently been coined to describe the activities and goals of such clubs. The hyphen accentuates a tendency, then bourgeoning, to conflate "Semitism" with Jewishness.

According to biblical ethnology, Jews were presumed to be descended from Noah's son Shem, who is identified in Genesis 11 as the ancestor of Abraham. By the mid-nineteenth century, this idea had converged with a new philological framework for distinguishing "Indo-European" languages (i.e., Sanskrit, Greek, German) from "Semitic" languages (i.e., Hebrew and Arabic) and other types of languages. A confusion of linguistic difference with increasingly popular theories of racial difference ultimately developed into the idea of a race of "Semites," which included Jews and Arabs. Among *antisemitisch* ideologues, Jewish "Semites" represented the backwardness and degeneracy over which Indo-European "Aryans" were destined to triumph. Scholars today continue to recognize distinct Indo-European and Semitic language groups. However, the idea of distinct "Semitic" and "Aryan" races is no longer considered credible.

The noun *antisemitismus* was used by the 1880s to connect agitation against Jews in the German context to threats against Jews in other parts of Europe and to historical instances of anti-Jewish hostility stretching back to antiquity. And this is the sense of "anti-Semitism" that became conventional: a hatred of Jews, Judaism, or Jewishness or an insistence on their subordination, which has existed from antiquity to the present. In the late twentieth century, some scholars began to remove the hyphen in English, attempting to de-emphasize the discredited idea of racial "Semitism."

The term "antisemitism" may only make sense in the context of late-nineteenth-century European philological and racial theories and their Nazi legacy. But it is now also a broader, indispensable political category. Modern Jewish politics swings, both left and right, on this hinge. Antisemitism today is the word used by Jews to describe what they worry about when they worry that they won't be safe or they will be disadvantaged because they are Jews. Beliefs about antisemitism—what should count, its causes and extent—are often decisive when Jews and others make political judgments about the State of Israel, diaspora Jewish institutions, antidiscrimination laws, and the meaning of Jewish history.

The idea of antisemitism is also an important intellectual provocation. In century after century, there have been attacks on Jews, accusations of Jewish malevolence, legal restrictions, and expulsions. Instances are evident in almost every geographical region, even where it would be difficult to find actual Jews. Deciding how these disparate cases relate means making difficult interpretive judgments about how to map an immeasurable territory.

In order to cope with this difficulty, some scholars simply assume that there is a connection between all instances of anti-Jewish hostility from antiquity to the present. Others insist that each instance should be isolated in its own context for the purpose of historical research. Regardless, it is a somber truth that human beings have constructed meaningful worlds, over and over again, with Jews, Judaism, or Jewishness as a guiding negative principle. Those who wish to think seriously about this fact cannot be paralyzed by its resistance to tidy analysis.

The idea of antisemitism, then, plays an important role as a tool for the protection of Jews against hostility and subordination. But it also makes intellectual demands. It demands reflection on how the shadows of human thought, symbolism, and story are cast. Where is Jewishness portrayed as the darkness by contrast to the light? When are Jews depicted as a pernicious force that explains the presence of evil in the world? How is Judaism used as a critical category to identify what is retrograde, deracinating, or base? The idea of antisemitism demands that we investigate how language, images, structures, and institutions are used to constitute an antagonist: villainy, the demonic, the enemy, the conspiratorial cabal, the exploitative interloper, "the Jew." Thinking carefully about antisemitism means confronting critically, and mitigating, this exercise of our humanity.

## About the author

**Jeffrey I. Israel** is a professor of religion at Williams College in Williamstown, Massachusetts.

## Suggestions for further reading

*In this book*
See also chapters 35 (Did Jews kill Jesus?) and 50 (What is the Holocaust?).

*Elsewhere*
Lipton, Sara. *Dark Mirror: The Medieval Origins of Anti-Jewish Iconography*. New York: Metropolitan Books, 2014.

Nirenberg, David. *Anti-Judaism: The Western Tradition*. New York: W. W. Norton & Company, 2013.

Ury, Scott, and Guy Miron. *Antisemitism and the Politics of History*. Waltham, MA: Brandeis University Press, 2023.

# 44
# Are Jews White?

## Sabina Ali

The question "Are Jews White?" carries several assumptions. It assumes that all Jews are the same and that all Jews are of European descent. Yet Jews include people of different cultural, ethnic, and racial backgrounds. Another assumption is that there is a single yes or no answer for all times and places, treating Whiteness as a static, unchanging racial category rather than a category that depends on geographical location, time period, and historical circumstances.

In the US, the majority of Jews are of European background and are considered White. However, at least 15 percent of Jews in the US identify as Jews of color. Jews of color include people who self-identify, or are perceived by others, as part of a non-White racial group or multiple racial groups, such as Black/African American, Asian American, Latinx, and multiracial or biracial. They can also identify by nationality (such as Cherokee, Ethiopian, and Iranian); by cultural, ethnic, or geographic categories (such as Sephardi and Mizrahi); or by other categories (such as transracial adoptees and converts).

Jews of color have often been overlooked and undercounted in research for several reasons. For example, multiracial people, Jewish and non-Jewish, have long pointed out that standard census and survey categories fail to capture their racial identities. Also, people of West and Central Asian and North African backgrounds are still often categorized as White, even though many do not identify that way. Other survey methods, such as choosing common Jewish last names or neighborhoods, skew toward European-descent names and geographies.

Beyond surveys and data collection, it is important to consider Jews who exist on the margins of what is considered normative White Jewishness. This includes Jews of African descent, such as Black Jews who have adopted or converted to Judaism, whether many generations ago or recently. It also includes Black Hebrews and Israelites, who see themselves at the center of biblical history, despite being typically treated as exotic, militant, nationalistic sects outside the boundaries of mainstream Jewishness. For example, Ethiopian Hebrews (distinct from Ethiopian Jews) reject the idea of conversion because they view their religion as a return to Judaism. At the same time, they share similarities with many mainstream White Jewish groups, such as following strict kosher dietary practices.

As for the second assumption, it is essential to remember that race is constructed differently in different locations and across time. For example, Jews were persecuted in and expelled from the Iberian Peninsula in the fourteenth and fifteenth centuries based on ideas about blood purity, and the Nazis weaponized racial discourse to target Jews. However, in the Americas, European-descended Jews were legally considered White—they could not be enslaved, they were included in naturalization laws, and they could marry other White people without breaking miscegenation laws. Since the colonial period, Jews in the Americas have engaged in settler-colonial projects and considered themselves White. For example, many were involved in and benefited from plantation economies, embraced the discourse of Manifest Destiny, and integrated into White frontier heritage in their settlement of the West.

It is also helpful to see how race works differently in different places by looking at racial dynamics in Israel. Along with Israel's apartheid practices and violent and genocidal oppression of Palestinians, Israel has also engaged in systemic discrimination against its Mizrahi Jewish citizens (those of West and Central Asian and North African backgrounds). Early European Jewish elites in Israel held Orientalist ideas about Mizrahi Jews, viewing them as primitive, superstitious, ignorant, and violent. Consequently, Israel marginalized Mizrahi Jews, forcing many to live in overcrowded camps along the buffer zones of the state and subjecting them to structural discrimination in education, employment, and political representation, as well as the suppression of their languages, cultural practices, and religious customs. Although Mizrahi Jews and other racialized groups, like Ethiopian Jews, continue to face discrimination in Israel, their Jewishness makes them embedded in Israel's settler-colonial project in ways that even Palestinian Arab citizens of Israel—who might be racially similar—are not.

Thinking about Jews and race requires a reflection on who is recognized as Jewish and who has the authority to decide, as well as how racial ideas are shaped by a variety of social, cultural, historical, political, and geographical factors. Jews are not a single, unified group, and Jewishness has never been stable or fixed.

## About the author

**Sabina Ali** (she/her) is a PhD candidate in the Department of Religious Studies at Indiana University, Bloomington.

## Suggestions for further reading

*In this book*

See also chapters 45 (Are Jews European or Middle Eastern or something else?), 46 (What is the relationship between Blacks and Jews?), 47 (Is Judaism a religion or an ethnicity?), 49 (Can you tell if you're Jewish from your DNA?), and 51 (What role did race play in the Holocaust?).

*Elsewhere*

Goldstein, Eric L. *The Price of Whiteness: Jews, Race, and American Identity*. Princeton, NJ: Princeton University Press, 2006.

Haynes, Bruce D. *The Soul of Judaism: Jews of African Descent in America Ethnicity*. New York: New York University Press, 2018.

Kaye/Kantrowitz, Melanie. *The Colors of Jews: Racial Politics and Radical Diasporism*. Bloomington: Indiana University Press, 2007.

Koffman, David S. *The Jews' Indian: Colonialism, Pluralism, and Belonging in America*. New Brunswick, NJ: Rutgers University Press, 2019.

Liebman, Laura. *Once We Were Slaves: The Extraordinary Journey of a Multi-Racial Jewish Family*. New York: Oxford University Press, 2021.

Shohat, Ella. "Sephardim in Israel: Zionism from the Standpoint of its Jewish Victims." *Social Text* (19/20) (Autumn 1988): 1–35.

Weisenfeld, Judith. *New World A-Coming: Black Religion and Racial Identity during the Great Migration*. New York: New York University Press, 2016.

# 45
# Are Jews European or Middle Eastern or something else?

## Aziza Khazzoom

Judaism originated in the Middle East, but some groups migrated to Europe. Thus, the question can be rephrased: Did Jews who lived in Europe become European, or did they remain Middle Eastern? The question interfaces with recently popular arguments that Jews belong in Israel because they are indigenous and addresses the degree to which Jews cohere as a people. The answer depends on how one measures group belonging and on how mutable or stable one perceives it to be.

When people get a DNA test to find out if they have Jewish ancestry, they treat "Jewish" as a biological condition, something that can be easily measured, even parsed (e.g., "I am 25 percent Jewish"). From that perspective, one would assess whether European Jews are still Middle Eastern by asking to what degree the gene pool was Europeanized through intermarriage and conversion in Europe. Arguably, this strategy implies a singular Jewishness that cannot be overwritten by historical and cultural difference.

But we also think of "Jewish" as a history and set of religious and cultural practices. These are more mutable. In this approach, even if European Jews originated in the Middle East, their long residence in Christian Europe and the impact of European events make them European regardless of their genes. Middle Eastern Jews also experienced histories and intellectual movements alongside other Middle Easterners. Thus, on the sites of culture, history, and even religious philosophy and liturgy, Jews often have more in common with their host populations than with each other. There are European Jews, and there are Middle Eastern Jews, and they don't always cohere into one population.

Finally, "Jewish" can mean identity. In this approach, Jews are Jews because they say they are Jews, and they cohere as a group because they identify as one. Identity is interesting because it is so malleable. Groups often consciously act to "construct" their identities, such as when Asian

Americans went to court to get themselves classified as White or when the Israeli state promoted a common Hebrew culture to erase cultural differences generated by exile and create a unified Jewish society.

Identity construction is where the Middle Eastern/European question gets complicated. Prior to Europe's Enlightenment, Jews, even European Jews, were conceived as "eastern," "Asiatic," or "oriental" and therefore backward and suspicious. But starting in the late eighteenth century, Western European Jews were offered full citizenship if they could assimilate into Christian Europe. Jews initiated cultural change projects in response, altering their bodies, professions, sexuality, and religious thought to become what was believed to be European.

Through international Jewish educational initiatives, the project spread to Eastern Europe and the Middle East. It affected Zionism, but in complicated ways, as Zionism sought to join the European family of nations *through* moving Jews back to their Middle Eastern roots. Though most Jews promoted westernization projects, others resisted, often launching easternization or hybridization projects in response. From this perspective, Jews do cohere as a population with complex stances around Middle Easternness and Europeanness. But this history also challenges the categories, reading "European" and "Middle Eastern" not as objective descriptions so much as tools in the antisemitic treatment of Europe's Jews.

So are Jews Middle Eastern or European or something else? It depends on the criterion, but one of the more interesting features of Jewish history is how Jews have purposefully moved between the categories, sometimes adopting them and sometimes challenging them. In this respect, accurately classifying Jews is less important than asking how Jews can continue to rethink the global categories that underlie racial and ethnic difference both within Jewish communities and across the globe.

## About the author

**Aziza Khazzoom** is an associate professor in Middle Eastern languages and cultures at Indiana University, Bloomington.

## Suggestions for further reading

### In this book
See also chapters 41 (What is Judeo-Islamic civilization?), 43 (What is antisemitism?), 44 (Are Jews White?), 47 (Is Judaism a religion or an ethnicity?), and 49 (Can you tell if you're Jewish from your DNA?).

*Elsewhere*
Kahn, Susan Martha. "The Multiple Meanings of Jewish Genes." *Culture, Medicine and Psychiatry* 29 (2005): 179–192.

Khazzoom, Aziza. "The Great Chain of Orientalism: Jewish Identity, Stigma Management, and Ethnic Exclusion in Israel." *American Sociological Review* 68(4) (2003): 481–510.

# 46
# What is the relationship between Blacks and Jews?

## Henry Goldschmidt

The short answer, in five seconds rather than five minutes, is *it depends*. Given the extraordinary internal diversity of both Black and Jewish communities in the United States and elsewhere, there is no simple answer to this question. Contrary to popular discussions of the issue—which tend to posit a "golden age" of Black-Jewish partnership in the African American civil rights movement, followed by recurring conflict in the decades since—there is no single story of Black-Jewish relations. The violence that rocked the Brooklyn neighborhood of Crown Heights in 1991, for example, must be understood in terms of the distinctive histories and concerns of the Lubavitch Hasidic community and their predominantly Afro-Caribbean neighbors. These are not the same Blacks or Jews who marched with Rev. Dr. Martin Luther King Jr. and Rabbi Abraham Joshua Heschel in Selma, Alabama, in 1965. To take Selma and Crown Heights as two chapters in one story is to falsely imagine Blackness and Jewishness as static, monolithic identities.

But to emphasize the diversity of Blacks and Jews is not to dodge the question entirely. In this brief essay, I will make three broad generalizations about Black-Jewish relations in the United States—to be taken not as simple truths but as heuristic principles that generally point toward the truth.

Perhaps above all, it is essential to understand that most Jews are considered racially White. Of course, not *all* Jews are White. A 2020 survey by the Pew Research Center found that 8 percent to 17 percent of American Jews identify as people of color in one way or another, and approximately 2 percent identify as Black. The fact that about 150,000 out of an estimated 7.5 million American Jews are Black must be central to any discussion of Black-Jewish relations. We are *not* talking about clearly bounded, mutually exclusive communities. But that said, the vast majority of American Jews are White. Their interactions with their Black neighbors—including interactions with Black Jews—are thus shaped by patterns of racial hierarchy and segregation that are woven into every aspect of American life. This is not to say that all Jews are more privileged than their Black neighbors or to discount Jewish experiences of marginalization, but it is to say that most relationships between Blacks and Jews are relationships between Blacks and Whites.

At the same time, however, Jewish Whiteness has a complex history, which has left many White Jews ambivalent about their racial identity. This second principle stands in tension with the first but does not contradict it. Jews have been legally classified as White since the founding of the United States, but from the mid-nineteenth through the mid-twentieth century, Jewish immigrants faced racialized forms of antisemitism that viewed "Hebrews" as biologically inferior to native-born Whites. And in the same period, many American Jews embraced racialized understandings of their own peoplehood, grounded in what they often described as distinctive "Jewish blood." This racialized Jewishness has largely given way to unambiguous Jewish Whiteness since the mid-twentieth century, but its legacy shapes relationships between Blacks and Jews. Some White American Jews feel a sense of solidarity with Black Americans as fellow victims of racial exclusion, while others work to distinguish themselves from Black Americans through racist stereotypes of Black indolence in contrast to an idealized image of Jewish immigrants who "pulled themselves up by their own bootstraps." In both cases—or rather, both ends of this spectrum—Jews' perceptions of their Black neighbors are inextricably tied to the fraught history of Jewish Whiteness.

On the other side of the coin, Black Americans' perceptions of their Jewish neighbors are often shaped by a long history of African American and Afro-Caribbean identification with the biblical Israelites. Many Black Christians have felt a profound connection with ancient Israel since at least the late eighteenth century, when enslaved Africans began to read and preach the Exodus narrative as a story of their own redemption in the Americas. This sense of affinity is now shared by Black Americans of diverse religious backgrounds, including many Christians, Jews, Muslims, Rastafarians, and others. It informs a range of perceptions of contemporary Jews, from arguably antisemitic claims that the "real Jews" are Black, to a philosemitic appreciation of Jewish values, to a political commitment to the State of Israel. As with the ambivalence of Jewish Whiteness, Black identification with ancient Israel does not dictate a single approach to Black-Jewish relations, but it nevertheless shapes encounters between Blacks and Jews.

Black-Jewish relations in the United States are thus shaped by the overarching realities of race and by the distinctive histories of both Blacks and Jews. These histories are not destiny, but they cannot be ignored.

## About the author

**Henry Goldschmidt** is a cultural anthropologist, community educator, interfaith organizer, and scholar of religion. He is currently the Director of Programs at the Interfaith Center of New York, where he develops and facilitates education and social action programs for a range of audiences, including religious and civic leaders, K–12 teachers and students, social service and mental health professionals, and the general public.

## Suggestions for further reading

*In this book*
See also chapters 44 (Are Jews White?) and 47 (Is Judaism a religion or an ethnicity?).

*Elsewhere*
Adams, Maurianne, and John Bracey, eds. *Strangers and Neighbors: Relations Between Blacks and Jews in the United States.* Amherst: University of Massachusetts Press, 2000.

Chireau, Yvonne, and Nathaniel Deutsch, eds. *Black Zion: African American Religious Encounters with Judaism.* New York: Oxford University Press, 2000.

Goldschmidt, Henry. *Race and Religion Among the Chosen Peoples of Crown Heights.* New Brunswick, NJ: Rutgers University Press, 2006.

Goldstein, Eric L. *The Price of Whiteness: Jews, Race, and American Identity.* Princeton, NJ: Princeton University Press, 2008.

Salzman, Jack, and Cornel West, eds. *Struggles in the Promised Land: Towards a History of Black-Jewish Relations in the United States.* New York: Oxford University Press, 1997.

# 47
# Is Judaism a religion or an ethnicity?

Jeffrey I. Israel

Jews are a human population living mostly in the United States and Israel. They share a sense of embodied continuity—descent—from an ancient community that lived in Judea in the fifth century BCE. This is the community that built and administered the Second Temple in Jerusalem, established a calendar of public rituals, and codified a canon of Hebrew literature and law, which have been transmitted across generations of Jews as sources of Jewish culture. Jewishness passes from parents to children through a chain of inherited memories colored by these sources or the experiences of those who have carried them through history. Jewishness can also inhere after a public commitment—conversion—that is accepted by an authorized body of Jews. Throughout their history, Jews have been compelled to explain to others exactly what kind of group they are, or they have been shunted into the categories preferred by others. The idea that Jews are characterized by their adherence to a "religion" called "Judaism" is a product of these processes. So is the idea that Jews are best categorized as an "ethnicity."

Strictly speaking, it is appropriate to list Judaism as a species of the genus religion, along with Christianity, Buddhism, Islam, Hinduism, and others. Judaism is not usually a term used to describe ethnicity. But the adjective "Jewish" is often used this way: Jewish food, Jewish neighborhood, Jewish language, Jewish folklore, and Jewish homeland are all phrases that seem to describe ethnic data. However, Jews are neither essentially a religious group nor essentially an ethnic group. Many modern Jews are indifferent to the religion of Judaism or explicitly reject it. They may nevertheless maintain a sense of descent connecting them to the Jews of antiquity; draw, with varying degrees of competence and intensity, from the classical sources of Jewish culture; and maintain close social bonds with other Jews who share a sense of collective memory. While Judaism is now a familiar term appearing on every list of "world religions," being an adherent of the religion of Judaism is not a necessary condition for being a Jew in the modern world.

Even in the premodern world, Jews may have unselfconsciously observed Jewish law and participated in Jewish rituals, but they did not think of themselves as practicing the religion of Judaism. In fact, Judaism was essentially a derogatory category in Christian discourse used to mark the antithesis of whatever is good, pure, and universal. As the scholar Daniel Boyarin has put it, "'Judaism' is not a *Jewish* term." Jews started to use "Judaism" as a Jewish term when modern politics produced opportunities for specifically religious toleration. Jewish thinkers and activists then hoped to promote Jewish eligibility for political emancipation by making Jews recognizable as adherents of a venerable religion that ought to be tolerated.

So Judaism is indeed a religion, but it is not always clear what it has to do with Jews. It is the term used to describe what is ostensibly their religion. But so many Jews say that they are not religious or that religion is unimportant to their Jewishness that a distance remains between Jews and Judaism. On the other hand, if Judaism is often marginal to Jews, this is not because being a Jew is essentially a matter of ethnicity. There are ethnic distinctions that Jews make among themselves: Ashkenazi Jews descend from Jews who lived in Eastern Europe, Sephardi Jews descend from Jews who lived in Spain, Mizrahi Jews descend from Jews who lived in predominantly Arabic-speaking lands. These divisions account for differences of language, regional origin, cuisine, dress, historical consciousness, music, and more. They crisscross unpredictably with national cultures: There are French Jews, Egyptian Jews, Mexican Jews, and so on. If Jews share a sense of descent from ancient Judeans, what they share is not ethnic, since the variations of Jewish ethnicity derive from more recent cultural experiences. Usually, more specificity is necessary to determine the ethnic character hidden under "Jewish."

All of the categories used to classify Jews fail. Jews are not essentially or necessarily a religious group, an ethnic group, or a national group, for instance. Whether and how to fit into these categories is a fundamental question of modern Jewish politics, which is still contested. Claims that privilege one category over another are always more prescriptive than descriptive. Even when scholars set out to study Jews by privileging one of these categories, they inevitably take sides in what remains contested among Jews. They thereby participate in the politics of the group that they set out only to describe. There is no stability to be found in the idea of culture either. The founding Judaic community produced *sources* of culture, but no Jewish culture is separable from its embodied temporal and regional inflection. The Jewishness that Jewish cultures share is almost like the element of life in biology: It animates every living being, but it cannot be perceived outside of the lives that it animates.

## About the author

**Jeffrey I. Israel** is an associate professor of religion at Williams College in Williamstown, Massachusetts.

## Suggestions for further reading

*In this book*
See also chapters 21 (What are the differences among Ashkenazi, Sephardi, and Mizrahi Jews?), 24 (What does it mean to be a secular Jew?), and 45 (Are Jews European or Middle Eastern or something else?).

*Elsewhere*
Baker, Cynthia. *Jew*. New Brunswick, NJ: Rutgers University Press, 2016.

Batnitzky, Leora. *How Judaism Became a Religion: An Introduction to Modern Jewish Thought*. Princeton, NJ: Princeton University Press, 2011.

Boyarin, Daniel. *Judaism: The Genealogy of a Modern Notion*. New Brunswick, NJ: Rutgers University Press, 2018.

# 48
# Does Judaism pass down through the mother?

## Deena Aranoff

Many Jews today believe that Jewishness is passed down through the mother. What is the origin of this emphasis on the maternal line? In biblical narratives, unique family blessings and divine inheritance are passed within family systems, but the text emphasizes the male head of household as the carrier of the lineage. For example, Moses's marriage to the daughter of the priest of Midian, Judah's marriage to a Canaanite woman, and Joseph's marriage to Asenath in Egypt do not incur biblical censure. To be sure, biblical stories emphasize the virtue of endogamy—that is, marriage within the larger family clan. In addition, women in biblical stories play a significant role. However, marriage to women outside the clan does not disrupt the family line. The only type of mixed marriage that is prohibited in the Bible, and somewhat inconsistently, is marriage to people from nations with whom there is a history of prolonged conflict and cultural contagion, such as the Canaanite nations, Ammonites, or Moabites. One does not detect in these prohibitions, however, a general sense that the ethnic line of Israel is matrilineal.

The first hints of a generalized concern with the maternal line appear in biblical texts pertaining to the return to Judea under Persian rule. There we encounter censorship of "foreign wives" among the people (Ezra 10:2). Distress about the disruptive impact of mothers from other geographic regions and the consequent mixed character of Judean households is described as a crisis of language: The Judeans' children "do not know how to speak Judaite" (Neh. 13:24). This lament for the mixed cultural-linguistic state of the household reflects a general concern among Judean elites: With neither monarchy nor military, and with the voice of prophecy on its last legs, what are the cultural threads that might sustain this fledgling Judea? Households emerged as key building blocks of the reestablished Judea, and as such, we see the first efforts to monitor its constituent members.

The significance of the maternal relation, while fretted over in these late biblical texts, however, is not codified in Jewish law until the writings of the rabbis. The Mishnah posits the matrilineal principle as fact, stating that the child of a non-Jewish woman is not Jewish (Mishnah Qiddushin 3:12). It does not provide the basis for this principle. In sum, the maternal line was a postbiblical development that reflects the diasporic condition, even in the land of Israel, and arises with the recognition of the household in the making of Jewish culture.

What is the basis for the gradual emergence of the matrilineal principle in Jewish history? We might trace the emphasis on the maternal line to a foundational aspect of human experience—namely, the way in which some of the most enduring aspects of culture are produced in the household and in the context of maternal care in particular. The mother is a source of the child's social and cultural markings. In relation to her, we find the beginnings of language as well as social, religious, and cultural formation. Child-rearing meets the basic needs of the child, but it is also the process through which culturally inflected patterns of thinking and acting are reproduced in the child. Interactions with the mother, and with all the persons who populate a child's early environment, produce patterns that organize the child's lifelong behavior. Family relations function as a matrix within which a repertoire of culturally constituted Jewish behaviors, of both the individual and the collective, is forged. Thus, beyond its biological dimension, the maternal line represents the cultural matrix of early childhood and its centrality in what anthropologist Clifford Geertz called the "cultural finishing" of the person; child-rearing situates the child in a cultural and social milieu that includes a notion of one's ancestors and a sense of one's mythic origins as well as future destinations. The maternal relation is the loom on which the child is woven into the fabric of culture, language, religion, and memory.

Some Jews today have embraced the notion of patrilineal lineage in the determination of Jewishness. Claims of patrilineal Jewishness are often accompanied by an emphasis upon the markedly Jewish culture of the household environment as the carrier of that Jewishness. Thus, in this new iteration, matrilineal descent is construed more broadly to signify Jewishness as it is transmitted in early household relations—that is, being "raised Jewish."

## About the author

**Deena Aranoff** is the faculty director of the Richard S. Dinner Center for Jewish Studies at the Graduate Theological Union in Berkeley, California.

She teaches rabbinic literature, medieval patterns of Jewish thought, and the broader question of continuity and change in Jewish history. Her recent publications engage with the subject of childcare, maternity, and the making of Jewish culture.

## Suggestions for further reading

*In this book*

See also chapters 26 (Can you convert to Judaism?), 27 (Can Jews marry non-Jews?), and 47 (Is Judaism a religion or an ethnicity?).

*Elsewhere*

Aranoff, Deena. "Mother's Milk: Child-Rearing and the Production of Jewish Culture." *Journal of Jewish Identities* 12(1) (2019): 1–17.

Baskin, Judith. "Jewish Private Life: Gender, Marriage, and the Lives of Women." In *The Cambridge Guide to Jewish History, Religion, and Culture*, edited by Judith Baskin and Kenneth Seeskin, 357–380. New York: Cambridge University Press, 2010.

Cohen, Shaye J. D. "The Origins of the Matrilineal Principle in Rabbinic Law." *AJS Review* 10(1) (1985): 19–53.

# 49
# Can you tell if you're Jewish from your DNA?

Rachel B. Gross

DNA testing can tell you about your ancestry, which many people consider an important part of their identity. Genetic testing shows that Jewish populations from particular geographic regions share significant genetic ancestry. The largest regional group sharing genetic ancestry is Ashkenazi Jews, whose ancestors come from Central and Eastern Europe and who make up about 80 percent of Jews worldwide.

Genetic studies have found that Jews around the world seem to share common origins, including Ashkenazi Jews; Sephardi Jews, whose ancestors come from Spain and Portugal; Mizrahi Jews, from the Middle East; and Jews from other regions. Several studies have examined the Cohen Modal Haplotype (CMH), a set of markers found on the Y chromosome of many Ashkenazi and Sephardi men who identify as *Cohanim* (plural of *Cohen*), descendants of the ancient Israelite priestly class. These studies seem to provide scientific support for familial and religious origin stories.

Other population studies have sought to find the historical origins of Jewish groups. A 2013 study of Ashkenazi Jews' mitochondrial DNA (identifying maternal ancestry) revealed four common matrilineal ancestors. Genetic research has also explored the Khazar hypothesis, a discredited idea that Ashkenazi Jews are descended from Khazars, a nomadic Turkic people. Genetic studies have also demonstrated considerable genetic "mixing" of Jewish and local non-Jewish populations around the world, limiting the reliability of individual genetic test results to give certain answers about one's ancestry.

Today, we interpret the results of DNA testing within our contemporary views of identity in terms such as race, ethnicity, nationality, culture, and religion. While we now think of race and religion as separate categories, they were entwined forms of identity for most of human history. Most people were born into the social and geographic communities of their ancestors and rarely traveled beyond them. Jewishness encompassed all of these forms of identity, and this was not unique to Judaism.

Modern categories of identity were shaped by political and philosophical changes in Europe around the seventeenth through the nineteenth centuries. For most of the last two thousand years, the majority of Jews have lived as minorities in Christian or Muslim lands. These Jewish communities were largely self-governed, and their religion and their local politics were intertwined. Gradually, the Enlightenment and the rise of nation-states in Europe led to the political emancipation of Jews. Jewish community leaders lost political control of their communities, and free White Jewish men gained the rights of citizenship within nation-states.

As European Jewish communities lost their political autonomy and many Jews gained individual rights, Jews needed new ways to articulate their differences from non-Jews. Jewish community leaders focused on "religion," which was understood as individual practices and beliefs. Other Jewish practices, often with regional origins (such as culinary, musical, and artistic traditions) or social habits (such as a particular sense of humor) were understood as Jewish "culture." (These cultural traditions were often shaped by and not always easily separated from religious traditions. Jewish cuisines, for instance, were shaped by Jewish religious dietary laws.) Both Judaism, the religion, and Jewishness, the culture, could be engaged with on a voluntary basis. Nonetheless, Jews and others continued to think of Jews as connected through shared ancestry, which was sometimes described as a race, ethnicity, or "nation."

In the mid-twentieth century, Nazis deemed Jews and other minorities to be inferior races in need of elimination. After World War II, when the horrors of the Holocaust were revealed, the world largely turned away from describing Jews as a race. By the mid- to late twentieth century, American Jews were long accustomed to describing Judaism and Jewishness as a religion and a culture, individual matters of belief, practice, and choice. Still, Jews continued to think of themselves as connected by ancestry.

While we generally think of Judaism as a religion today, interest in DNA studies demonstrates an abiding interest in understanding Jews as a racial or ethnic group. In the twenty-first century, DNA testing has become a popular aspect of genealogical research, promoted by companies like Ancestry.com. On the individual level, genetic testing is most useful and reliable when combined with other forms of family history research, such as confirming or refuting stories about family origins, and it can help connect dispersed relatives.

At the same time, genetic testing and increasing digitization of family history records have complicated the idea of who is a Jew. Today, many people learn from DNA tests that they have Ashkenazi Jewish ancestry, including adoptees and people whose families kept secrets. This sometimes leads individuals to participate in Jewish communities or take on other markers of Jewish affiliation.

The responses to DNA testing highlight how Jews and others continue to think of Jewishness in biological terms as well as the limits of doing so. While DNA testing can broaden who is included as a Jew, it also establishes boundaries, raising questions about the Jewishness of converts to Judaism or those adopted into Jewish families. DNA testing cannot tell you if you identify as Jewish, but it can be one tool among many in interpreting the role that ancestry plays in your identity.

## About the author

**Rachel B. Gross** is an associate professor and the John and Marcia Goldman Chair in American Jewish Studies in the Department of Jewish Studies at San Francisco State University. She is a religious studies scholar who studies twentieth- and twenty-first-century American Jews. Her book *Beyond the Synagogue: Jewish Nostalgia as Religious Practice* (New York University Press, 2021) is a 2021 National Jewish Book Award finalist in American Jewish Studies and received an Honorable Mention for the 2021 Saul Viener Book Prize, given by the American Jewish Historical Society. She is currently working on a religious biography of the twentieth-century American Jewish writer Mary Antin.

## Suggestions for further reading

*In this book*
See also chapters 21 (What are the differences among Ashkenazi, Sephardi, and Mizrahi Jews?), 44 (Are Jews White?), 45 (Are Jews European or Middle Eastern or something else?), and 47 (Is Judaism a religion or an ethnicity?).

*Elsewhere*
Fox, Dory. "Jewish Genetic Potency: The Meaning of Jewish Ancestry in the 21st-Century United States." *American Jewish History* 104(1) (January 2020): 59–86.

Goldstein, Eric L. *The Price of Whiteness: Jews, Race, and American Identity*. Princeton, NJ: Princeton University Press, 2006.

Gross, Rachel B. *Beyond the Synagogue: Jewish Nostalgia as Religious Practice*. New York: New York University Press, 2021.

Imhoff, Sarah, and Hillary Kaell. "Lineage Matters: DNA, Race, and Gene Talk in Judaism and Messianic Judaism." *Religion and American Culture: A Journal of American Culture* 27(1) (Winter 2017): 95–127.

Sorkin, David. *Jewish Emancipation: A History Across Five Centuries.* Princeton, NJ: Princeton University Press, 2019.

# Holocaust

# 50
# What is the Holocaust?

## Helene Sinnreich

The Holocaust was the deliberate, systematic, and state-sponsored campaign of persecution and genocide orchestrated against the Jews of Europe by the Nazi regime and its allies between 1933 and 1945.

After the rise to power of Adolf Hitler and the Nazi Party, Jews in Germany were cast as enemies of the state and began to be stripped of their rights and property through a series of discriminatory laws and policies. The Nuremberg Laws, enacted in 1935, stripped Jews of their citizenship and prohibited marriage and sexual relations between Jews and non-Jews. Subsequent laws systematically excluded Jews from many professions and businesses. These laws isolated and marginalized Jews across Germany.

Beginning in 1933, the Nazi regime had begun establishing concentration camps as centers for forced labor, imprisonment, and torture. Many individuals, both Jews and non-Jews, were sent to concentration camps in the early part of the Nazi regime, including Nazi political opponents, homosexuals, and others. People were targeted based on politics, ideology, or behavior.

Antisemitism, which was deeply ingrained in the ideology of Nazi Germany, resulted in boycotts against Jews and eventually escalated into violence. During the infamous Kristallnacht, or "Night of Broken Glass," in November 1938, Jewish homes, businesses, and places of worship were destroyed. Many Jews were imprisoned or sent to concentration camps at that time.

The situation for Jews worsened with the outbreak of World War II in 1939 as Nazi forces expanded their control over much of Europe. This expansion facilitated the implementation of more extreme measures against Jews and other groups the Germans held to be racially inferior, such as disabled people, Roma, and Sinti. Persecution of Jews expanded to include not only the loss of rights, citizenship, and property but also the loss of freedom of movement and eventually mass murder.

Jews in occupied Europe were persecuted in multiple ways. In addition to the passing of laws that stripped them of many of their rights and property, they were forced to mark themselves in public by wearing Stars of David on their clothing. Additionally, in many cases, they were forced to live in designated areas of cities called ghettos. These areas were often closed off from the non-Jewish population and, due to overcrowding and limited access to food, resulted in starvation and widespread disease.

Following the invasion of the Soviet Union in 1941, the Nazis and their collaborators initiated the ultimate expression of antisemitism, the "Final Solution," a euphemism for the genocide of European Jewry. The Nazis aimed to annihilate the Jewish population entirely. To carry out this systematic mass murder of Jews, the Nazis employed industrialized methods of mass murder, including gas chambers, crematoria, and firing squads. In the Soviet Union, German soldiers and their allies massacred people with machine guns and gassed them with truck engines.

Eventually, gassing structures were installed in some concentration camps. Jews from all over Europe were sent to these extermination camps, where mass murder was carried out on an industrial scale. The most notorious of the extermination camps was Auschwitz-Birkenau, where an estimated 1.1 million people, the vast majority of whom were Jews, were murdered. Other camps, such as Treblinka, Sobibor, and Belzec, were similarly designed for the sole purpose of mass killing.

Despite the overwhelming horror and suffering inflicted by the Holocaust, there were acts of resistance, courage, and resilience among its victims. Jews attempted to survive the Nazi brutality in numerous ways. Jewish partisan groups fought back against their oppressors in forests, ghettos, and even concentration camps. In addition to Jewish uprisings, some Jews went into hiding or sought to illicitly escape Nazi borders. In many cases, they were assisted by rescuers and members of the non-Jewish resistance.

The end of World War II in 1945 marked the liberation of the surviving inmates of the concentration camps and the exposure of the full extent of the horrors of the Holocaust to the world. By the war's end, six million Jews had perished, which comprised two-thirds of European Jewry.

The aftermath of the Holocaust led to a grappling by the world of how to understand, prevent, and punish the perpetrators of such a crime against a vast number of people. The Nuremberg Trials, held in the aftermath of the war, sought to hold Nazi leaders accountable for their crimes against humanity. Other trials of perpetrators and collaborators followed. One legacy that arose from the Holocaust was an attempt to define this type of violence intended to destroy a group of people, resulting in the coining of the term "genocide."

## About the author

**Helene Sinnreich** is a professor and head of the Department of Religious Studies at the University of Tennessee, Knoxville.

## Suggestions for further reading

*In this book*
See also chapters 38 (What are Jewish-Christian relations?), 43 (What is antisemitism?), 51 (What role did race play in the Holocaust?), 52 (How did Jews resist during the Holocaust?), 53 (How do Jews commemorate the Holocaust?), 54 (Is it OK for art, film, or books to depict the Holocaust?), and 55 (How do Jews think about God and the Holocaust?).

*Elsewhere*
Rhodes, Richard. *Masters of Death: The SS Einsatzgruppen and the Invention of the Holocaust*. New York: Vintage Books/Random House, 2003.

Roseman, Mark. *The Wannsee Conference and the Final Solution: A Reconsideration*. New York: Henry Holt, 2002.

Sinnreich, Helene J. *The Atrocity of Hunger: Starvation in the Warsaw, Łódź, and Kraków Ghettos During World War II*. New York: Cambridge University Press, 2023.

# 51
# What role did race play in the Holocaust?

## Mark Roseman

Whoopi Goldberg was recently critiqued for saying that the Holocaust was not about race because both Nazis and Jews were White. Her concept of race was certainly too narrowly drawn from today's North American context. The Nazis talked of Jews as a race in ways that had nothing to do with the color line. But Goldberg's comments alert us to ambiguities in the nature of Nazi persecution. Were Jews really seen as a "race"? A religion? A global conspiracy? How different was anti-Jewish policy from other Nazi racial measures—and from preexisting Christian Jew-hatred?

In early twentieth-century Europe, "race" was a bio-buzzword with multiple meanings. For "racial hygienists" (the German term for eugenicists), it was about the hereditary health of the home population and encouraging the best to breed. For imperial administrators, the issue was White prestige and keeping Germany's non-White colonial subjects at a distance. On the home front, the emancipation of Jews earlier in the nineteenth century had given rise to a countersentiment under the new label of "antisemitism." Antisemites increasingly drew on imperial notions of racial inferiority and the dangers of intermarriage. Race was thus both a putative scientific term for thinking about the quality of German stock and a political slogan for radical nationalist efforts to liberate "true" Germans from those deemed alien.

Following World War I, the new Nazi Party weaponized racial discourse, presenting Jews as parasites and the central threat to the German people. Once in power, the Nazis excluded Jews from key professions, defining anyone with at least one Jewish grandparent as Jewish (including converts to Christianity). Later, the 1935 Nuremberg Laws borrowed the notion of "mixed race" from US racial law and colonial practice and created elaborate distinctions between "full Jews," half Jews, quarter Jews, and Aryans. Because the claim of biological difference was entirely illusory, the Nazis could not reliably physically establish who was Jewish and so fell back on recorded religious affiliation of grandparents to determine identity.

The Nazis brutally induced German Jews to leave the country. From the outbreak of war, and with millions of Polish Jews falling into German hands, the Nazis increasingly sought to "solve" the Jewish problem with forced territorial solutions. In summer 1941, these morphed into mass murder and the European-wide genocide through shooting and gassing.

The war against the Jews was one part of a much broader racial agenda to purify society. The Nazis sought to eliminate inheritable diseases by forced sterilization, though the four hundred thousand Germans they sterilized often showed little evidence of hereditary conditions. From 1939, the Nazis began murdering the mentally ill. With increasing severity, they policed the interactions between Roma, Sinti, and the general population, a policy that eventually led to the deportation and murder of many Roma in Auschwitz and mass shootings in occupied Soviet territory. Nazi policy began to treat criminality as a biological condition, incarcerating repeat offenders in concentration camps. Meanwhile, ancestry tests were required of the majority population for marriage, employment, and more.

Did the Nazis see Jews as another race? The answer is complicated: they certainly used racial rhetoric to describe Jews. But no other "racial" group played the same negative role in the Nazi imagination. Adolf Hitler's hateful rhetoric of insects and bloodsuckers painted Jews as another species. Hitler himself sometimes called Jews an "anti-race," whatever that meant. Moreover, during the 1920s, and with increasing insistence from the mid-1930s, Jews were presented as an organized conspiracy working to bring Germany down. Where disabled people, say, were deemed a potential contaminant of the healthy organism, Jews were thought of as an organized global enemy. It was no accident that the shift to mass murder came with the murderous invasion of the Soviet Union, where the Nazis saw themselves fighting a political system they called "Judeo-Bolshevism."

Many Nazi tropes also echoed earlier Christian themes. The link between Jews and the demonic or the idea of Jews as materialist parasites, unwilling to work for the common good, were drawn from the Christian world and explain the resonance early Nazi antisemitism found in many churches. At the same time, the upheavals of the First World War, East-European Jewish migrations westward, the reaction to the Russian Revolution, and more had created a very particular global panic about Jews after 1918. It was in this atmosphere that Nazism had taken shape, and during World War II, a shared hatred of "Judeo-Bolshevism" would help the Nazis find collaborators across Europe in the war against the Jews.

Not all those caught up in this strange global panic spoke the language of race. In that sense it is clear there was more at play at the time, intersecting with the Nazis' racial-nationalism.

### About the author

**Mark Roseman** is a Distinguished Professor in History and the Pat M. Glazer Chair in Jewish Studies at Indiana University, Bloomington. He is author and editor of eleven books on the Holocaust and modern German history, including *Lives, Reclaimed: A Story of Rescue and Resistance in Nazi Germany* (Macmillan, 2019) and *Beyond the Racial State* (Cambridge University Press, 2017). He is general editor of the four-volume *The Cambridge History of the Holocaust*.

### Suggestions for further reading

*In this book*
See also chapters 38 (What are Jewish-Christian relations?), 43 (What is antisemitism?), and 50 (What is the Holocaust?).

*Elsewhere*
Bloxham, Donald. *The Final Solution: A Genocide.* New York: Oxford University Press, 2009.

Burleigh, Michael, and Wolfgang Wippermann. *The Racial State: Germany, 1933–1945.* New York: Cambridge University Press, 1991.

Hutton, Christopher. *Race and the Third Reich: Linguistics, Racial Anthropology and Genetics in the Dialectic of Volk.* New York: Cambridge University Press, 2005.

Pendas, Devin, Mark Roseman, and Richard Wetzell, eds. *Beyond the Racial State.* New York: Cambridge University Press, 2017.

Roseman, Mark. "The Holocaust in European History." In *Oxford Handbook of Modern Europe, 1914–1945*, edited by Nicholas Doumanis, 518–536. New York: Oxford University Press, 2016.

# 52
# How did Jews resist during the Holocaust?

Sean Sidky

Jews resisted the Nazis in an enormous variety of ways. There are too many forms to cover comprehensively here; instead, following recent scholarship, we will look at three categories of resistance: (1) social or cultural resistance, (2) individual acts of resistance, and (3) armed resistance.

First, social or cultural resistance includes the many ways Jewish communities strove to *be* communities under conditions of extreme oppression: Jews created hospitals, orphanages, and soup kitchens; in some ghettos, like Warsaw and Vilnius, there were musical and theater performances. Education was a priority for many, despite schools being prohibited in many areas under Nazi control. The historian Waitman Wade Beorn notes that of the forty-two thousand children in the Warsaw Ghetto in 1942, at least half of them were receiving some kind of secret education. In the hospitals and clinics of the ghettos, with some assistance from Jewish welfare organizations, doctors and nurses labored under terrible conditions to treat injuries and disease and prevent the spread of epidemics.

One prominent example of cultural resistance was a group known as the *Oyneg Shabes*. Coordinated by historian Emanuel Ringelblum, the *Oyneg Shabes* worked with other forms of organized cultural resistance to document their activities and Jewish life in the ghetto in general, an intentional form of resistance to the Nazi attempt at erasing Jewish culture. They sealed these documents in metal canisters and buried them beneath the ghetto before its liquidation; some of those canisters still remain unrecovered.

Second, individual acts of resistance bear no less significance than group actions, though they are often harder to document. In the early years of persecution, individual resistance included protests, petitions, and writing letters to friends and relatives overseas begging them to inform their communities of what was happening in Europe. As the persecution continued, the most prominent form of individual resistance was escape and hiding: It was common enough, for example, for Jews to pry up loose floorboards to escape from transport trains that the Nazi police gave special orders to secure floor planks in trains. Hundreds escaped by jumping from transports in Western Europe. Thousands more survived the war in hiding, across Germany and the occupied nations, with the aid of non-Jewish resisters.

Other acts of resistance are even less visible, especially in more extreme contexts: Jewish doctors in concentration camps, for example, were often coerced by the Nazis to perform damaging, invasive surgeries on inmates and have been regularly dismissed as collaborators. And yet recent work has shown that these doctors often took significant steps to try to minimize harm and ensure the recovery of their patients; this was itself a form of resistance and one that challenges our normal understanding of where and how resistance can take place.

Third, armed acts of resistance include some of the most recognizable actions that took place during the Holocaust. For nearly a month, beginning on April 19, 1943, several hundred inhabitants of the Warsaw Ghetto, armed with stolen guns, fought against the Nazis' final attempts at deporting the population of the ghetto. The Warsaw Ghetto Uprising is the most famous of these revolts, but the United States Holocaust Memorial Museum notes that there were armed uprisings in around one hundred ghettos, a quarter of all the ghettos in Eastern Europe. There were also armed uprisings at several major killing centers in Eastern Europe: at Treblinka and at Sobibor in 1943 and at Auschwitz-Birkenau in 1944, when inmates working in an on-site munitions factory and the *Sonderkommando* unit attempted to blow up one of the crematoria.

Additionally, some Jews who fled the ghettos and transports joined or started groups of armed guerrilla fighters known as Partisans. While many partisan groups made up of Soviet citizens or local nationalist groups were dismissive or even actively hostile toward the Jews, in some places, such as Belarus, both Jewish men and women either joined Soviet partisans or formed their own, such as the Bielski group, who maintained a large camp in the forests, both fighting the Nazis and sneaking into the ghettos to help others escape.

Although these forms of resistance differ widely, we can point to one way of thinking about Jewish resistance through the notion of *Amidah* (standing up): a term that aims to account for the vast ways people worked to preserve Jewish religion and culture prohibited by the Nazis. In the words of Waitman Wade Beorn, "In short, because the Nazis sought to destroy Jews physically, culturally, and spiritually, one can convincingly argue that anything they did to oppose this annihilation, even the act of staying alive, can be considered to be resistance."

A significant portion of this chapter was completed and aided by conversations during the 2024 writing retreat hosted by the United States Holocaust Memorial Museum's Jack, Joseph and Morton Mandel Center for Advanced Holocaust Studies.

## About the author

**Sean Sidky** is a visiting assistant professor of Judaic studies at Virginia Tech. His scholarship focuses on American Judaism, Jewish literature in Yiddish and English, and the Holocaust. He also writes about inclusive teaching, pedagogy, and course development. His work can be found in *Studies in American Jewish Literature, Genocide Studies and Prevention,* and a number of edited volumes. He teaches courses on Judaism, including history, religion, and culture; the Holocaust; religion in the United States; and popular culture.

## Suggestions for further reading

*In this book*
See also chapter 50 (What is the Holocaust?).

*Elsewhere*
Beorn, Waitman Wade. *The Holocaust in Eastern Europe: At the Epicenter of the Final Solution* (1st edition). London: Bloomsbury, 2018.

Gruner, Wolf. *Resisters: How Ordinary Jews Fought Persecution in Hitler's Germany* (1st edition). New Haven, CT: Yale University Press, 2023.

Siegel, S. J. "Treating an Auschwitz Prisoner-Physician: The Case of Dr. Maximilian Samuel." *Holocaust and Genocide Studies* 28(3) (December 1, 2014): 450–481.

von Fransecky, Tanja. *Escapees: The History of Jews Who Fled Nazi Deportation Trains in France, Belgium, and the Netherlands*. Translated by Benjamin Liebelt. New York: Berghahn Books, 2019.

# 53
# How do Jews commemorate the Holocaust?

## Laura Levitt

The Holocaust, *Shoah* in Hebrew, refers to the mass destruction of Jewish life in Eastern and Central Europe and beyond through the Nazi genocide between 1933 and 1945; it has been recognized and ritually marked by Jews ever since. Trying to capture the momentum and the power of these acts of recollection, respect, mourning, and moral outrage cannot be easily untangled from a now almost universal engagement with Holocaust memory. Holocaust museums and memorials, days of commemorating specific critical events, and other memorializing acts abound. Days of remembrance include *Kristallnacht*, the Night of the Broken Glass, on November 9, 1938; the liberation of the infamous death camp, Auschwitz, on January 27, 1947; and what we now call Yom HaShoah, Holocaust Remembrance Day, on the twenty-seventh day of Nissan, just after Passover on the Jewish calendar, that marks the anniversary of the Warsaw Ghetto Uprising in 1943. Yom HaShoah was itself first instituted as a National Day of Remembrance in the State of Israel in 1953, and over time has become a more widely recognized day of remembrance.

Alongside these dates, Jews around the world have come to bring Holocaust memory into other Jewish rituals and holy days. These include the fast day of Tisha B'Av, a day when Jews mourn the destructions of the First and Second Temples of ancient Judaism. This fast day has come to encompass any number of Jewish catastrophes. In North America, this holy fast day is commemorated in the summer and has become a regular part of the Jewish summer camp experience across the religious and secular Jewish spectrum. In the postwar period, it has been the site where many young Jews first learn about the Holocaust.

The Shoah has also been incorporated into Passover seders with various contemporary Haggadot, ritual texts created for use during the ritual meal that incorporate readings and reflections on the degradation of not only ancient Jewish enslavement in Egypt but also the experience of the Holocaust. The Holocaust is also remembered by individual survivors and their families in home rituals, including the naming of children after often multiple loved ones who perished in the Holocaust. Others have chosen to include the names of relatives who died without graves on their own gravestones. And in Melbourne, Australia, survivors of the Buchenwald death camp created an annual ball, where they dance to celebrate their liberation on April 11, 1945.

Since the end of the war, survivors have worked individually and communally to remember the lives of those lost. Collectively, they have created Yizkor books, or memorial books that reconstitute the memory of entire lost communities. Contributors from across the globe share maps, stories, images, photographs, recollections of places and people, songs, food, and customs of particular towns and villages destroyed by the Holocaust. Artists and writers also use their crafts to tell their stories, and the next generations continue to produce works of postmemory, or recollections passed between generations. Others are now experimenting with new technologies and social media to commemorate the Shoah. Since the 1990s, there has been a proliferation of Holocaust museums and memorials that add to generations of powerful films, video archives, and educational initiatives directed toward both Jewish and broader communities. Some US states even mandate Holocaust education in public schools.

The ubiquitousness of Holocaust memory as we currently know it was built on the legacy of survivors and their memories, but as survivors are aging and dying, what comes next? As memory moves into history, memorial efforts now include the creation of new technologies to keep the memories of survivors and their presence fresh, such as holograms and AI-driven avatars. Others have turned to the materiality of Holocaust memory, to tangible objects that were there then and that are here now, to connect to this past in new ways.

The challenge is how to keep new generations aware of this particular story of Jewish trauma and loss and what it teaches us about not only ongoing antisemitism but also the singling out of any minority groups as targets of fascistic, racist, and genocidal violence. The phrase "never again" has always carried both a specific and a more universal call to act against horrific acts of genocide, of communal, social, and cultural destruction. This slogan is about Jews and other victims of the Nazis, as well as a message about all victims of genocide. As scholar Michael Rothberg explains, this kind of multidirectional memory, of making connections to others, has enabled new forms of solidarity and alliances as opposed to competing legacies.

## About the author

**Laura Levitt** is a professor of religion, Jewish studies, and gender at Temple University in Philadelphia, Pennsylvania.

## Suggestions for further reading

*In this book*

See also chapters 50 (What is the Holocaust?), 52 (How did Jews resist during the Holocaust?), and 54 (Is it OK for art, film, or books to depict the Holocaust?).

*Elsewhere*

Ben-Moshe, Danny, Uri Mizrahi, and Andrew Wiseman, dir. *The Buchenwald Ball*. Los Angeles, CA: Blue Rose Production; Victoria, Australia: Pericles Film Productions, 2006.

Fox, Sandy. "Tisha B'Av, 'Ghetto Day,' and Producing 'Authentic' Jews at Postwar Jewish Summer Camps." *Journal of Modern Jewish Studies* 17(2) (2017): 156–172.

Gubkin, Liora. *You Shall Tell Your Children: Holocaust Memory in American Passover Ritual*. New Brunswick, NJ: Rutgers University Press, 2007.

Kugelmass, Jack, and Jonathan Boyarin. *From a Ruined Garden: The Memorial Books of Polish Jewry* (2nd expanded edition). Bloomington: Indiana University Press, 1998.

Rothberg, Michael. *Multidirectional Memory: Remembering the Holocaust in the Age of Decolonization*. Stanford, CA: Stanford University Press, 2009.

Shanker, Noah, and Daniel Leopard. "Pinchas-DiT: Simulation and the Imagined Future of Holocaust Survivor Memory." Invited contribution to *Lessons and Legacies* (volume 15), edited by Avinoam Patt and Erin McGlothlin. Evanston, IL: Northwestern University Press, 2024.

Is it OK for art, films, or novels to depict the Holocaust?
============================================================

Sean Sidky

Hardly a year goes by without new films, television shows, and novels about the Holocaust. Though generally well received, representations of the Holocaust face an unusually high level of scrutiny from critics, usually regarding historical accuracy. The most common critique is that historical inaccuracies in Holocaust representations, even in fiction, are unethical, distort history, or even lend fuel to the flames of Holocaust denial. Philosopher Berel Lang argues that history "sets the limits for representations of the Holocaust." That is, we should judge Holocaust representations first on how historically accurate they are. According to this argument, it is OK for art to represent the Holocaust as long as it in no way distorts or transforms historical fact in doing so. This leaves little room for anything like fiction, granting acceptability only to documentary realism.

However, as critic Peter Rainer noted of *Schindler's List* (1993), criticisms about Holocaust films seem to stem from "the deeper conviction that the Holocaust should not be dramatized at all—by anybody; that however one does so is a disservice, an obscenity." This argument, of which survivor Elie Wiesel was the most vocal proponent, suggests that the experience of the Holocaust—the concentration camp, in particular—was so dehumanizing, so extreme, so unlike anything the rest of us have ever experienced that it is beyond our capacity to understand, let alone to represent. This line of thinking would suggest that when any art, film, television show, or novel claims to be representing the Holocaust, they are *fundamentally* failing to understand and express the *reality* of the Holocaust. As Wiesel has claimed on several occasions, "A novel about Treblinka is either not a novel or not about Treblinka." Wiesel has even suggested that survivors themselves are unable to fully express their experiences. This position reflects a common understanding of the nature of trauma and traumatic experiences as impossible to fully express even by those who went through them, let alone to be understood by anyone who did not experience that trauma directly.

Yet even those who hold this position do not stop writing: Writers Cynthia Ozick, Aharon Appelfeld (himself a survivor), and Wiesel, for example, have each stated that despite believing that the Holocaust should not be represented, they still felt the need to try—to keep writing, even insufficiently. While we can critique a given representation for its historicity, its morality, or its taste, it becomes a much more difficult task to talk about whether it is OK for *any* art to represent the Holocaust. As literature scholar Lawrence Langer writes, "All Holocaust art involves a transaction between fact and imagination, between the details of destruction and various techniques for facing or effacing their grotesque features." After all, no one is asking whether it was OK for Jews to create art *during* the Holocaust, such as the poetry written by Abraham Sutzkever hiding in the forests of Vilnius, the drawings done by students in the art classes taught in secret by Friedl Dicker-Brandeis in Theresienstadt, or the paintings of Charlotte Salomon, made in hiding in France.

So instead of asking whether it is OK for art to represent the Holocaust, we might instead ask whether it is possible for humanity to confront, or come to terms with, an event like the Holocaust *without* all of the interpretive tools available to us: writing, speaking, artistic expression. This is the argument offered by survivor Imre Kertész, who writes, "The concentration camp is imaginable only and exclusively as literature, never as reality. (Not even—or rather, least of all—when we have directly experienced it)." Kertész even suggests that artistic, literary, or "stylized" representations were necessary in order for the Holocaust to enter into public consciousness at all, to move beyond a specific thing that happened to the Jews to something that implicates the entire world. No representation can fully depict all the details of an event, whether a documentary film, a history book, or a graphic novel; art always involves making choices about perspective, focus, where to place emphasis, and what can be left unsaid. In this sense, even if we think it is morally problematic, artistic representation of the Holocaust is inevitable: Even those who believe it is *impossible* to represent the Holocaust artistically recognize that when faced with a tragedy of such immense proportions, all we can do is try our best to comprehend it, with whatever tools we have available to us.

## About the author

**Sean Sidky** is a visiting assistant professor of Judaic studies at Virginia Tech. His scholarship focuses on American Judaism, Jewish literature in

Yiddish and English, and the Holocaust. He also writes about inclusive teaching, pedagogy, and course development. His work can be found in *Studies in American Jewish Literature, Genocide Studies and Prevention*, and a number of edited volumes. He teaches courses on Judaism, including history, religion, and culture; the Holocaust; religion in the United States; and popular culture.

## Suggestions for further reading

*In this book*
See also chapters 50 (What is the Holocaust?) and 53 (How do Jews commemorate the Holocaust?).

*Elsewhere*
Felman, Shoshana, and Dori Laub. *Testimony: Crises of Witnessing in Literature, Psychoanalysis, and History*. New York: Routledge, 1992.

Kertész, Imre, and John (John Kenneth) MacKay. "Who Owns Auschwitz?" *The Yale Journal of Criticism* 14(1) (March 2001): 267–272.

Lang, Berel. *Holocaust Representation: Art Within the Limits of History and Ethics*. Baltimore, MD: Johns Hopkins University Press, 2000.

Lang, Berel, ed. *Writing and the Holocaust*. New York: Holmes & Meier, 1988.

Langer, Lawrence L. *Using and Abusing the Holocaust*. Bloomington: Indiana University Press, 2006.

Rainer, Peter. "Commentary: Why the 'Schindler's List' Backlash?: Charges That the Holocaust Has Been 'Spielbergized' May Conceal the Deeper Belief That It Shouldn't Be Dramatized at All." *Los Angeles Times*, January 30, 1994. https://www.latimes.com/archives/la-xpm-1994-01-30-ca-16952-story.html.

Wiesel, Elie. "Does the Holocaust Lie Beyond the Reach of Art?" *The New York Times*, April 17, 1983. https://www.nytimes.com/1983/04/17/movies/does-the-holocaust-lie-beyond-the-reach-of-art.html.

Wiesel, Elie. "The Holocaust as Literary Inspiration." In *Dimensions of the Holocaust: Lectures at Northwestern University*, edited by Elliot Lefkovitz, 5–19. Evanston, IL: Northwestern University Press, 1977.

Wiesel, Elie. "Why I Write." In *Confronting the Holocaust: The Impact of Elie Wiesel*, edited by Alvin H. Rosenfeld and Irving Greenberg, 200–206. Bloomington: Indiana University Press, 1978.

# 55
# How do Jews think about God and the Holocaust?

## Barbara Krawcowicz

In 1966, Richard Rubenstein, a young, radical Jewish theologian, rhetorically asked, "We stand in a cold, silent, unfeeling cosmos, unaided by any purposeful power beyond our own resources. After Auschwitz, what else can a Jew say about God?" He continued, "I believe the greatest single challenge to modern Judaism arises out of the question of God and the death camps." The theologian Emil Fackenheim declared, "The events that are associated with the dread name of Auschwitz . . . call everything into question: for the believing Jew, for the unbelieving Jew. . . . Only one thing is as yet clear. The Jew may not authentically think about religion . . . as though Auschwitz had not happened."

These two North American theologians saw in the Holocaust an event that—by itself or in conjunction with sociocultural changes of the modern era—necessitated a profound rethinking of the core categories of Jewish religious tradition. Many shared this conviction. There was no agreement as to the answers, but there was a shared sense of urgency of the questions, the most fundamental of which was this, in Rubenstein's words: "How can Jews believe in an omnipotent, beneficent God after Auschwitz?"

Why, however, should Auschwitz prompt this question with particular urgency? Jewish history, after all, saw other catastrophes. From the destruction of the Temples to medieval massacres, to the expulsion from Spain, to Eastern European pogroms—many generations confronted disasters, and Jewish tradition, beginning from the Hebrew Bible itself, contains a plethora of responses to the question of why God would allow or even will suffering upon his people.

The problem is, argue some, that these traditional explanations do not work in the case of the Holocaust. Consider, for example, the notion of sin, centrally linked to that of suffering in Jewish tradition, which asserts quite often that suffering comes either as a divine punishment for sin or as a God-given opportunity to cleanse oneself from it. But to use these concepts in front of the burning children, as one theologian put it, to tell *them* that God was punishing or cleansing them from sin is a *blasphemy*. It is *obscene*, said another, to think that God was in any way involved in the near-total destruction of European Jewry. And yet traditional Jewish responses to the question of God and evil appear to inescapably lead in this direction. The *unprecedented* character of the Holocaust, its *uniqueness*, is signaled by this incongruency between traditional theological language and the reality of destruction. When post-Holocaust theologians asserted that the Holocaust was unique, they were saying that tradition—as they saw and understood it—could not provide the answers a post-Holocaust Jew required.

Among new answers proposed, two became prominent: first, Fackenheim's idea to add another commandment to the traditional list of divinely given 613. The 614th commandment said: you shall not give Hitler posthumous victories. These words expressed a heightened sense of the importance of Jewish religious and national continuity after the Holocaust. It was a sentiment widely shared by secular and religious Jews alike, including traditionalists who rejected the idea of altering the list of God-given commandments but wholeheartedly agreed about the necessity of continued Jewish religious existence and of rebuilding at least something of what was lost.

Another idea that gained popularity was that of Eliezer Berkovits, who used a version of a free-will theodicy: an argument, in a nutshell, that says God has to limit his omnipotence and interference in human affairs because otherwise, human freedom—an essential part of what it means to be human—would have been impossible. Tragically, there is a price to be paid for that. Simultaneously, Berkovits reached into Jewish textual tradition and mined it for those voices that questioned explanations of evil in terms of sin. The biblical Job was the most prominent example, and Berkovits referred to post-Holocaust Jews as "brothers of Job": brothers of those who were murdered and who must now embrace both "holy belief" and "holy disbelief," faith and doubt of the victims themselves. In other words, Jews could still believe in an omnipotent, beneficent God after Auschwitz, but theirs had to be a deeply troubled faith. This new emphasis on what one scholar described as antitheodic strains in Jewish tradition may be the most lasting theological legacy of Jewish struggles with God in the post-Holocaust age.

Intense theological debates about God and the Holocaust have gradually fizzled out. That is not to say that the Holocaust became less important but rather that the focus shifted from theological considerations to commemorative practices. Creating various ways of commemoration and mourning proved more important than finding answers to perhaps ultimately unanswerable theological questions.

## About the author

**Barbara Krawcowicz** is an assistant professor at the Institute of Religious Studies of Jagiellonian University in Kraków, Poland.

## Suggestions for further reading

*In this book*
See also chapters 25 (Do Jews believe in God?), 53 (How do Jews commemorate the Holocaust?), and 54 (Is it OK for art, film, or books to depict the Holocaust?).

*Elsewhere*
Braiterman, Zachary. *(God) After Auschwitz: Tradition and Change in Post-Holocaust Jewish Thought*. Princeton, NJ: Princeton University Press, 1998.

Krawcowicz, Barbara. *History, Metahistory, and Evil: Jewish Theological Responses to the Holocaust*. Brookline, MA: Academic Studies Press, 2021.

Morgan, Michael L. *Beyond Auschwitz: Post-Holocaust Thought in America*. New York: Oxford University Press, 2001.

Rubenstein, Richard. *After Auschwitz: History, Theology, and Contemporary Judaism*. Indianapolis: Bobbs-Merril, 1966.

# Zionism and Israel

# 56
# What is Zionism?

## Jacob Beckert

Zionism can be seen as a national liberation movement, a colonial enterprise, a quest for cultural revival, or a religious obligation. Understanding Zionism involves examining its founding ideals and its complex, contentious legacy.

In the late 1800s, distressed by persistent antisemitism and inspired by nationalism, a group of Eastern European Jews sought to settle in Palestine, then part of the Ottoman Empire. Few Jews lived in the Holy Land at the time, but they maintained a connection to the area through liturgy, hopes of a messianic return, and pilgrimages. However, this new group, calling themselves the Lovers of Zion, aimed to form a new, self-sufficient Jewish community in Palestine and established farming villages.

In Western Europe, a secular Jewish journalist named Theodor Herzl independently envisioned a Jewish return to the Holy Land. Herzl initially believed that Jewish assimilation would end antisemitism, but he reevaluated this stance after the false accusations of treason against a Jewish French military officer. Herzl believed that by establishing a Jewish commonwealth outside of Europe, Europeans would see Jews as an enlightened group capable of self-governance. Influenced by contemporary European ideals, which valued colonizing and civilizing supposedly empty parts of the world, Herzl thought that only by leaving Europe would Jews be regarded as equally civilized.

After learning that a group of Jews sought to settle in Palestine, Herzl decided it would make the ideal location for his commonwealth. Herzl and the Lovers of Zion were unlikely bedfellows: Herzl was ignorant of much of Jewish tradition and revered European culture, while the Lovers of Zion were religious and less committed to European culture. Together, they created a movement called Zionism, which sought to obtain permission from a powerful state or empire to settle Jews and create a semisovereign Jewish polity in Palestine. Zionists also sought to redefine Judaism, transforming it from a religious/ethnic group into a nationality comparable to other European nationalities.

A diverse coalition, the Zionist movement soon split into several factions. Some advocated for immediate settlement, while others preferred to first obtain sponsorship from a more powerful nation. Many hoped to create a secular state, yet others believed in the need to infuse Jewish religion into its legal framework. Cultural, or spiritual, Zionists believed the focus on sovereignty was a mistake, advocating instead for a small, idealistic Jewish community to revitalize Hebrew and create an authentic Jewish culture.

Zionism would have remained a fleeting phenomenon without the support of Great Britain. At war with the Ottoman Empire, the British government endorsed the idea of a "Jewish National Home" in Palestine in part because they believed global Jewish support might bolster their military efforts. For the British, Zionism was a useful tool in their imperial ambitions, promoting economic development and increasing British influence in the region. Additionally, many in the British government supported Zionism for Christian religious reasons, believing that a Jewish return to Palestine was a necessary precondition for the return of Jesus.

As part of the victorious powers in World War I, Britain gained control over Palestine and created a legal framework to support the creation of a Jewish national home. While Palestine was predominantly populated by Arab Muslims and Christians, the framework ensured the Zionist movement had rights to aid in the governing of British Palestine. Equally significant, Zionists were given important economic concessions, along with the ability to issue immigration visas to Jews. Within Palestine, a new leader, David Ben-Gurion, became Zionism's preeminent figure and in the 1940s introduced the concept of "statism"—the belief that Zionism's primary goal was to create an independent nation-state that would be completely sovereign and serve as the central institution for the Jewish people worldwide. This concept soon became the dominant force within the Zionist movement.

The Zionist movement's legal and economic power, along with its demands for sovereignty, led to another, very different understanding of Zionism among the Arab population of Palestine. Most Arabs in Palestine resented the British giving Jews in Palestine political rights and economic power denied to Arabs. While some Arabs recognized the historical Jewish connection to the land, for many, the actual process of Zionist settlement felt akin to European colonialism.

This resentment stoked intercommunal conflict and escalated to war when the UN established a Jewish state, renamed Israel, in 1948. In the war, many Arabs in Palestine lost their lives, and many more were displaced. Their descendants became stateless refugees. Others became Israeli citizens but were relegated to second-class status. Resentment grew in later conflicts, especially after the 1967 War, when Israel occupied territories home to millions of stateless Palestinians.

Many ideas promoted by early Zionist leaders still shape the beliefs of self-identified Zionists today, though for most Zionists the central defining feature is an overriding sense of supporting the existence of the modern State of Israel. Like Herzl, most see a Jewish state as essential to addressing antisemitism. Ben-Gurion's statism is also key, with Israel's sovereignty central to many Zionists, along with the belief that the state represents Jewish interests globally. Jewish institutions in Israel and abroad are often built on the cultural Zionist idea that authentic Jewish culture stems from Israel and sustains Jews worldwide. A Zionist today may focus on various aspects, such as blending religion with state, upholding democratic values, or continuing what they see as early Zionist ideals through settlement in occupied territories. Yet for most, the core ideas remain an amalgamation of those of the early leaders.

In addition, like the British, many support Zionism for reasons parallel to Zionists' self-definition—they see the movement as a tool for bringing Western culture or influence into the Middle East. Increasingly, many Western Christians also support Zionism out of messianic Christian belief.

To opponents of Zionism, however, the consequences to non-Jewish Arab populations—death, displacement, and loss of political power—overshadow the movement's aspirations and achievements. They believe the ongoing conflict and humanitarian issues within Israel, the territories occupied by Israel, and the Palestinian diaspora represent the true core of Zionism—rather than the ideals of its founders. Understanding these diverse perspectives and recognizing the historical and ideological foundations of Zionism are essential for understanding its modern-day manifestations and implications.

## About the author

**Jacob Beckert** is a historian specializing in the history of capitalism and development in Mandatory Palestine. His research focuses on American Jewish investment during the 1920s and 1930s, examining how these investments, despite being framed as nonpolitical and purely capitalist, intensified intercommunal conflicts between Jews and Arabs.

## Suggestions for further reading

*In this book*
See also chapter 57 (What is anti-Zionism?).

*Elsewhere*
Brenner, Michael. *In Search of Israel: The History of an Idea*. Princeton, NJ: Princeton University Press, 2018.

Khalidi, Rashid. *The Iron Cage: The Story of the Palestinian Struggle for Statehood*. Boston: Beacon Press, 2006.

Khalidi, Walid. *Before Their Diaspora: A Photographic History of the Palestinians, 1876–1948*. Washington, DC: Institute for Palestine Studies, 1984.

Morris, Benny. *The Birth of the Palestinian Refugee Problem Revisited* (2nd edition). New York: Cambridge University Press, 2004.

Penslar, Derek J. *Zionism: An Emotional State*. Chicago: Rutgers University Press, 2023.

Seikaly, Sherene. *Men of Capital: Scarcity and Economy in Mandate Palestine*. Stanford, CA: Stanford University Press, 2016.

# 57
# What is anti-Zionism?

## Shaul Magid

Zionism and anti-Zionism were born at about the same time. When Zionism arose in Europe with its aspirations for national Jewish self-determination and perhaps an eventual Jewish nation-state, many Jews, especially in Europe and the United States, responded negatively. These various negative responses amount to what is called anti-Zionism.

For most of its history, at least until the State of Israel was established in 1948, anti-Zionism was a position held by many Jews for many different reasons. I limit myself here to *Jewish* anti-Zionism. Non-Jews who opposed the establishment of a Jewish state were not quite anti-Zionist; anti-Zionism was largely an internal Jewish discourse about the best alternative for the future of the Jews in light of either persecution or assimilation.

One stream of anti-Zionism grew out of responses to the failure of Jewish emancipation in the nineteenth century in Europe to create societies that embraced Jews fully as citizens and as Jews. Some Jews preferred integration (or assimilation) and adapted to European norms in countries where they resided. Some constructed forms of Judaism that became known as Liberal or Reform Judaism. These communities mostly opposed Jewish nationalism and preferred, for example, to be "Germans of the Mosaic persuasion"—that is, to define Judaism exclusively as a religion. They assimilated culturally yet retained some semblance of Jewish difference through liberal Judaism.

Another important anti-Zionist expression of Jewishness arose among the many Jews who aligned with socialist or communist parties. These Jews sought to take part in a universal workers' revolution and eschewed the notion of nationalism altogether. Even some of those communists and socialists who lived in Mandate Palestine, including in the early socialist kibbutz movement, were not in favor of a Jewish state.

Most Orthodox and ultra-Orthodox Jews in Europe were anti-Zionist for theological reasons. They believed that exile was part of Jewish destiny until the coming of the Messiah. They viewed Zionism as a transgression and blasphemy. Even those who settled in the land were opposed to Zionism.

The Reform, socialists, and ultra-Orthodox were anti-Zionists because the establishment of a Jewish state would undermine what they each sought to achieve: for the Reform, integration and equality in their countries of residence; for the socialists, a Marxian future with no nations; and for the ultra-Orthodox, fidelity to tradition. Three very different communities believed the same thing: A Jewish state was a mistake.

In the United States, most Jews were opposed to, or ambivalent about, Zionism until the early 1940s. Jews were integrated in American culture, and therefore Zionism or anti-Zionism wasn't about the failure of emancipation. Rather, most American Jews, at least until the 1930s, viewed Zionism as a threat to their Americanism. The Pittsburgh Platform of 1885, the first official statement of the Reform movement on this question, stated explicitly that Jews were "no longer a nation" but carriers of a religious tradition and no longer aspired to return to the land of Israel.

After the establishment of the State of Israel in 1948, most of these forms of anti-Zionism all but disappeared. Reform largely abandoned its anti-Zionist stance even before 1948. Jewish socialists mostly could not survive the rise of Stalin and the eventual collapse of communism and could not easily translate their universalist beliefs to another generation. Two major forms of anti-Zionism remained. The ultra-Orthodox anti-Zionism remained committed to its theological principles. In Israel, small pockets of anti-Zionism also emerged, such as the group Matzpen after the 1967 War and the onset of the occupation.

Today, there are additional iterations of anti-Zionism. One is often called "post-Zionism," which includes some Israelis and diaspora progressives who identify as Zionists as well as some who do not. In Israel this includes those who have defined their Jewishness in opposition to Israel's polices of occupation and domination, and in the diaspora, it includes young progressives. There is a wide spectrum in this camp, from those who simply think that Zionism has helped produce an untenable situation of domination, to those who hold Israel is an apartheid state, to those who do not want the state to exist at all.

Another form of anti-Zionism has grown in the US and Europe since October 7, 2023, moving from an earlier phase of "distancing from Israel" to becoming openly antagonistic toward it. Sometimes this movement couples with the pro-Palestinian solidarity movement and campus protests and the movement for Boycott, Divestment, Sanctions. Contemporary Jewish anti-Zionists do not fully share a vision of the future for the State of Israel. One state? No state? A different state? What they seem committed to is the dismantling of Israel's culture of domination, based on the unacceptable premise, as they see it, that Jewish freedom must come at the expense of the Palestinian minority.

## About the author

**Shaul Magid** is a professor of modern Judaism at Harvard Divinity School and a senior research fellow at the Center for the Study of World Religions at Harvard. An author of many books and articles, his latest book is *The Necessity of Exile* (Ayin Press, 2023). He is a member of the Academy for Jewish Research and the American Society for the Study of Religion.

## Suggestions for further reading

*In this book*
See also chapters 20 (What are the differences among Reform, Conservative, Reconstructionist, and Orthodox Judaism?) and 56 (What is Zionism?).

*Elsewhere*
Beinart, Peter. *Being Jewish After the Destruction of Gaza: A Reckoning.* New York: Knopf, 2025.

Boyarin, Daniel. *The No-State Solution: A Jewish Manifesto.* New Haven, CT: Yale University Press, 2023.

Butler, Judith. *Parting Ways: Jewishness and the Critique of Zionism.* New York: Columbia University Press, 2012.

Feld, Marjorie. *The Threshold of Dissent: History of American Jewish Critics of Zionism.* New York: New York University Press, 2024.

Levin, Geoffrey. *Our Palestine Question: Israel and American Jewish Dissent, 1948–1978.* New Haven, CT: Yale University Press, 2023.

Magid, Shaul. *The Necessity of Exile: Essays from a Distance.* New York: Ayin Press, 2023.

Rosen, Brant. *Wrestling in the Daylight: A Rabbi's Path to Palestinian Solidarity.* Charlottesville, VA: Just World Books, 2012.

Selzer, Michael. *Zionism Reconsidered: The Rejection of Jewish Normalcy.* New York: Macmillan, 1970.

Sharan, Shlomo, and David Bukay. *Crossovers: Anti-Zionism and Anti-Semitism.* New Brunswick, NJ: Transaction Publishers, 2010.

# 58
# What is the role of Judaism in the State of Israel?

## Alexander Kaye

Among Jews in the State of Israel, the question of the role of Judaism has always been a matter of debate. There are three broad schools of thought on this matter, which have their origins in the beginnings of the Zionist movement. One school, political Zionists with intellectual ancestors like Theodor Herzl, believes that Israel should represent the right of the Jews to self-determination. This view interprets Judaism primarily as a national or ethnic identity. The secure perpetuation of national existence is the primary goal. Another school, with origins among cultural Zionists like Ahad Ha'am (the pen name of Asher Ginsburg), thinks of Judaism primarily in cultural terms and wants the State of Israel to be a vehicle for the flourishing of Jewish spiritual life. In this view, the mere survival of the nation is not sufficient; the nation exists to promote Jewish values. The most striking example of the success of this approach is the revival of Hebrew as an everyday spoken language. Yet another group views Judaism in theological terms and thinks of the establishment of the State of Israel as part of a divine plan. In this view, the state represents a stage in the process of messianic redemption.

How have these historical positions worked out in practice?

In its founding document, the Declaration of Independence, Israel is defined as a Jewish state in the national sense. The country, geographically, is defined as "the birthplace of the Jewish people" and the state as the vehicle through which the people can exercise their "natural right" to be "masters of their own fate, like all other nations, in their own sovereign State." These statements reflect the national concerns of the Jews who today make up around 75 percent of Israel's roughly 9.5 million citizens. Indeed, Israel has become home to an astonishing variety of Jewish religious communities, global in origin, which produce a vibrant and eclectic array of intellectual and cultural output in the fields of religious and academic scholarship, liturgy, music and literature, visual and performing arts, and more.

At the same time, the Declaration of Independence explicitly protects the rights of non-Jews too, ensuring "complete equality of social and political rights to all its inhabitants irrespective of religion, race or sex" and guaranteeing "freedom of religion, conscience, language, education and culture." This pattern of recognizing a special place in law and culture for a majority ethnic-national group while protecting the civil rights of all individuals is common among constitutional democracies with large ethnic majorities.

The official status of Judaism in Israel is a "civil religion." That is, many of the representations of traditional Jewish religious practice have been incorporated into the symbols of the state. For example, the official language is Hebrew, the national calendar echoes the rhythm of the Jewish year, and the menorah appears prominently on the state's seal. At the same time, the Arabic language also has a special status in Israel, and any citizen, Jewish or not, has the right to vote, run for office, serve in any branch of government, and practice any (or no) religion as they see fit. In these respects, Israel is also far from unique. Many countries, for example, have the Christian cross or Muslim crescent on their flags while protecting religious minorities in law.

One area of Israeli law in which Jewish identity is specifically privileged is immigration. Under the 1950 "Law of Return," individuals who are Jewish, or have at least one Jewish parent or grandparent, have fast-track legal access to Israeli citizenship. For others, becoming an Israeli citizen can be very hard indeed. Critics of this law consider it discriminatory that Jews from anywhere in the world can immigrate to Israel while there are millions of Christian and Muslim Palestinians whose ancestors lost their homes in Israel during the 1948 War and are prevented from returning to those homes by Israeli law. Defenders of the law note that granting citizenship on the basis of national or ethnic origin is not unique to Israel and is consistent with Israel's legitimate claim to the project of self-determination for the Jewish people.

Further questions about the place of Judaism in Israel center on questions of religion and power. Because of the nature of Israeli democracy, which relies heavily on coalition building to form government, relatively small political parties can hold a lot of control. As a result, some groups like ultra-Orthodox Jews, with highly traditionalist views of society and gender, have been able to hold a great deal of authority over certain aspects of life—including the institutions that control matters of marriage and divorce—for all Jews in Israel, including the vast majority who are outside of that community.

Other debates focus on questions of nationalism. As Israel's occupation of the Palestinian territories nears its sixtieth year and the Israeli-Palestinian conflict seems to have entered a new stage of brutality and intransigence, Jews in Israel are drawing on their own Jewish traditions in two very different directions. Mirroring a trend toward chauvinistic religious nationalism around the world, some Israeli Jews have developed a new kind of Jewish nationalism. Often drawing on new interpretations of Jewish mystical traditions, they might emphasize the exclusive rights of Jews to Israel and place Jewish nationalist priorities ahead of democratic concerns. By contrast, other Israeli Jews are calling for increased empathy based on the long history of Jewish persecution and powerlessness, as well as the many Jewish religious teachings about the importance of kindness to the "stranger." According to these religious impulses, the Jewish character of the State of Israel can only be fulfilled if it supports calls for equality and insists on being a "state for all its citizens."

## About the author

**Alexander Kaye** is the director of the Schusterman Center for Israel Studies at Brandeis University, where he occupies the Karl, Harry, and Helen Stoll Chair in Israel Studies and is an associate professor in the Department of Near Eastern and Judaic Studies. He received a PhD in Jewish history from Columbia University and a BA and MPhil in history from the University of Cambridge. He is the author of *The Invention of Jewish Theocracy: The Struggle for Legal Authority in Modern Israel* (OUP, 2020).

## Suggestions for further reading

### In this book
See also chapters 56 (What is Zionism?) and 57 (What is anti-Zionism?).

### Elsewhere
Almog, Shmuel, Jehuda Reinharz, and Anita Shapira, eds. *Zionism and Religion*. Hanover, NH: University Press of New England, 1998.

Cohen, Asher. "Religion, Society, and Politics in Israel." In *The Oxford Handbook of Israeli Politics and Society*, edited by Reuven Y. Hazan, Alan Dowty, Menachem Hofnung, and Gideon Rahat, 161–178. New York: Oxford University Press, 2021.

Kaye, Alexander. *The Invention of Jewish Theocracy: The Struggle for Legal Authority in Modern Israel*. New York: Oxford University Press, 2020.

Kedar, Nir. *Law and Identity in Israel: A Century of Debate*. New York: New York University Press, 2019.

Liebman, Charles S., and Eliezer Don-Yehiya. *Civil Religion in Israel: Traditional Judaism and Political Culture in the Jewish State*. Berkeley: University of California Press, 1983.

# 59
# How is ancient Israel related to the State of Israel today?

Rachel Havrelock

To what degree does the State of Israel revive or resemble the society of ancient Israel? On the one hand, it's a strange question—like measuring modern Italy against the Roman Empire or comparing Iran to the Persian Empire but with a long history of diaspora in between—but on the other hand, the Tanakh (Hebrew Bible) has played a key role in the international recognition of Israel and in the shape of Israeli geography and culture. Even the name of the state and that of its citizens as Israelis signals the desire to recall the ancient people of Israel (*Bene Israel*), also known as Israelites. Gesturing toward ancient Israelites with these names is a means of suggesting that the modern state reanimates biblical kingdoms.

When the Zionist movement began in Europe in the late nineteenth century, it aspired to conclude Jewish experiences of diaspora and establish some form of political sovereignty in a homeland. Jewish national thinkers introduced harsh critiques of diasporic practices like studying Talmud in yeshivas, working in trades rather than agriculture, and a general avoidance of militarism. But if the goal was a Jewish homeland, then, without diasporic traditions, what would be Jewish about it? Emphasis on the "land" in "homeland" quickly led early Zionists to the Tanakh as both an atlas for an unknown place and a template for sovereign Jewish politics. The Bible offered additional benefits due to its familiarity to Christians, whose approval (when it came) largely derived from beliefs that Jewish people were modern manifestations of biblical Israelites, a legitimate folk whose unusual status in the world might be rectified by political autonomy.

Among the early Zionist proponents of the Bible, David Ben-Gurion, the first prime minister of Israel, stands out for his enthusiasm. In his advocacy among Western powers and Jewish communities, Ben-Gurion leveraged the notion that a modern country would revive the ancient kingdom of Israel and activate practical redemption through the establishment of state institutions. Thoroughly believing these tenets, he infused biblical language and themes into Israel's Declaration of Independence, marked the land with biblical excavations and place names, and endowed educational curriculum and national holidays with imagery from the Bible. Ben-Gurion further recognized the need for a national mythology to bind immigrants from across the world and endow the struggles of establishment with a sense of higher purpose. His chosen mythology centered on the biblical Exodus, with the Zionist leader Theodor Herzl playing the role of the visionary Moses guiding the people from oppression and Ben-Gurion serving as the commander Joshua, who oversaw the campaigns to conquer the land. Although this framing of Israel's founding war of 1948 became dominant, it did not come to the fore until Israel's tenth anniversary in 1958.

By the end of Israel's first decade, most of the Jewish population had immigrated to Israel after the 1948 War and therefore had not participated in its battles. Newly minted Israelis spoke a Babel-variety of languages, had different ethnicities, and held class positions largely based on the status of their country of origin. Prime Minister Ben-Gurion surveyed the situation and saw the need for a shared culture to boost civic bonds. To create this culture, he convened the country's elite in a twice-monthly study group that applied biblical themes to Israeli life and interpreted contemporary events in biblical language. The prime minister's study group, which has continued in some form until the present, initiated the project with the book of Joshua, which narrates a genocidal conquest against the peoples of Canaan by tribes of Israel returning to an unfamiliar homeland. Despite the fact that the study group included many professors of Bible and archaeology, it was not an academic exercise. Participants were expected to actively disseminate its conclusions in Israel and abroad. This had the effect of projecting a scenario of perennial military contest onto the already precarious and tense Israeli-Palestinian relationship and coding it as an inevitable war between Israelites and Canaanites.

The centralization of Israeli culture around the Bible, Hebrew language, and military service initiated by Ben-Gurion held until 1967, when the war that brought the Golan Heights, the West Bank, the Gaza Strip, and the Sinai Peninsula under Israeli control elicited varying positions among Israelis. Military occupation of these territories inspired the birth of both the peace and the settler movements. Initially, each of these antithetical movements ventured its own biblical interpretations that varied from the official government line. The writer and Israel Prize winner S. Yizhar, for example, penned a treatise "Against Joshua," rejecting the militarism of

Israeli culture long justified by biblical references. In contrast, the Israeli movement to expropriate and settle Palestinian land embraced biblical texts, particularly the book of Joshua, as a charter for armed takeover.

Paralleling evangelical Christian counterparts in the United States, Israeli settlers relate to the Bible through a lens of increasing literalism. Where Ben-Gurion and his associates interpreted by way of analogy— modern Israelis are *like* the ancient people of Israel—the settler movement figures itself *as* the ancient people reborn in order to rule all territory mentioned in the Tanakh, reestablish the Jewish kingdom, and hasten the coming of the Messiah. Even as this orientation toward the Bible is employed by Israeli government officials at home and abroad, its fundamentalist approach and accompanying violence have repelled many other sectors of Israeli society from the Bible. In many ways, the post-1967 contest over biblical interpretation has been resolved with a small, powerful group seizing the Tanakh and others dispensing with it as irrelevant to the contemporary moment.

## About the author

**Rachel Havrelock**, a professor of English at the University of Illinois Chicago, has worked extensively on Jewish national interpretations of the Bible. She is the author of *The Joshua Generation: Israeli Occupation and the Bible* (Princeton University Press, 2020), *River Jordan: The Mythology of a Dividing Line* (University of Chicago Press, 2011), and numerous articles about nationalism and biblical literature. While conducting research, Havrelock lived and studied at Tel Aviv University and Bir Zeit University. With artists Yuri Lane and Sharif Ezzat, she created the hip-hop play *From Tel Aviv to Ramallah*, which has toured across the world. Havrelock serves on the International Advisory Committee of the trilateral Jordanian-Palestinian-Israeli NGO Ecopeace Middle East, committed to environmental peacemaking.

## Suggestions for further reading

*In this book*
See also chapters 56 (What is Zionism?), 57 (What is anti-Zionism?), and 58 (What is the role of Judaism in the State of Israel?).

*Elsewhere*
Boyarin, Daniel. *Unheroic Conduct: The Rise of Heterosexuality and the Invention of the Jewish Man*. Berkeley: University of California Press, 1997.

Feige, Michael. *Settling the Hearts: Jewish Fundamentalism in the Occupied Territories*. Detroit, MI: Wayne State University Press, 2009.

Havrelock, Rachel. *The Joshua Generation: Israeli Occupation and the Bible*. Princeton, NJ: Princeton University Press, 2020.

Zerubavel, Yael. *Desert in the Promised Land*. Stanford, CA: Stanford University Press, 2018.

# Judaism and Social Issues

# 60
# What are Jewish ethics?

## William Plevan

The very term "Jewish ethics" is a relatively modern one to designate an area of Jewish thought and practice. There is no biblical or Talmudic term that corresponds exactly to the term "ethics" as we use it today (Modern Hebrew uses the term *mussar*, which in the Bible means "discipline"). At the same time, ethics in the sense we mean it today has clearly been a central component of Jewish thought and practice since ancient times. The field of Jewish ethics, then, includes several different kinds of discussions and genres of literature. While these different discussions often overlap, it helps to divide the field of Jewish ethics into three areas: (1) interpersonal norms and rules, (2) ethical wisdom and character, and (3) broad principles or values. In each of these areas, contemporary Jews from a variety of backgrounds draw on classical Jewish texts such as the Bible and Talmud as well as later sources to address issues of ethical concern.

The first area of Jewish ethics consists of norms and rules that guide interpersonal conduct. The Bible is replete with commandments that regulate social, political, economic, and family life. The rabbis of the Talmud and subsequent commentaries and codes developed a system of Jewish law (halakhah) that governed interpersonal behavior and civil law as well as ritual practice. During the medieval period, when Jews largely lived in autonomous communities, rabbinic authorities were often able to instill halakhic norms in communal life. In the area of *tzedakah*, almsgiving, they applied Talmudic rules about the collection and distribution of funds to communal charities. In the area of civil law, such as contract disputes and torts, rabbis had mixed success in imposing halakhic norms because the people often found non-Jewish courts and customs more favorable.

Depending on their religious outlook, today's Jews approach ancient and medieval halakhic norms differently. Many Jews today look to these ancient and medieval halakhic texts as sources for moral guidance and inspiration in ethical matters while also relying on contemporary insights from both Jewish and non-Jewish sources. Orthodox and traditional

Jewish communities continue to view halakhah as an authoritative system of norms and ostensibly rely on rabbinic experts for guidance, though individuals may at times deviate from such practices. While Jewish civil law ceases to function as a legal system, many Jews, whether orthodox or liberal, look to its norms and principles as guides for ethical conduct in business practices.

A second area of Jewish ethics is wisdom and character ethics. The earliest Jewish examples of this form of ethical writing can be found in several biblical books (Proverbs, Ecclesiastes, Job, and many parts of Psalms) that offer instruction on wise and righteous conduct, reflect on the value of wisdom, and consider the nature of divine reward and punishment. The Talmudic tractate *Pirkei Avot* (Sayings of the Fathers) offers guidance for rabbinic sages on cultivating the virtues of Torah learning, reverence for God, and proper judicial conduct. Commentaries on *Avot* from the medieval period to today interpret and expand on these ethical insights. Beginning in the medieval period, Jewish pietists wrote and taught about cultivating ethical character traits (*middot*) such as humility, compassion, and appropriate speech, another form of Jewish ethical literature that is produced by Jews from a variety of backgrounds today. Many Jews in the medieval period wrote ethical wills to offer guidance to their children on wise and moral conduct, a practice that some Jews maintain today.

A third area of Jewish ethics is discussion of broad principles and values. Whether such principles were a significant feature of premodern Jewish ethics is something debated by scholars, but in the modern period, many Jewish scholars and leaders identified such principles as important features of Jewish ethics, often drawing them from biblical passages, Talmudic legal categories, or the literature on ethical *middot*. European Jewish Reformers in the nineteenth century, for example, looked to the biblical prophets to argue that social justice and ethical humanism are central to Jewish thought and practice. Many Jews today cite the biblical notion that human beings are created in the divine image (Gen. 1:27) as the Jewish basis for human equality. Another prominent example is the increased prevalence of the term *tikkun olam*—"mending the world"—among North American Jews. The term originally appears in the Talmud as a legal principle in cases where existing legal standards would create social disruption. Today, Jews use the term to refer to a general Jewish commitment to social justice, shared responsibility, and the common good.

## About the author

**William Plevan** is a visiting assistant professor of contemporary Jewish thought at the Reconstructionist Rabbinical College and its 2023–2024 Democracy Fellow. He writes and teaches on contemporary Jewish theology, ethics, and political thought and is currently working on a book on the ideal of community in Martin Buber's thought. His essay on Buber's approach to virtue ethics was recently published in *Jewish Virtue Ethics* (SUNY Press, 2023). He received rabbinical ordination from the Jewish Theological Seminary and a PhD in religion from Princeton.

## Suggestions for further reading

*In this book*
See also chapter 6 (What is Jewish law?).

*Elsewhere*
Claussen, Geoffrey D. *Jewish Ethics: The Basics*. London: Routledge, 2024.

Claussen, Geoffrey D. *Modern Musar: Contested Virtues in Jewish Thought*. Philadelphia, PA: The Jewish Publication Society, 2022.

Dorff, Elliot N., and Louis E. Newman, eds. *Jewish Choices, Jewish Voices*. Philadelphia, PA: The Jewish Publication Society, 2008.

Krasner, Jonathan. "The Place of Tikkun Olam in American Jewish Life." *Jewish Political Studies Review* 25(3/4) (2013): 59–98.

Reimer, Jack, and Nathaniel Stampfer, eds. *Ethical Wills and How to Prepare Them: A Guide to Sharing Your Values from Generation to Generation* (2nd edition). Woodstock, VT: Jewish Lights, 2015.

Thompson, Jennifer A., and Allison Wolf, eds. *Applying Jewish Ethics: Beyond the Rabbinic Tradition*. Lanham, MD: Lexington Books, 2023.

# 61
# What does Judaism say about social justice?

## Aryeh Cohen

When we talk about what "Judaism" says, the assumption is that we are looking for an answer that represents a univocal tradition, but Jewish texts and communities have approached social issues in a variety of ways in different historical periods. Moreover, "social justice" is a modern term, which was coined in the nineteenth century and popularized by the philosopher John Stuart Mill. It has no real corollary in ancient or medieval Jewish Aramaic or Hebrew sources. Even the contemporary Hebrew term for social justice is just a translation of the English: *tzedeq hevrati*.

If we take as a starting point that social justice is the demand for equity and equal access to resources and power, then we can find statements about social justice in many places in the Jewish tradition. For example, biblical and rabbinic texts make legal statements about labor or housing that demand a certain type of social justice. Jewish law allows artisans and laborers to contract with each other so that they each work on a specific day, so one cannot monopolize the market for a specific trade. The Talmud also prescribes consequences for a person who breaks such a contract (Baba Bathra 8b–9a). There are also philosophical statements that undergird the laws and point to the theology or religious theory behind them. For example, the Talmud says that a worker can decide to stop working for their employer even at midday because they "are My slaves and not slaves to slaves" (Baba Qama 116b). That is, labor should not be servitude, and Jews are only servants of God. The Talmud also recounts strict laws about not withholding wages (Baba Metzia 111a) that are grounded in the Torah (Lev. 19:13; Deut. 24:14) as well as moral judgments for those who do: A person who withholds wages is like one who spills blood. These statements recur in modern Jewish texts when the idea of organizing labor enters the market. For example, US and Israeli rabbis apply the concept of artisans contracting with each other to permit unions and strikes.

Jewish texts do not name housing as a specific need of the poor until the twelfth century, but since then, Jewish leaders have continued to uphold that principle. The twelfth-century jurist Maimonides reinforced his legal decision on housing with the moral flourish that "one cannot be left to languish in the street"—an ethical demand, not a legal one.

Jewish texts suggest two larger philosophical explanations for what might be called social justice legislation. One is for the betterment of the world (*mipnei tiqun olam*), and the other is for the ways of peace (*mipnei darkhei shalom*). The former is most often applied to internally Jewish legal matters and the latter to intergroup relations. These motivational statements come to justify everything from leniency in divorce law, to the equal obligation of burying both Jews and non-Jews, to supporting impoverished Jews and non-Jews. Although some have argued that understanding *tikkun olam* as a social justice prescription is a twentieth-century phenomenon, the scholar David Seidenberg has collected all the *tikkun olam* texts and shown conclusively that "the roots of the social justice interpretation of tikkun olam" date back to the tenth century.

On many fronts and for different reasons, traditional texts and interpreters have argued for a social justice view. This may be in part because of the essentially communitarian bent of Rabbinic Judaism. Soup kitchens and mutual aid and burial societies were always understood as a solid obligation according to Jewish law. The Jewish ethics (*mussar*) movement reinforced notions of labor justice by directives such as the following: When you check to see if matzah (unleavened bread eaten on Passover) is kosher, don't only check the flour and water; check to see how much the bakers are being paid.

At the same time, it is important to note that while the rabbinic tradition is not inherently capitalist, it is also not inherently socialist. It believes in private property and private business. Some Jewish socialists have drawn from halakhic tradition, but so have Jewish capitalists, and most of the socialists were and are secular.

Secular Judaism, which flourished outside the tradition and the traditional texts, has had a lot to say about social justice, but it is mainly in the vein of US liberalism—with a burst of socialist and communist organizing in the early twentieth century, which gave way with entry into the middle and upper classes to bourgeois liberalism. In sum, while the Jewish tradition does not speak with one voice, it does have a lot to say about social justice.

## About the author

**Aryeh Cohen** is a professor of rabbinic literature at the Ziegler School of Rabbinic Studies of the American Jewish University. His research and scholarship sit at the intersection of Talmud, Jewish ethics, and social justice activism. His latest book, *Justice in the City: An Argument from the Sources of Rabbinic Judaism* (Academic Studies Press, 2013), emerges from and articulates these same concerns. Dr. Cohen is a co-convener of the Black Jewish Justice Alliance and a member of Clergy for Black Lives. From 2016 to 2022, Dr. Cohen was the Rabbi in Residence at Bend the Arc: Jewish Action, a national social justice organization. From 2012, Dr. Cohen was a board member of CLUE (Clergy and Laity United for Economic Justice), and from 2018 to 2020 he was co-chair of the board. Dr. Cohen is the president of the Society of Jewish Ethics, commissioner on the Los Angeles City Ethics Commission, and member of the Los Angeles District Attorney's Interfaith Advisory Board.

## Suggestions for further reading

*In this book*
See also chapters 3 (What is the Talmud?), 6 (What is Jewish law?), 24 (What does it mean to be a secular Jew?), 42 (Who was Moses Maimonides?), and 60 (What are Jewish ethics?).

*Elsewhere*
Adler, Rachel. *Engendering Judaism: An Inclusive Theology and Ethics*. Philadelphia, PA: The Jewish Publication Society, 1998.

Cohen, Aryeh. *Justice in the City: An Argument from the Sources of Rabbinic Judaism*. Brighton, MA: Academic Studies, 2012.

Jacobs, Jill. *There Shall Be No Needy: Pursuing Social Justice Through Jewish Law and Tradition*. Woodstock, VT: Jewish Lights, 2010.

Seidenberg. David Mevorach. "History and Evolution of *Tikkun Olam*, According to the Textual Sources." *Journal of Jewish Ethics* 7(44928) (2021): 129–163.

# 62
# What's the connection between Jews and feminism?

Steven Kaplin

It has been common among both Jews and feminists to assume that Judaism and feminism are inherently at odds: Judaism and traditional Jewish life is too patriarchal to be acceptable to feminists; feminism is too modern, too critical, and too not-Jewish to be acceptable to a tradition-focused group like Jews. Though widespread, this perception of Jews and feminists is demonstrably misguided.

Intellectually, theologically, socially, textually, ritually, artistically, politically, historically, and economically, Jews and feminism not only overlap but have mutually shaped one another. At the most basic level, contemporary Jewish life, in its equally diverse forms and geographic locales, would be unrecognizable without the influence of feminism. Women leaders, including rabbis, have made Judaism what it is today. Contemporary feminism would not be itself without the many Jewish feminists who participate in its various manifestations. It is as difficult to imagine, for example, feminist movements without famous Jewish leaders such as Emma Goldman, Betty Friedan, and Gloria Steinem. The influence of Jews can be seen clearly in women's suffrage and labor movements, organizing around birth control and sexual freedom, and the many religious transformations of the late twentieth and early twenty-first centuries.

Although Jews were active in prior women's and feminist movements, Jewish feminism as such began with second-wave feminism and the women's liberation movement in the late 1960s in the United States. Jewish women were overrepresented, and many became well-known figures in the movement. Bella Abzug, for instance, was elected as a representative in Congress, famously voting for the Equal Rights Amendment and participating in the National Women's Political Caucus. A more radical example was Shulamith Firestone, who wrote *The Dialectic of Sex: The Case for Feminist Revolution* and argued that the elimination of sexism would require not only the entrance of women into male spaces (like Congress) but the complete restructuring of all societies engaged in sexual difference. Jewish women like Abzug and Firestone are representative of the fact that Jewish women were influential in many areas of feminism, not solely within Jewish communities.

The Jewish legacy of second-wave feminism has carried over to later trends in feminist thought and organizing, including LGBTQ+-centric feminism, multiracial feminism, and international feminism. Lesbian Jewish feminists, for instance, have played an important role in bringing mainstream religious acceptance to queer-identifying folks: The now-widespread practice of placing an orange on the Passover seder plate, originally representing lesbian women and now largely representing women in general, is a prime example of Jews connecting broader feminist ideals with Judaism. As another example, Melanie Kaye/Kantrowitz's *The Color of Jews* argues that Jewish feminist women are particularly well positioned to think through the complexities of race in America because, as Jews, they are accustomed to thinking about victimhood and inequality, while as feminist women, they have both the analytical tools and personal perspectives to recognize that Jews are not alone in their victimhood nor above/outside the oppression of others. Instead, Jewishness and feminism *together* create a positionality from which Jews can better engage in broader efforts toward racial equality. In each of these two examples, out of many others, Jewishness and feminism are not only connected but mutually enriching.

Within Judaism itself, Jewish feminism has arguably been the most important movement of the last half century. Jewish feminists have drastically changed Jewish norms regarding theology, history and tradition, texts, community, ritual, and ethics. Mixed seating in synagogues, gender-neutral God-language, and women in rabbinical and other leadership roles serve as obvious examples, but the impact of feminism can also be seen in the expansion of Jewish education for women and girls, in the creation of reproductive (e.g., first menstruation, pregnancy, miscarriage, and menopause) rituals, in the leadership of Orthodox women as halakhic advisers, and in the adoption of recent texts, written by and for women, into both formal and informal religious practices. In contemporary Judaism, both Orthodox and not, feminism is mainstream.

Despite—or perhaps because of—Jewish feminism's widespread integration into Judaism generally, remaining feminist questions about Judaism and Jewish life often feel particularly fraught. What, for instance, is the Jewish feminist position on Black Lives Matter? Or Israel's 2023 invasion into Gaza? In cases such as these, some Jewish feminists report feeling competing inclinations toward solidarity with Jewish people, and particularly Jewish women, who are facing oppression and, in contradiction, toward people, and particularly women, who are facing oppression from Jews or groups that include Jews. In this, Jews and feminism connect in yet another form.

## About the author

**Steven Kaplin** is a PhD candidate in religious studies at Indiana University. He specializes in the study of American Judaism, particularly in the intersections between Jewish feminism, spirituality, and thought in the twentieth and twenty-first centuries.

## Suggestions for further reading

*In this book*
See also chapters 15 (Why does gender matter in Jewish law?), 61 (What does Judaism say about social justice?), 64 (How do Jewish traditions portray trans and nonbinary identities?), and 65 (What does contemporary Judaism say about sexualities?).

*Elsewhere*
Antler, Joyce. *Jewish Radical Feminism: Voices from the Women's Liberation Movement*. New York: New York University Press, 2018.

Firestone, Shulamith. *The Dialectic of Sex: The Case for Feminist Revolution*. New York: Quill, 1993.

Fishman, Sylvia Barack. *A Breath of Life: Feminism in the American Jewish Community*. New York: Free Press, 1993.

Kaye/Kantrowitz, Melanie. *The Colors of Jews: Racial Politics and Radical Diasporism*. Bloomington: Indiana University Press, 2007.

Plaskow, Judith. *The Coming of Lilith: Essays on Feminism, Judaism, and Sexual Ethics, 1972–2003*. Boston: Beacon Press, 2005.

# 63
# What does Judaism say about the climate crisis?

## Dustin Atlas

There are two main reasons to ask, "What does Judaism say about the climate crisis?" The first is to find out something about Judaism. The second is to see if Judaism has anything to offer the conversation about ecological catastrophe. While different, these are not entirely distinct: What Judaism "is" will affect any contributions to conversations. Conversely, the specific things Judaism has "said" about the crisis can illuminate Judaism.

Judaism, of course, does not "say" anything about the climate crisis, or if you prefer, it says a lot of different things. And as is often the case with religious systems, these statements draw on a past that is as invented as it is discovered. But where climate is concerned, there is perhaps more inventing than normal. Because as Hans Jonas—the most important Jewish ecological thinker—notes, all ancient systems of religion and philosophy were developed when "man's inroads into nature, as seen by himself, were essentially superficial and powerless to upset its appointed balance. (Hindsight reveals that they were not always so harmless in reality.)" In other words, when the basics of Rabbinic Judaism were developed, the idea that humans could seriously disrupt "nature" was ridiculous. Nature was big, and humans were small.

For this reason, basically everything Judaism has to say about the ecological crisis is a new position that seeks to connect itself to an older text with varying success. While there is perhaps no reason for Judaism to say anything, many Jews feel the need to have a response to a crisis that endangers their intellectual and religious worlds. Further, there is a felt need to respond to people who blame the ecological crisis on religions, such as Lynn White, who says that the contemporary ecological crisis is a direct result of a "Judeo-Christian teleology" that pushed aside (good) animistic "pagans" and replaced them with the (bad) belief that it's "God's will that man exploit nature for his proper ends." Out of these two needs (to say something and to defend Judaism) come several responses. Four of these are prominent:

1. *Stewardship:* The belief that God made humans to care for the land; the land is God's, and we are its caretakers, much as God is portrayed as a shepherd. This is likely the most common position.
2. *Ritual innovation:* Taking an element out of Jewish ritual or liturgy and applying it to ecology. For instance, some argue for giving nature itself a rest on Shabbes (Sabbath) or applying the Jubilee year to nature itself (ceasing to exploit it every seven years).
3. *Ecological mysticism:* Drawing on the pantheistic elements in Kabbalistic and even rabbinic texts, using them to suggest that all of nature is divine and should be cared for. Less mystical approaches stress the embodied element of the Shekhinah (God's feminine form) and use that to suggest care for the earth.
4. *Existential responses:* Claiming that humans have a religious and moral obligation to sustain human life and flourishing and that this cannot be done without a similarly flourishing ecological system. A subspecies of these responses are those that claim that Judaism can't help us prevent disaster but might help us live with it.

It is an open question if any of these responses are viable, but one thing they all share is an attempt to appropriate a response from a tradition that had little to say about ecology and rework this response until it seems like it will work in the present.

This process of combining discovery with invention is hardly unique to the ecological question—it is arguably the standard way religions address problems—but it is clearer here than in many other areas of inquiry, precisely because the ecological question is very much a function of modern technology and economics and the ways these forces have changed what it means to be human.

Thus, this question of what Judaism has to say about ecology raises a number of questions in turn. But foremost among them is this: Why should we expect a religious system to have something to say about modern global problems like this one? The ecological crisis involves, by definition, all people (indeed, all living beings) and not just Jews. Does a Jewish response even make sense here? To answer this requires that we think carefully about the relationships not only between Judaism and non-Jews but also between Judaism and all other living beings.

## About the author

**Dustin Atlas** is an associate professor and the director of Jewish Studies at Queen's University. He writes about cats, ecology, death, apocalypse, and imperfection.

## Suggestions for further reading

*In this book*
See also chapters 5 (What is Kabbalah?) and 17 (What do Jews do on the Sabbath?).

*Elsewhere*
Jonas, Hans. *The Imperative of Responsibility: In Search of an Ethics for the Technological Age.* Chicago: University of Chicago Press, 1984.

Rubenstein, Mary-Jane. *Pantheologies: Gods, Worlds, Monsters.* New York: Columbia University Press, 2018.

Tirosh-Samuelson, Hava, ed. *Judaism and Ecology: Created World and Revealed Word.* Cambridge, MA: Harvard University Press, 2003.

White, Lynn, Jr. "The Historical Roots of Our Ecologic Crisis." *Science* 155(3767) (1967): 1203–1207.

Yaffe, Martin D., ed. *Judaism and Environmental Ethics: A Reader.* Lanham, MD: Lexington Books, 2001.

# 64
# How do Jewish traditions portray trans and nonbinary identities?

Joy Ladin

Traditional forms of Judaism have little to say about gender identity. The Torah and most of later Jewish law and legend identify human beings as male or female on the basis of their physical sex without regard to how they might identify themselves, following assumptions we now call "the gender binary" or "binary gender." Rabbinic texts include some discussion of people labeled "androginos" and "tumtum," people whose bodies are not clearly or simply male or female and today might be called "intersex." But as when men and women are the subject, those discussions identify intersex people in terms of their observable physical bodies rather than how they identify themselves.

Jewish tradition's assumption of binary gender and silence regarding gender identity can make it hard for those who identify as trans or nonbinary to find a place within it. Binary gender identities are assigned to infants at birth depending on their genitalia, but trans and nonbinary identities, broad categories that include many different relations to gender, are self-determined and self-identified. Because they are determined by how individuals understand themselves, they cannot be recognized until individuals openly express them. For trans and nonbinary people, gender identity isn't solely a question of bodies or how others interpret them: It is a process of self-discovery, of understanding and deciding how to identify oneself. For some, this discovery is made very young, around three or four, the age when nontrans children begin to identify themselves with the genders they have been assigned. For others, the self-discovery process takes many years, and for some, it is ongoing.

While Jewish tradition doesn't address how individuals identify in terms of gender, it does portray individuals who change their identities, sometimes drastically, and individuals who decide how to identify themselves to others. To take a few famous examples from the Torah, Abraham becomes Judaism's first patriarch after he decides to follow the divine voice that tells him to abruptly leave the life he has been living and embark on one that is new and uncharted. His grandson Jacob rejects his status as second-born son and takes the firstborn birthright and blessing away from his older brother Esau, defying their culture's assigned birth-order-defined gender roles. Purim celebrates the story of Esther, who stayed in the closet as a Jew in order to become queen of Persia and later risked her life by coming out in order to forestall a genocide against her people.

Judaism also continues to recognize self-determined identities through the ritual of conversion. Like gender transition, conversion begins when people who are not born Jewish self-identify as—determine they really feel or are—Jewish and concludes with official recognition of this self-determined identity, a process that, for physically male people, includes a body-altering operation: circumcision.

Because traditional Judaism makes no mention of gender identity or how individuals identify themselves in terms of gender, there are no laws or halakhah that address or forbid being transgender or nonbinary, though Orthodox rabbis have interpreted the prohibition against cross-dressing in Deuteronomy 22:5 and the commandment to be fertile in Genesis 9:7 as prohibiting gender transition. Even apart from these rulings, binary gender is so foundational to Orthodox Judaism and community that Orthodox Jews who identify as trans or nonbinary face significant social, legal, and ritual challenges. Most trans and nonbinary Orthodox Jews remain partly or completely closeted in Orthodox settings, though Orthodox LGBTQ+ advocacy groups such as Eshel and JQY are slowly increasing awareness and tolerance of trans and nonbinary identities in some Orthodox communities.

There has been far greater progress toward inclusion among non-Orthodox forms of Judaism, including ordination of openly trans and nonbinary rabbis, development of trans- and nonbinary-specific rituals and blessings, work on nongendered forms of Hebrew, and particularly thanks to the work of Keshet, SOJOURN, the Trans Halakha Project, and other advocacy groups, development of trans- and nonbinary-inclusive welcome statements, institutional policies, and educational and social programming in synagogues, Jewish community centers, camps, Hillel chapters, and day schools. In most Jewish communities and institutions, there is still work to be done for openly trans and nonbinary Jews to feel safe, comfortable, and valued for who they are. But for the first time in Jewish history, there are now some truly inclusive communities and institutions. Their examples show that despite traditional Judaism's investment in binary gender, full inclusion of trans and nonbinary Jews is possible wherever Jews are committed to achieving it.

## About the author

**Joy Ladin**, the first openly transgender employee of an Orthodox Jewish institution, is the author of *Once Out of Nature: Selected Essays on the Transformation of Gender* (Persea, 2024), National Jewish Book Award finalist *Through the Door of Life: a Jewish Journey Between Genders* (University of Wisconsin, 2012), Lambda Literary and Triangle Award finalist *The Soul of the Stranger: Reading God and Torah from a Transgender Perspective* (Brandeis, 2018), and eleven books of poetry, including, most recently, *Family* (Persea, 2024), *Shekhinah Speaks* (Selva Obscura, 2022), and National Jewish Book Award winner *The Book of Anna* (EOAGH, 2021). Her writing is available at joyladin.wordpress.com.

## Suggestions for further reading

### In this book
See also chapters 15 (Why does gender matter in Jewish law?), 62 (What's the connection between Jews and feminism?), and 65 (What does contemporary Judaism say about sexualities?).

### Elsewhere
Dzmura, Noach, ed. *Balancing on the Mechitza: Transgender in Jewish Community*. Berkeley, CA: North Atlantic Books, 2014.

Ladin, Joy. *The Soul of the Stranger: Reading God and Torah from a Transgender Perspective*. Waltham, MA: Brandeis University Press, 2019.

Strassfeld, Max K. *Trans Talmud: Androgynes and Eunuchs in Rabbinic Literature*. Oakland: University of California Press, 2022.

# 65
# What does contemporary Judaism say about sexualities?

## Jonathan B. Krasner

In modern Western society today, we take sexual orientation and sexual identity for granted. Sexual identity is a fundamental building block in the construction of the self. Categories like heterosexual, homosexual, and bisexual (and more recently, asexual) are as much existential as they are descriptive.

But sexual orientation as a distinct and intrinsic identity is actually a modern construct that emerged in the late nineteenth and early twentieth centuries. The terms "homosexual" and "heterosexual"—which were coined in the late 1860s but did not come into general usage until the mid-twentieth century—would have been foreign to biblical and rabbinic authors.

Classical Jewish texts focused on specific sexual acts rather than underlying orientations, framing them in terms of boundary-affirming values like purity, social hierarchy, and gender roles. For example, Leviticus 18:22 addresses the act of one man penetrating another "as one lies with a woman." The focus is on the disruption of gender roles rather than an individual's orientation. In the Talmud, female same-sex intimacy was dismissed as mere "licentiousness" (*Yevamot* 76a) because it did not threaten the social hierarchy. Had the rabbis been concerned with sexual orientation, they would have treated all types of same-sex intimacy similarly.

The understanding of sexual orientation and sexual identity that emerged with modernity presented rabbis and theologians with a dilemma: Reframing sexual acts as expressions of intrinsic identities challenged traditional Jewish interpretations. If sexual orientation is innate and immutable, how can prohibitions on same-sex acts align with Judaism's emphasis on justice and human dignity (*kavod habriyot*)?

Jewish thinkers and movements have approached this tension in two ways: Some resist the modern understanding of sexual orientation and maintain traditional prohibitions, while others reframe Jewish values to align with contemporary insights.

The resistance camp was exemplified by Moshe Feinstein, a leading twentieth-century Orthodox rabbi and halakhic authority. In *Igrot Moshe, Orah Hayyim* (1976), Feinstein dismissed homosexuality as "one of the most debased sins," denying that same-sex desire could be natural. More recently, Rabbi Aharon Feldman, head of Ner Israel Rabbinical College, acknowledges same-sex attraction as a real experience but insists that Jewish law remains concerned only with acts, not desires. In his correspondence with a Jewish man who was struggling with his sexuality, Feldman characterized homosexuality as a challenge to be mastered, urging celibacy for those unable to enter heterosexual marriages.

Resisters focused on the biblical and rabbinic prohibitions, but accommodationists also looked to classical Jewish texts for guidance. Many found inspiration in the Talmudic expansion of the Hebrew Bible's rationale for marriage as procreation. The Talmud elevates sexual pleasure and mutual concern and thereby acknowledges the fundamental importance of human dignity. The emphasis on *kavod habriyot* provided an opening for a more flexible approach to long-term, monogamous, same-sex relationships.

Unbound by *halakhah*, Reform and Reconstructionist Judaism were the quickest to embrace the modern understanding of sexual orientation as immutable. By the end of the twentieth century, both movements fully included LGBTQ+ Jews, sanctified same-sex unions, and admitted openly gay clergy. Drawing on values like creation in God's image and *kavod habriyot*, they reframed Jewish tradition to celebrate diversity and equality.

The Conservative movement, operating within the bounds of *halakhah* but open to reinterpretation, acted more cautiously. In the late 1980s and early 1990s, the movement's Committee on Jewish Law and Standards considered a responsum written by Rabbi Bradley Artson, which advocated for gay and lesbian equality, including the ordination of openly gay rabbis and the sanctification of same-sex unions, but it was not until 2006 that the committee approved a more modest responsum. It maintained the prohibition on male anal sex while affirming the dignity and sanctity of monogamous same-sex partnerships on the grounds that to do otherwise would violate *kavod habriyot*.

Within Modern Orthodoxy, a minority liberal flank seeks to reconcile Jewish law with the realities of sexual orientation. Rabbi Steven Greenberg, the first openly gay Orthodox rabbi, challenges traditional interpretations of Leviticus and Talmudic passages, arguing that prohibitions on male same-sex acts reflect ancient gender norms rather than divine moral principles. Organizations like Eshel, cofounded by Greenberg and Miryam Kabakov, advocate for LGBTQ+ inclusion within Orthodox spaces.

Other more centrist modern Orthodox thinkers have begun to show engagement with the concept of sexual orientation. The 2010 "Statement of Principles on the Place of Jews with a Homosexual Orientation in Our Community," signed by over 160 leaders, marked a significant shift. The statement distinguished between orientation and behavior, calling for dignity and inclusion of LGBTQ+ Jews within Orthodox spaces while upholding prohibitions on same-sex acts. However, more traditional Orthodox leaders rejected its premise of orientation as identity. Indeed, a dueling "Declaration on the Torah Approach to Homosexuality," also signed by scores of Orthodox leaders, declared that "the concept that God created a human being who is unable to find happiness in a loving relationship unless he violates a biblical prohibition is neither plausible nor acceptable."

Contemporary Judaism's approaches to queer sexualities reveal a spectrum of responses, reflecting the challenge of integrating modern constructs of sexual orientation with ancient traditions. Orthodox Judaism largely resists these constructs, emphasizing behavior over identity, while Reform, Reconstructionist, and Conservative movements accommodate modern understandings to varying degrees. These diverse responses underscore the evolving nature of Jewish thought as it seeks to balance fidelity to tradition with the realities of human experience.

## About the author

**Jonathan B. Krasner** is an associate professor and the Jack, Joseph, and Morton Mandel Professor of Jewish Education Research with a joint appointment in the Department of Near Eastern and Judaic Studies and the Jack, Joseph, and Morton Mandel Center for Studies in Jewish Education.

## Suggestions for further reading

*In this book*
See also chapters 2 (What is the Torah?), 3 (What is the Talmud?), 6 (What is Jewish law?), 62 (What's the connection between Jews and feminism?), and 64 (How do Jewish traditions portray trans and nonbinary identities?).

*Elsewhere*
Biale, David. *Eros and the Jews: From Biblical Israel to Contemporary America*. Berkeley: University of California Press, 2023.

Boyarin, Daniel. "Are There Any Jews in the History of Sexuality?" *Journal of the History of Sexuality* 5 (1995): 333–355.

Greenberg, David F. *The Construction of Homosexuality*. Chicago: University of Chicago Press, 2008.

Greenberg, Steven. *Wrestling with God and Men: Homosexuality in the Jewish Tradition*. Madison: University of Wisconsin Press, 2005.

Katz, Jonathan Ned. *The Invention of Heterosexuality*. Chicago: University of Chicago Press, 2007.

Shneer, David, and Caryn Aviv, eds. *Queer Jews*. New York: Routledge, 2002.

# 66
# How do Jewish traditions approach disability?

Andrea Dara Cooper

Disability has often been defined as an individual medical diagnosis involving impairment; the "problem" lies with a person's body, which is pathologized or deemed in need of treatment. In recent decades, disability activists and scholars have challenged this model, maintaining that disability is not simply a medical problem but rather a social construction. According to the social model, cultural attitudes and assumptions decide which bodies are "normal" and which are marginalized, and the built environment is disabling. More recently, disability activists have argued for a model that takes into account both impairment and social barriers to access.

How do these approaches resonate with Jewish texts, traditions, and practices? Scholar, rabbi, and activist Julia Watts Belser demonstrates how disability is a valued dimension of human difference and Jewish diversity. She observes that while religious communities "have more often tended to treat disability as a problem to be solved than a perspective to be embraced," Jewish sacred texts and traditions provide multiple examples of prominent figures, leaders, and community members with disabilities.

In the Hebrew Bible, Moses is presented with a disability, being "slow of speech and tongue." God maintains that Moses's speech disability does not affect his candidacy for leadership, appointing his brother Aaron to voice Moses's words to the people. Ultimately, Moses delivers a celebrated speech to the Israelites by himself in the book of Deuteronomy. While some early commentators interpreted this to mean that Moses was "healed" of his speech impairment, the narrative can also be read as evidence that the people eventually learned how to listen to Moses and embrace his speech.

Other biblical texts present disability in a less positive light. For example, many troubling metaphors align the Israelite people's stubbornness and ignorance with deafness or blindness. Aside from the obvious problems with such negative associations, scholars point out that using disability as a trope to convey a theological lesson threatens to efface the actual lived experiences of people with disabilities.

Many Talmudic sources assert the inherent value of people with disabilities, taking for granted that they are created *b'tzelem Elohim*, in the "divine image." At the same time, a number of these sources deny that people with disabilities can fulfill certain legal obligations. Since halakhah (Jewish law) is foundational to Judaism, the question of whether or not a person can observe specific *mitzvot* (commandments) has historically been of utmost importance. There is a useful analogy here to gender: Today, scholars of gender point out that the Talmud already recognized multiple genders, and this can be a resource for contemporary readers to challenge assumptions about gender as a binary or fixed category. But even while recognizing many genders, the rabbis nevertheless were preoccupied with figuring out which category—male or female—each person fit into for reasons related to halakhah. Just as Jewish legal obligations presume a gender binary (despite the rabbis recognizing multiple genders), many halakhic obligations to do with specific timing and abilities assume that people with disabilities present a problem to the legal system; they have to somehow fit into that system, even though the sources acknowledge that the system doesn't account for all bodies and experiences.

Disability scholars and activists challenge approaches that present disability as a problem to be dealt with or solved. They emphasize drawing on disability as a resource rather than a detriment.

In contemporary Jewish life, people with disabilities demonstrate the importance of innovation within practice, ritual, and prayer, illustrating how these developments contribute to the ongoing creative reshaping of Jewish tradition. This can involve enhanced accessibility of synagogues not only for entering buildings but also for welcoming people with disabilities to the *bima*, the platform from which the Torah is read and the service is led. Deaf Jews, for example, have reinterpreted traditional prayers such as the *Shema*, which calls the Jewish community to "hear," to focus instead on giving attention to God's oneness.

Indeed, innovation has long been central to Jewish tradition. The rabbis in late antiquity maintained that each generation experiences the revelation of Torah anew, regenerating it and giving it new meaning. Similar to feminist scholars' and theologians' point that reframing and remaking Jewish traditions has always been central to Judaism, disability scholars writing from a Jewish perspective emphasize the importance of reinterpreting sacred texts and practices through a disability lens. For example, the Jewish practice of keeping the Sabbath as a day of rest resonates with principles of disability justice, helping challenge the widespread assumption that our worth is measured by our work and productivity. As Belser maintains, disability can be a generative force and a source of embodied knowledge in Judaism.

## About the author

**Andrea Dara Cooper** is an associate professor and Leonard and Tobee Kaplan Scholar in Modern Jewish Thought and Culture in the Department of Religious Studies at the University of North Carolina at Chapel Hill, where she researches and teaches on religion and culture, Jewish studies, gender, and philosophy. She is the author of *Gendering Modern Jewish Thought* (Indiana University Press, 2021).

## Suggestions for further reading

*In this book*
See also chapters 15 (Why does gender matter in Jewish law?), 17 (What do Jews do on the Sabbath?), 62 (What's the connection between Jews and feminism?), and 64 (How do Jewish traditions portray trans and nonbinary identities?).

*Elsewhere*
Abrams, Judith. *Judaism and Disability: Portrayals in Ancient Texts from the Tanach Through the Bavli.* Washington, DC: Gallaudet University Press, 1998.

Imhoff, Sarah. *The Lives of Jessie Sampter: Queer, Disabled, Zionist.* Durham, NC: Duke University Press, 2022.

Olyan, Saul. *Disability in the Hebrew Bible: Interpreting Mental and Physical Differences.* New York: Cambridge University Press, 2008.

Watts Belser, Julia. "Judaism and Disability." In *Disability and World Religions: An Introduction*, edited by Darla Y. Schumm and Michael Stoltzfus. Waco, TX: Baylor University Press, 2016.

Watts Belser, Julia. *Loving Our Own Bones: Disability Wisdom and the Spiritual Subversiveness of Knowing Ourselves Whole.* Boston: Beacon Press, 2023.

# 67
# What's the deal with Jews and comedy?

## Jennifer Caplan

The history of modern comedy is inextricably linked with the history of modern Judaism, particularly in North America. There is no singular answer to why comedy became known as what Steve Allen once called a "Jewish cottage industry," but we can draw some inferences from the histories of both Jews and humor to understand their relationship.

What is funny, and how do we know? The methodological approach known as "humor theory" dates to at least the eighteenth century and has developed alongside the art form of comedy. A few elements from humor theory help us understand the relationship of Jews to humor. One key point is that humor (and Jewish humor in particular) is deeply tied to language. A great deal of humor comes from the way words sound, work together, and take on a variety of meanings. For that reason, it is difficult—or even impossible—to compare humor across space and time. Additionally, humor is very positional, meaning that something may be funny (or not) both based on your position in society and in relation to the person telling the joke.

Those points matter because when teasing out the history of Jews and humor, it is tempting to try to trace the origins back to the Bible or the Talmud. That requires assumptions and probably misapprehensions about what someone in a very different time, place, and language found humorous. It is safer, therefore, to keep things as contemporary as possible, so we will look only as far back as nineteenth-century Eastern Europe. The stories of Yiddish writers such as Sholem Aleichem and S. Y. Abramovich offer a good baseline for why North American comedy came to be so linked to Jews. This is because they rely on similar humor forms, notably humor based in juxtaposition and humor based in superiority, and because so much of the rhythms and cadences of North American humor are based on the sounds and rhythms of Yiddish. Both "shm-reduplication" (i.e.,

"Yiddish shmiddish") and a particular type of subject-verb inversion ("you want I should . . ."; "this you tell me . . .") come from patterns common to the English spoken by native Yiddish speakers.

From this vantage point, comedy becomes just another example of American Jews capitalizing on a new industry unhindered by a European-style guild system keeping Jews out. Jewish immigrants such as Samuel Goldwyn, Louis B. Mayer, William Fox, and the Warner Brothers built the original film studios. Jews owned, operated, and performed in many vaudeville theaters in the 1910s and 1920s, and there was overlap between those Jews who learned comedy in the Yiddish-language films and theaters and those who came up through English-language venues. Today's stand-up comedy developed from the comedy acts in vaudeville and burlesque variety shows, which faded just as the hundreds of Jewish resorts in the Catskill Mountains were being built. In the 1930s and 1940s, performers who found their theaters closing could perform for resort guests, and as television became the dominant entertainment medium in the 1950s, these same comedians honed their acts in the Catskills and brought them to the small screen on everything from late-night talk show appearances, sketch comedy shows like Sid Caesar's *Your Show of Shows* or Milton Berle's *Texaco Star Theatre*, and eventually ensemble shows like *Saturday Night Live*.

Like the early film studios, all of the original television networks were owned by Jews. As more and more homes across the country (not just in big cities) had televisions, viewer tastes began to change, and Jewish executives began to fear oversaturating the airwaves with Jewish performers. This concern about "surplus visibility" meant that for most of the later twentieth century, Jewish characters were missing from comedy. As the original Jewish owners retired or died, corporations bought the networks; so by the 1990s, Jewish comedians playing Jewish characters were back in force and have remained visible into the twenty-first century.

During the 1970s and 1980s, comedy had begun to change, however, and it has continued to diversify since that period. Jews may still be disproportionately represented in comedy (since Jews today make up .2 percent of the global population), but they no longer constitute 80 percent of professional comedy, as Steve Allen once estimated they had. Furthermore, Jewish culture has become more diverse, so while that Eastern European, Yiddish influence is still strongly felt, it is no longer the only image of Jews or Jewishness we find in comedy. Jews and humor will, therefore, forever remain linked, but they are no longer inextricable.

## About the author

**Jennifer Caplan** is an associate professor and the Jewish Foundation of Cincinnati Chair in Judaic Studies at the University of Cincinnati. She is the author of *Funny, You Don't Look Funny: Judaism and Humor from the Silent Generation to Millennials* (Wayne State University Press, 2023) and is currently working on a monograph on Jewish characters in the DC and Marvel universes.

## Suggestions for further reading

*In this book*
See also chapters 23 (What languages do Jews speak?) and 47 (Is Judaism a religion or an ethnicity?).

*Elsewhere*
Allen, Steve. *Funny People*. New York: Stein and Day, 1981.

Brook, Vincent. *Something Ain't Kosher Here*. New Brunswick, NJ: Rutgers University Press, 2003.

Caplan, Jennifer. *Funny, You Don't Look Funny: Judaism and Humor from the Silent Generation to Millennials*. Detroit, MI: Wayne State University Press, 2023.

Dauber, Jeremy. *Jewish Comedy: A Serious History*. New York: W. W. Norton & Co, 2017.

Freud, Sigmund. *Jokes and Their Relation to the Unconscious*. New York: W. W. Norton & Sons, 1990.

Friedman, Hershey. *God Laughed: The Source of Jewish Humor*. New York: Routledge, 2014.

Oring, Elliot. *The First Book of Jewish Jokes: The Collection of L. M. Büschenthal*. Bloomington: Indiana University Press, 2018.

Telushkin, Joseph. *Jewish Humor*. New York: William Morrow, 1998.

Wisse, Ruth. *No Joke: Making Jewish Humor*. Princeton, NJ: Princeton University Press, 2013.

# 68
# Where do stereotypes about Jews and money come from?

## Samuel Hayim Brody

The Jews are not the only people in history to be accused of illicit trade practices. They are not even the only people to have their group name transformed into a verb meaning "cheat, deceive, rip off." Examples include *gyp* (derived from *gypsy*, already an insulting exonym for the Romani people); *welch* (applied by the Anglos and Normans to the Celtic Welsh who resisted their invasion); and *Indian giver* (applied by European traders to Native Americans because of confusion over whether exchange constituted gift-giving or trade). The Jewish example is *to Jew down*. Despite how obvious these insults are, many continue to use them as if they are neutral or even positive expressions (who doesn't love a good deal, after all?). Yet as this comparison shows, these phrases are always generated by dominant groups and applied to oppressed ones.

Between the eleventh and fourteenth centuries, Western Europe underwent a period of rapid commercial development. Cities expanded, and more people became merchants and had contact with money, banking, and trade. All of this had long been common in other parts of the world, including the Islamic Mediterranean, one of Europe's primary trading partners. Still, it was a shock to the system of sleepy Latin Christendom, and church authorities were conflicted about how to deal with it.

One response was to found mendicant orders, bringing the energy and devotion of the monastery to the newly bustling cities. The Franciscans developed a theology to push the boundaries of what Christianity had historically considered permissible trade practices while at the same time placing renewed stress on the dangers of "usury" (now sometimes defined as *excessive* interest rather than as any price for money whatsoever). Frequently, this was done by painting usury as the practice of suspicious outsiders, such as Jews and Lombards (Italian merchant-bankers). Eventually, both groups suffered expulsion from entire regions as punishment for the practice.

How much moneylending were Jews actually doing? For most, desperately poor, the answer was none. A few did some, and a very few wealthy individuals did a lot. Jews certainly did not do *more* moneylending than Christians, despite the legend among both groups that Jews were forced into the despised profession through bans on landholding or guild membership. The history is complex, depends on time and location, and cannot be captured by the popular story "In the Middle Ages, Jews were forbidden to own land . . ." Shakespeare's Shylock, written at a time when no Jews lived in England, represents the peak of the stereotype's power. At no time was the stereotype derived from knowledge of Jewish sources themselves, even if "business secrets of the Talmud" remains an enduringly popular genre in places such as China and South Korea. The Talmud, like Catholic canon law and Islamic *fiqh*, contains many regulations of business practices but, alas, no "secrets" for getting rich quick.

Beginning in the seventeenth century, absolutist rulers, newly willing to openly embrace raison d'etat as a policy basis, began to readmit Jews to their realms under the assumption that they would benefit the economy. In the eighteenth and nineteenth centuries, as Enlightenment philosophy led Europeans to debate granting Jews civil rights, the question often turned on whether Jews could be "productivized"—turned toward more respectable pursuits, such as agriculture and manual labor. Jews, too, engaged in these debates, with Jewish liberals, socialists, and Zionists all endorsing their own versions of "productivization." Such framings were salient only in Christian Europe; in the Islamic world, the Jewish occupational profile did not appear distinct enough to warrant comment.

As the nineteenth century became the twentieth, the stereotype metastasized into a justification for murderous antisemitism on a new scale. Important thinkers on both the left and the right identified Jews with capitalism itself and saw the spread of capitalism as a form of global "Judaization"—the world becoming "Jewish." When capitalism failed, many suffering in the economic crisis identified the "invisible hand" of the market as a Jewish one. Such scapegoating fueled the growth of fascism in many countries, even as fascists also associated Jews with the communist threat, in a kind of photo-negative of the classic stereotype.

Today, despite post–World War II claims of progress beyond such stereotypes, we are arguably seeing a resurgence of this pattern. When liberalism is ascendant and capitalism and markets are seen as good, Jews are tolerated; when crisis comes, Jews are targeted. Liberals believe this proves the salutary philosemitism of liberalism. Socialists believe this proves that capitalism's instability is deadly for Jews. Critical study of the nature and prevalence of the popular association between Jews and money is necessary to drain this image of its power.

## About the author
**Samuel Hayim Brody** is an associate professor in the Religious Studies Department at the University of Kansas. He is author of *Martin Buber's Theopolitics* (Indiana University Press, 2018) and, with Julie Cooper, an editor of *The King Is in the Field: Essays in Modern Jewish Political Thought* (University of Pennsylvania Press, 2023).

## Suggestions for further reading
*In this book*
See also chapter 43 (What is antisemitism?).

*Elsewhere*
Dorin, Rowan. *No Return: Jews, Christian Usurers, and the Spread of Mass Expulsion in Medieval Europe*. Princeton, NJ: Princeton University Press, 2023.

Hanebrink, Paul. *A Specter Haunting Europe: The Myth of Judeo-Bolshevism*. Cambridge, MA: Harvard University Press, 2018.

Mell, Julie. *The Myth of the Medieval Jewish Moneylender* (2 volumes). New York: Palgrave Macmillan, 2017.

Trivellato, Francesca. *The Promise and Peril of Credit: What a Forgotten Legend About Jews and Finance Tells Us About the Making of European Commercial Society*. Princeton, NJ: Princeton University Press, 2019.

# 69
# What does Jewish tradition say about war?

Geoffrey D. Claussen

There is no singular Jewish tradition that "says" anything in particular about any of the issues under discussion in this book, including questions about war. But Jews in diverse historical contexts have constructed a wide range of Jewish traditions about war, framing their ideas with reference to Jewish identities, histories, and texts.

Some Jews, for example, have seen the Hebrew Bible as a source of moral authority, and they have drawn on biblical traditions in formulating their ideas about war. They have necessarily been selective, however, since the Bible contains a strikingly wide range of perspectives. Some biblical authors believed that the sacrifice of human life in war, regardless of guilt, could secure divine favor, while others depicted God ordaining war to ensure justice. Many biblical texts highlight God's commandments for the Israelites to wipe out enemy nations, such as the Canaanites, whose land the Israelites were to inherit, but other biblical texts seem to discourage the human initiation of war.

The rabbinic literature of the first millennium CE, which some Jews have viewed as essential to Jewish tradition, drew on some of these biblical texts and developed its own diverse ideas about war. Some rabbinic texts praise the heroic Israelite warriors of the Bible and the divine commandments to destroy enemy nations, while others depict war as God's prerogative and discourage human participation. Rabbinic texts also imagine limits on the wars that later generations of Jews could carry out; one tradition, for example, indicates that the people of Israel were prohibited by God from "going up as a wall" to the land of Israel, seemingly outlawing any war to establish Jewish control of the land, an idea that may have been especially compelling to some rabbis after the failures of Jewish revolts against Roman rule in Palestine.

Modern Jews have constructed a wide range of Jewish traditions about war, sometimes drawing on the sorts of traditions named here and sometimes drawing on other understandings of Jewish history and identity reflecting particular contexts and political agendas. During the US Civil War, for example, Jewish preachers in the American South drew on biblical texts in arguing for the South's right to defend themselves and the institution of slavery; in the North, other preachers drew on biblical texts in arguing for war that would destroy the institution of slavery. During World War I, some Jewish thinkers pledged allegiance to the nationalist causes of the countries in which they lived and argued that their Jewish identities positioned them to defend those causes, while Jewish pacifists argued that war and nationalism were forms of idolatry and contrary to God's message in the Torah.

The Zionist movement produced many new Jewish approaches to war. Some Zionists valorized the use of military force to gain control over land in Palestine, appealing to militaristic models from Jewish history, while others cautioned against militarism, often appealing to what they understood as humanitarian Jewish values. After the State of Israel was founded, some Zionists came to view the state and its army as holy and its wars as part of a messianic mission to ensure Jewish control of the land of Israel, while others appealed to Jewish texts or history in justifying those wars as a matter of self-defense. Jewish critics of Israeli military campaigns, meanwhile, have often appealed to Jewish history, critiquing Israel for victimizing others in ways that Jews have historically been victimized. Others have appealed to ethical principles found in traditional Jewish sources that might significantly limit war, such as recognizing all people as created in God's image and prioritizing saving human lives.

These are just a few of the many ways that Jews have constructed Jewish traditions regarding war. While many have claimed that their views represent the authentic teaching of "Jewish tradition," "Jewish ethics," or "Judaism," the critical study of these traditions indicates that Jewish tradition does not "say" anything about war in a singular voice. Rather, Jews in particular historic contexts have sought to advance particular ideas about war and have often claimed that these ideas represent the view of tradition.

## About the author

**Geoffrey D. Claussen** is a professor of religious studies, Lori and Eric Sklut Professor in Jewish Studies, and the chair of the Department of Religious Studies at Elon University. His recent books include *Modern*

*Musar: Contested Virtues in Jewish Thought* (JPS, 2022) and *Jewish Ethics: The Basics* (Routledge, 2025).

## Suggestions for further reading

*In this book*
See also chapters 1 (Why are texts sacred to Jews?), 2 (What is the Torah?), 56 (What is Zionism?), and 57 (What is anti-Zionism?).

*Elsewhere*
Claussen, Geoffrey D. *Jewish Ethics: The Basics*. New York: Routledge, 2025.

Eisen, Robert. *The Peace and Violence of Judaism: From the Bible to Modern Zionism*. New York: Oxford University Press, 2011.

Firestone, Reuven. *Holy War in Judaism: The Fall and Rise of a Controversial Idea*. New York: Oxford University Press, 2012.

Niditch, Susan. *War in the Hebrew Bible: A Study in the Ethics of Violence*. New York: Oxford University Press, 1993.

# 70
# How have Jews approached slavery?

## Jonathan K. Crane

The most common Hebrew term for "slave" is *'eved*, from the verb *la'avod*, meaning "to work." Whereas other workers are paid for their labor, a slave is not. And unlike most other workers, a slave is a member of the master's household and is thus subject to the master's power over personal matters like marriage.

Slavery is a foundational concept in Judaism. In a temporal sense, it appears in some of the earliest layers of the Judaic textual tradition. The Bible has many stories about slaves and slavery, though there is no consistency in how these stories present the topic. For instance, the first mention of the term "slave" is when Noah curses Ham's son, Canaan, to be the slave of his brothers (Gen. 9:25–26). Though Noah does not specify what this means, it is clear that he views enslavement as a kind of punishment. By contrast, when Abraham sends his slave to secure a wife for his son Isaac, the slave negotiates with Rebecca's father, Bethuel, at length and with professional sophistication (Gen. 24)—a story suggesting slaves can exercise great agency and influence the future of the Jewish people. The last several chapters of Genesis relate the story of Joseph being sold into servitude in Egypt and his eventual ascension to great power. Such stories indicate that in the ancient world, slavery was a complex yet familiar institution.

Slavery is also a foundational concept in Judaism in a theological sense. Consider, for example, the fact that slaves are included in the commandment to rest on the Sabbath (Ex. 20:8–11; Deut. 5:12–15). And as narrated through Exodus, Leviticus, Numbers, and Deuteronomy, the story of the exodus of Jews from enslavement in Egypt indicates slavery's centrality to Judaism's theology. While Moses figures significantly as a human leader who brings the Jews out of bondage, the story is told, retold, and ritualized at Passover with God as the nation's ultimate liberator.

To this day, many Jews begin their mornings reciting a prayer (*Birkot HaShachar*) thanking God for not making them a slave.

There is also a slew of laws about slavery, who may be enslaved, and for how long. The Bible distinguishes non-Jewish slaves from Jewish slaves, male from female, pauper from war captive. According to Exodus 21 and Leviticus 25:39–46, for example, non-Jewish persons could be owned in perpetuity, while the Jewish ones could not, and different punishments were to be meted out for injuring or killing non-Jewish versus Jewish slaves. In late antiquity, the rabbis similarly laid down laws about how various people could be enslaved, how they were to be treated, and if they qualified, how they were to be redeemed, manumitted, or released to freedom (see, for example, BT *Arachin* 29a; *Pirkei Avot* 2.7). Not only could manumission be achieved through a variety of mechanisms (e.g., a third party paying for a slave's outstanding debt, a man's marriage to a free woman, being sold across international lines), but some sources from the Bible to modern *responsa* and sermons insist that the formerly enslaved—and even their progeny—are due reparations for their years of service.

That such discussions about slavery continued through the millennia suggests that Jews have had an ongoing relationship with the institution. Historical scholarship reveals that Jews participated in the capture, transportation, sale, and ownership of humans. Many invoked biblical sources to justify their participation in the slave industry. In the US context during the century leading up to the Civil War, debate about the meaning of those sources became increasingly fraught: Various Jews, African Americans, and Anglo-Protestants vied to claim that theirs was the rightful interpretation of the Exodus story of liberation. Some claimed that it was particularist and pertinent only to them; others insisted that it was a universal story. Though in the aftermath of that war Jews disengaged completely from overt slavery, they continued wrestling with the stories and strictures of enslavement and liberation to figure out how to relate them to the contemporary moment. Many took inspiration from those sources to become involved in transforming and dismantling Jim Crow legislation and mass incarceration—or what many viewed as slavery by another name.

This leads to one of the biggest challenges facing Jews today. What can and should be done with those foundational Jewish texts, theologies, liturgies, and histories that demonstrate the existence and even acceptance of slavery? How should those narratives and laws be understood today? Yes, there are countervailing and foundational Judaic stories, laws, and values that champion compassion, dignity, duty, and perhaps human rights—but how can it be argued that those should take priority over the similarly foundational ones that endorse slavery? What's at stake here are questions of historical fact (what was), historiography (the stories told about what happened), the meaning of those facts and stories, and the self-esteem derived from contending with their complexity.

## About the author

**Jonathan K. Crane**, PhD, rabbi, serves as the Raymond F. Schinazi Scholar in Bioethics and Jewish Thought at Emory University's Center for Ethics. A professor of medicine, Crane is a past president of the Society of Jewish Ethics, founder and coeditor of the *Journal of Jewish Ethics*, and author or editor of *Narratives and Jewish Bioethics* (Palgrave, 2013); *The Oxford Handbook of Jewish Ethics and Morality* (Oxford, 2022); *Beastly Morality: Animals as Ethical Agents* (Columbia, 2022); *Eating Ethically: Religion and Science for a Better Diet* (Columbia, 2018); *Judaism, Race, and Ethics: Conversations and Questions* (Penn State, 2020); *Modern Jewish Ethics Since 1970: Writings on Methods, Sources, and Issues* (Brandeis, 2025); and *Immoral Medicine: Defending American Biomedical Research at the Trial of Nazi Doctors* (forthcoming).

## Suggestions for further reading

### In this book
See also chapters 60 (What are Jewish ethics?) and 61 (What does Judaism say about social justice?).

### Elsewhere
Cohn, Haim H. "Slavery." In *Encyclopedia Judaica* (2nd extensively revised edition, volume 18), edited by Michael Berenbaum and Fred Skolnik, 667–670. New York: Macmillan Reference, 2006.

Crane, Jonathan K. "Not Just: Judaism and Reparations." *Journal of Jewish Ethics* 9(1) (2023): 82–109.

Hezser, Catherine. *Jewish Slavery in Antiquity*. New York: Oxford University Press, 2005.

Hoberman, Michael. "'God Loves the Hebrews': Exodus Typologies, Jewish Slaveholding, and Black Peoplehood in Antebellum America." *American Jewish Archives Journal* 67(2) (2015): 47–69.

Schorsch, Jonathan. *Jews and Blacks in the Early Modern World*. New York: Cambridge University Press, 2004.

# 71
# What do Jews think about abortion?

## Samira K. Mehta

Jewish law, or halakhah, permits abortion. That said, it is important to note that while Jewish law supports abortion rights, halakhah is primarily focused not on women's rights but rather on the preservation of Jewish life. For a consideration of feminist rationales for abortion, one must turn to Jewish ethics.

From the standpoint of Jewish law, there are three important points when it comes to abortion: the status of the embryo/fetus in Jewish law, the conditions under which a therapeutic abortion may take place, and the conditions under which a nontherapeutic abortion may take place.

Some branches of Christianity, such as the Catholic Church, see life as beginning at conception and therefore forbid abortion. While this discourse dominates conversations about abortion in the United States, in Jewish law, the fetus is not considered a person with full legal rights. For instance, the biblical book of Exodus notes that if a pregnant woman is attacked and then miscarries, the attacker owes a fine but is not guilty of murder. By contrast, if the pregnant person is severely injured, the penalty is akin to that of murder. Jewish tradition interprets this text as seeing a value in a fetus but not a value equivalent to that of a person.

In addition, the Talmud makes several references to fetuses. The Talmud states that for the first forty days after conception, the fetus is "mere water." After those forty days, the text treats the fetus like it is part of its mother's body: "A fetus is the thigh of the mother." Furthermore, the Talmud notes that if a pregnant woman converts to Judaism, when her baby is born, it is Jewish. This indicates that the fetus is not understood as a separate life from that of the pregnant parent at the moment of conversion.

Further evidence that pregnancy is not indicative of a unique life actually comes from Talmud rulings on livestock. If a man sells a cow and the cow turns out to be pregnant, the purchaser does not owe the seller for a second cow. All of these sources are taken to indicate that while the fetus has a legal status, it is not equivalent to that of a person. Rather, the fetus is considered as either a part of its mother or, at most, a potential person, but it does not hold the same full personhood as its mother.

Because of this valuing of life over potential life, Jewish law generally permits therapeutic abortion. Abortion is not only permitted but mandated to save the life of the mother, because potential life must be sacrificed to save existing life—even during labor, as long as the head has not emerged from the birth canal.

Where Jewish law on abortion gets complicated is when the mother's life is not at risk. Jewish law is clear that abortion is permitted if pregnancy or childbirth will severely damage maternal health, with most contemporary Jewish movements counting mental health as equally important to physical health. That said, there are debates about how severe the risk to maternal health needs to be before abortion is permitted. Jewish law generally also permits abortion if genetic testing shows evidence of a fatal disability.

Most debates in Jewish law focus on what are considered nontherapeutic abortions. This means that rabbis may disagree about how severe the damage to a pregnant person's physical or mental health must be before abortion is permitted. They also may debate the permissibility of abortion in the case of nonfatal fetal abnormalities or if an additional child will severely tax family resources.

These debates about Jewish law have not tended to support on-demand abortion, based in a pregnant person's wish to not be pregnant for reasons other than medical concern or severe economic trouble.

Debates in Jewish law aside, American Jews have generally supported legal abortion with very few restrictions. Eighty-three percent support a woman's right to an abortion. Some see it as a religious freedom issue. While many consult their rabbis when seeking an abortion, many others would not see a need to do so or would turn to them for support, not for permission.

Most recently, Jewish ethicists have looked beyond halakhic discussions to Jewish thought and Jewish women's lived experiences to expand the conversation around abortion to more fully take into account women's experiences of abortion grounded in their Jewish beliefs, identities, and practices.

Pieces of this essay were previously published in *The Conversation*.

## About the author

**Samira K. Mehta** is the director of Jewish studies and an associate professor of women's and gender studies and Jewish studies at the University of Colorado Boulder. She is the author of *Beyond Chrismukkah: The Christian-Jewish Interfaith Family in the United States* (UNC Press, 2018) and *The Racism of People Who Love You: Essays on Mixed Race Belonging* (Beacon, 2023) and is currently completing a book called *God Bless the Pill: Contraception and Sexuality in American Religion*.

## Suggestions for further reading

*In this book*
See also chapters 6 (What is Jewish law?), 3 (What is the Talmud?), 60 (What are Jewish ethics?), 62 (What's the connection between Jews and feminism?), and 65 (What does contemporary Judaism say about sexualities?).

*Elsewhere*
Kranson, Rachel. "From Women's Rights to Religious Freedom: The Women's League for Conservative Judaism and the Politics of Abortion: 1970–1982." In *Devotions and Desires: Histories of Sexuality and Religion in the 20th Century United States*, edited by Gillian Frank, Bethany Moreton, and Heather White, 170–192. Chapel Hill: University of North Carolina Press, 2018.

Mehta, Samira K. "Jewish Law Has Always Been Clear: Emergency Abortions Are an Essential Right." *The Forward*, June 27, 2024. https://forward.com/opinion/628053/emergency-abortion-supreme-court-jewish-tradition/.

Mehta, Samira K. "There Is No One 'Religious View' on Abortion: A Scholar of Religion, Gender and Sexuality Explains." *The Conversation*, June 13, 2022. https://theconversation.com/there-is-no-one-religious-view-on-abortion-a-scholar-of-religion-gender-and-sexuality-explains-184532.

Raucher, Michal. "The Cultural and Legal Reproduction of Poverty: Abortion Legislation in Israel." *Journal of Feminist Studies in Religion* 30(1) (2014): 147–156.

Raucher, Michal. "From Justification to Justice: Calling for a New Conservative Movement Position on Abortion." In *Masorti: The New Journal of Conservative Judaism* 67(1) (Winter 2022–2023): 55–77.

# Index

abortion, 235–236
Abraham (the patriarch), 42, 94, 113, 141, 213–214, 232
Abzug, Bella, 207–208 (see also: feminism)
Adam (biblical figure), 13, 122
afterlife (see: death)
alcohol, 34, 39–40, 127 (see also: wine)
ancestry, Jewish, 147, 159–160
   and citizenship in Israel, 91–92
   Cohen Modal Haplotype (CMH), 159
   and DNA, 159–161
   Khazar hypothesis, 159
   and race, 160
Ancient Hebrew (see: Hebrew; languages, Jewish)
angels, 99–101
Antiochus IV Epiphanes, 27, 36, 43 (see also: Greece; Second Temple period)
antisemitism, 40, 100, 102–103, 124–125, 141–143, 165–166, 168–169, 227
   accusation of Jews as Christ-killers, 110, 115–116
   blood libel, 124–125
   Christian, 100, 110, 116, 124–125, 154, 168–169
   in Nazi Germany, 142, 145, 165–166, 169
   in political judgments about the State of Israel, 142
   racialized forms, 151, 168
   as response to Jewish emancipation, 168
   and Zionism, 148, 185, 187
*antisemitismus*, 142 (see: antisemitism)
anti-Zionism, 189–191
apocalyptic figure, Jesus as, 112–113
Arabic, 71, 74–75, 131, 141, 193
Aramaic, 15, 74–75
Artson, Bradley, 217 (see also: Conservative Judaism; sexual orientation)
*Ashkenaz*, 68 (see also: Ashkenazi Jews)

Ashkenazi Jews, 68–70, 154, 159–161
   denominations, 65, 68
   food, 31, 68
   genetic ancestry, 159–161
   Khazar hypothesis, 159
   languages, 74
   non-Jewish Eastern European influence, 68
   Yiddish, 68, 74–76, 223–224
assimilation, Jewish, 28–29, 43, 87, 91–92, 104, 148, 185, 189, 227
atonement (see: Yom Kippur)
authority
   divine authority of Hebrew Bible, 3
   of halakhah, 21–23, 201–202
   of kings of ancient Israel, 96
   non-Jewish political, 22
   of Pontius Pilate, 115–116
   rabbinic, 24–25, 51, 201
   rejection of traditional, 51, 71, 81
   textual, 3–4, 9, 229
*autos-de-fé*, 103 (see also: Inquisition, Spanish)

Ba'al Shem Tov (see: ben Eliezer, Israel, the Ba'al Shem Tov; Hasidic Judaism)
Babylonia, rabbinic movement in, 9–10 (see also: Talmud, Babylonian)
baptism, forced, 102–103 (see also: conversion to Christianity: forced; crypto-Jews; Inquisition, Spanish)
bar mitzvah, 45–46
bat mitzvah, 45–46
belief
   in angels and demons, 99–100
   belief *that* vs. belief *in*, 81
   about death, 93–94
   distinction between religion and culture, 160
   in God, 80–81, 181
   influence of political emancipation, 65

239

belief (*continued*)
  in Jesus, 109–110
  in the Messiah, 96–98
  in resurrection, 93
  unbelief in Jesus, 109–110
Belser, Julia Watts, 220, 222 (see also: disability)
ben David, Anan, 71 (see also: Karaites)
ben Eliezer, Israel, the Ba'al Shem Tov (1698–1760), 16, 51 (see also: Hasidic Judaism)
ben Jehuda Leib Frank, Jakob (Jakub; 1726–1791), 104 (see also: crypto-Jews; Frankists)
Ben-Gurion, David
  centralization of Israeli culture around the Hebrew Bible, 195–197
  statism, 186–187
  Zionism of, 186–187
*Bereshit Rabba*, 12–13 (see also: midrash)
Berkovits, Eliezer, 181 (see also: Holocaust)
Biblical Hebrew (see: Hebrew; languages, Jewish)
biblical law, 6–7, 21–22 (see also: halakhah; Torah)
  in the Qur'an, 131
  terms to describe non-Israelites, 90
biblical texts, 3–4, 6–7 (see also: Hebrew Bible; Jewish texts)
  differences of interpretation between Christians and Jews, 121–123
  on disability, 220–221
  and Karaite Judaism, 71–72
  on matrilineal lineage, 156–157
  midrashic interpretation of, 12–13
  and non-Jews, 86, 90–91
  on war, 229–230
  and Zionism, 197
birth
  and abortion, 236–237
  celebrations of, 42–43
  gender identities assigned at, 213
  virgin birth of Jesus, 121–122
birth control, 207
Black Hebrews, 144–145
Black Israelites, 144–145
Black Jews, 144, 150–151
Black-Jewish relations, 150–152
blood libel, 124–125 (see also: antisemitism; Jewish-Christian relations)
b'mitzvah, 45–46

Brandeis, Louis (US Supreme Court Justice), 28
*brit milah* (see: circumcision)
*b'tzelem Elohim* (see: divine image)

Canaanites, 90, 156, 196, 229
canon, 4, 118–119, 130 (see also: Jewish texts)
capitalism, stereotypes about Jews and, 227
Chabad Lubavitch, 16, 97 (see also: Hasidic Judaism)
  and Kabbalah, 16–17
  on the Messiah, 97
charity, 22
children
  bar, bat, and b'mitzvah, 45–46
  circumcision, 42–43
  Hanukkah, 27–28
  impact of intermarriage, 77, 86–87, 91, 156
  parallel celebrations to circumcision for girls, 43
Chrismukkah, 28
Christian Bible, 118, 121–122 (see also: New Testament)
Christian temperance movement, 40
Christianity, 110, 116, 118–119, 121–123 (see also: Christian Bible; Jesus of Nazareth)
  abortion in, 235
  and antisemitism, 100, 110, 116, 124–125, 154, 168–169
  conversion to, 102–103
  Jewish-Christian relations, 121–129, 154
  Messianic Jews, 127–129
circumcision, 42–43, 214
citizenship
  in Europe, 148, 160, 189
  in Israel, 91–92, 145, 187, 192–194
  Law of Return in Israel, 92, 193
  loss of citizenship in Nazi Germany, 165
  in nation-states, 22, 160
civil religion, status of Judaism in modern State of Israel, 193
clergy, Jewish (see: rabbis)
climate crisis, 210–211
Cohen, Hermann (1842–1918), 97
Cold War, 28, 125
colonialism, 86, 145, 168, 185–187, 196–197 (see also: settler colonialism)
comedy, 223–224 (see also: humor)
commandments, 4, 21, 33, 42–44, 45, 54, 80, 83–84, 90, 201, 214, 221, 229, 232

commentary, rabbinic, 15, 21, 24 (see also: Talmud, Babylonian)
Communism, 37, 125, 189–190, 227
Conservative Judaism, 66–67, 217–218
   commitment to gender egalitarianism, 46, 66
   and halakhah, 22, 217
   on intermarriage, 87
   ordination of gay and lesbian rabbis, 25–26, 217
   ordination of women, 25–26
   rabbis in, 25
   Sabbath, 55, 66
   on sexualities, 217–218
   on tattoos, 57
continuity crisis, 77–78, 84, 87 (see also: intermarriage)
*conversa*, 102 (see also: crypto-Jews)
conversion to Catholicism (see: conversion to Christianity)
conversion to Christianity, 102–104
   of crypto-Jews, 102–104
   forced, 37, 69, 102–103
   among Messianic Jews, 127
   Spanish Inquisition, 37, 103
conversion to Judaism, 52, 83–85, 91, 153, 161
   analogy to trans identities, 214
   biblical examples of, 86
   circumcision, 43, 83, 214
   debates of early Christians about, 119
   Ethiopian Hebrews' rejection of the idea of, 145
   genetics and, 147, 161
   impact on a fetus, 235
   institutionalization of, 91
   intermarriages, 87, 147
   Jews of African descent, 144
   rituals, 83, 214
   in the Second Temple period, 83
   state-sponsored, 84, 92
   and Talmud, 84, 86, 91
*conversos* (see: crypto-Jews)
creation of the world, 12–13, 16, 61
crucifixion, 115–116
crypto-Jews, 102–104
crypto-Judaism (see: crypto-Jews)
cultural Judaism (see: Judaism: cultural)

Daf Yomi (reading practice), 10 (see also: Talmud, Babylonian)
Day of Atonement (see: Yom Kippur)
Dead Sea Scrolls, 99

death, 30, 93–94, 174, 180
   of Jesus, 109–110, 112–113, 115–116, 121
demons, 99–101
denominations, Jewish, 22, 65–67
   Ashkenazi, 68
   Conservative Judaism, 66–67, 217–218
   demographics, 67
   Humanistic Judaism, 81
   Orthodox Judaism, 66–67
   Reconstructionist Judaism, 46, 66–67
   Reform Judaism, 65–67
   in relation to halakhah, 22
   Renewal movement, 67
Deuteronomy, 4, 6, 22, 36, 90, 130–131, 204, 214, 220, 232
diaspora, 52, 69, 71–72, 74–75, 76, 104, 190, 195
dietary laws (see: kashrut)
disability, 220–222, 236
divine attributes (see: *sefirot*)
divine commands (see: commandments)
divine energy (see: *sefirot*)
divine image, 220, 221
divine inheritance, 156
divine intervention, 30, 39
divine name (see: name of God)
divine punishment, 13, 180–181, 202
divine realm, 16, 100
divine revelation, 3–4, 130, 131, 214
DNA (see: ancestry, Jewish)
Dönme of Salonica, 103 (see also: crypto-Jews)
dreidel, 28 (see also: Hanukkah)
Duhm, Bernhard L. (1847–1928), 122–123

ecological crisis (see: climate crisis)
Edict of Expulsion (1492), 69, 103 (see also: crypto-Jews; Inquisition, Spanish)
education
   assimilationist, 148
   discrimination against Mizrahi Jews in, 69, 145
   feminist impact on, 208
   as form of resistance under Nazi Germany, 171
   Hasidic rejection of secular, 66
   about Holocaust, 175
   in Israel, 196
   Jewish texts, 4, 137
   *Mishneh Torah*, 137
   programming in synagogues, 25, 214
   rabbinical, 25

Egypt, Jews in
  in Genesis, 94, 156, 232
  Karaite diaspora, 72
  Maimonides, 136
  in Passover Haggadot, 30, 174–175
*Ein Yaakov*, 13 (see also: ibn Habib, Jacob; ibn Habib, Levi)
Eleazer, 36 (see also: Maccabees, Books of the)
emancipation, Jewish political
  changed communal and political autonomy, 65, 160, 195
  in Europe, 65, 84, 86, 141, 154, 160, 168, 189
  failure of, 189–190
  in Muslim-majority lands, 65
endogamy, in biblical stories, 156 (see also: matrilineal lineage; patrilineal lineage)
equality (see also: feminism; social justice)
  celebration of, 217
  gender and LGBTQ+, 13, 46, 48–49, 66, 217
  human, 202
  in political and social rights, 193–194, 207
  racial, 208
  and social justice, 204–205
ethical monotheism, 80
ethics, Jewish, 21–22, 80, 201–202, 205, 236
Ethiopian Hebrews, 145
Ethiopian Jews, 145
ethnicity, Jewish, 68–69, 77, 81, 144, 147–148, 153–154, 159–160, 192–193
  and law, 193
  and matrilineal lineage, 156
  postethnic Judaism, 91
  and race, 159–160
  and Zionism, 192–193
European Jews, 147–148 (see also: Ashkenazi Jews)
  and Holocaust, 165–166
  and intermarriage, 87
  Orientalism toward Mizrahi Jews, 145
  political emancipation of, 65, 84, 86, 141, 154, 160, 168, 189
  settlement in Palestine, 185
evil, 36, 61, 100, 142, 181
exegesis (see also: midrash)
  Karaite, 72
  marginalized, 49
  midrash, 12
Exile, 61, 103, 189–190

Exodus, 6, 12, 30, 33, 151, 196, 232–233, 235
Ezra-Nehemiah, 6–7
  and matrilineal lineage, 156

Fackenheim, Emil, 180–181
Feinstein, Moshe, 217
Feldman, Aharon, 217
feminism, 13, 46, 48–49, 207–209, 235
Ferdinand II, King of Aragon (r. 1479–1516), 102 (see: Inquisition, Spanish)
Firestone, Shulamith, 207–208 (see also: feminism)
food, 78, 81 (see also: kashrut)
  Ashkenazi, 31, 68
  Hanukkah, 28
  Holocaust commemoration through, 174
  kosher, 33–34, 36, 66
  limited or lack of access to, 166
  Mizrahi, 31
  *pareve*, 33–34
  Passover, 30–31, 34, 208
  Sabbath, 55
Frankists, 104 (see also: ben Jehuda Leib Frank, Jakob; crypto-Jews)
fundamentalism, of biblical interpretation in sectors of Israeli society, 197
funerals, 93 (see also: death)

Gager, John, 119
Garden of Eden, 13, 93, 122
Gemara, 21 (see also: commentary, rabbinic; Mishnah; Talmud, Babylonian)
gender, 48–50, 213–215, 216–217
  as analogy to disability, 221
  ancient gender norms, 217
  in bar, bat, and b'mitzvah ceremonies, 45–46
  binary, 49, 213–215, 221
  egalitarianism, 46, 66–67
  essentialism, 48, 50
  and halakhah, 48–50, 213–214, 217
  in Hasidic Judaism, 51–52
  in Reform Judaism, 65–66
  role in intermarriage, 87
  roles, 51, 216
  and Talmud, 49, 216–217
  trans and nonbinary identities, 213–215
  transition, 214
  in ultra-Orthodox Judaism, 66
gender studies, 48–50
genealogy (Foucault), l, 48–49

Genesis, 6, 12–13, 33, 39, 42, 54, 93–94, 122, 141, 202, 214, 232–233
genizah, 4 (see also: Jewish texts)
Gentiles (see: non-Jews)
Geonim, families of, 71 (see also: Karaite Judaism)
*ger*, 91 (see also: non-Jews)
Germany, Nazi, 165–166, 168–169, 171–173, 174 (see also: Holocaust)
God, 80–81, 181
   belief in, 80–81
   divine attributes, 15
   and the Holocaust, 81, 180
   Moses Maimonides on, 137
   meaning of, 81
   name of, 60–62
   and the presence of evil, 181
   in state of exile, 61
   unbelief in, 81
Gospels, 109, 112–113 (see also: Jesus of Nazareth; New Testament)
   on the death of Jesus, 115–116
   relationship with Qur'an, 130
*goy* (see: non-Jews)
Greece
   Antiochus IV Epiphanes, 27, 36, 43
   influence on conceptions of God, 60
   Jews under, 27, 43
   Judeo-Greek, 74–75
Greenberg, Steven, 217–218
*Guide of the Perplexed, The*, 137 (see also: Maimonides, Moses)

Ha'am, Ahad, 192
Haggadah, 30–31 (see also: Passover)
   and the Holocaust, 174–175
   Messianic Haggadot, 128
halakhah, 3, 9–10, 12, 21–25, 43, 48–50, 51, 84, 92, 100, 113, 136–137, 154, 157, 201–202, 204–205, 213–214, 217, 221, 233, 235–236
   denominational differences, 22, 65–67, 217
   kashrut, 33–34, 36
Halevi, Judah, 100, 134
Hannah Rachel Vermermacher, Maiden of Ludmir (1805–1888), 52
Hanukkah, 27–29, 36
Haredi (see: ultra-Orthodox Judaism)
Hasidic dynasty of Vien, 52 (see also: Hasidic Judaism)
Hasidic Judaism, 6, 16, 25, 51–52, 66, 100
   ben Eliezer, Israel, the Ba'al Shem Tov (1698–1760), 16, 51
   Chabad Lubavitch, 16, 97, 150
Hasidism (see: Hasidic Judaism)
Hasmoneans, 27 (see also: Hanukkah)
Havdalah, 39, 55 (see also: Sabbath)
Hebrew (language), 4, 58, 131, 141, 193, 214 (see also: languages, Jewish)
   Biblical, 74–75
   meanings of name of God, 60–61
   Modern, 75–76, 128
   revival of, 186, 192
   sacredness of, 4, 131
Hebrew Bible, 3–4, 6–7, 121–123 (see also: Torah)
   angels and demons in, 99
   circumcision, 42–43
   and disability, 220
   in early Islamic sources, 134
   and halakhah, 21
   and Karaite Judaism, 72
   and kashrut, 33, 36
   Mishnah and Talmud as continuation or extension of, 4, 9
   name of God, 60–61
   references to God, 80–81
   relationship to the Qur'an, 130–131
   role in modern State of Israel, 195–197
   Sabbath, 54
   and slavery, 232–233
   and war, 229
   and Zionism, 194–196
Hebrew Christians (see: Messianic Jews)
*Hebrew Hammer, The* (2003), 28 (see also: Hanukkah)
Heraclius (r. 610–641 CE), 102 (see also: conversion to Christianity; crypto-Jews; Iberian Peninsula)
Hertz, J. H., 62
Herzl, Theodor, 185, 192, 196
Heschel, Abraham Joshua, 54, 62
heterosexuality, 216–217 (see also: sexual orientation)
holidays (see: Hanukkah; Passover; Purim; Sabbath; Sukkot)
Holocaust, 165–166, 168–175, 177–178, 180–182
   Auschwitz-Birkenau, 57, 166, 169
   concentration camps, 165–166, 169, 172
   genocide, 166, 169

Holocaust (*continued*)
    ghettos, 166, 172
    Jewish resistance, 166, 171–173
    Nuremberg Laws (1935), 165, 168
    other persecuted groups, 165, 169
    post-Holocaust trauma, 58, 175, 177–178, 180
    tattoos, 57
homosexuality, 216–218 (see also: sexual orientation)
Humanistic Judaism, 81 (see also: secular Jews)
humor (see: comedy)

Iberian Peninsula, 37, 68–69, 74, 102–103, 145
Ibn Ezra, Abraham, 72 (see also: Karaite Judaism)
ibn Habib, Jacob, 13
ibn Habib, Levi, 13
identity, Jewish, 144–145, 147–148, 159–160
    ethnic, 68–69, 77, 81, 144, 147–148, 153–154, 159–160, 192–193
    genetic, 147, 159
    racial, 144–145, 147–148, 151, 159
    religious, 153–155
    secular, 77–78
    tattoos, 58
immigrants (see: immigration, Jewish)
immigration, Jewish
    Law of Return in modern State of Israel, 92, 193
    to Palestine (pre-1948), 186
    to the State of Israel, 72, 84, 91–92, 193, 196
    to the US, 58, 87, 151, 224
impurity of death, 93
injustice (see: ethics, Jewish; racism; social justice)
Inquisition, Spanish, 37, 102–103
    *autos-de-fé*, 103
    Ferdinand II, King of Aragon (r. 1479–1516), 102
    Isabella I, Queen of Castile (r. 1474–1504), 102
interfaith marriage (see: intermarriage)
intermarriage, 77, 86–88, 91, 156
intermediary beings (see: angels; demons)
interpretation, biblical, 12–13, 65–67, 121–122, 124
    allegory, 137
    *peshat*, 72
    supersessionism, 122, 124
    typology, 122

intertextuality, 13 (see also: midrash)
Isabella I, Queen of Castile (r. 1474–1504), 102 (see also: Inquisition, Spanish)
Islam, 130–135
    Judeo-Islamic civilization, 133–135
    Qur'an, 130–131
Israel, ancient, 93–94, 96, 151, 195–197
Israel, modern State of, 22–23, 84, 91–92, 97, 142, 145, 151, 174, 186–187, 189–197, 230
    citizenship, 91–92, 145, 187, 192–194
    immigration, 72, 84, 91–92, 193, 196
    Law of Return, 92, 193
    occupation of Palestine, 97, 145
    racism, 97, 145, 186–187, 193
Israelites, ancient, 3, 30, 42, 90, 99–100, 151, 159

Jerusalem Temple (see also: Second Temple period)
    destruction of, 3, 7, 9, 30, 65
    rededication of, 27
Jesus movement, 118 (see also: Christianity)
Jesus of Nazareth, 30, 96, 109–110, 112–113, 115–116, 121
Jewish ancestry (see: ancestry, Jewish)
Jewish denominations (see: denominations, Jewish)
Jewish ethics (see: ethics, Jewish)
Jewish holidays (see: Hanukkah; Passover; Purim; Sabbath; Sukkot)
Jewish identity (see: identity, Jewish)
Jewish languages (see: languages, Jewish)
Jewish law (see: halakhah)
Jewish mysticism (see: Kabbalah)
Jewish resistance to the Holocaust, 166, 171–173 (see also: Holocaust)
Jewish texts, 3–4, 6–7
    formation of canon, 4
    midrash, 12–13
    Mishnah, 3–4, 7, 9–10
    Oral Torah, 3–4, 7, 9
    sacredness of, 4
    study of, 4
    Talmud, 4, 7, 9–10, 21
    Torah, 3–4, 6–7
    Written Torah, 3–4, 6–7
Jewish-Christian relations, 10, 40, 68–69, 87, 96–97, 102–103, 121–129, 154, 160, 193, 227
    Black Christian–Jewish relations, 151
    Christian antisemitism, 100, 110, 116, 124–125, 154, 168–169

Christian theology of supersessionism, 122, 124
Christian Zionism, 125–126, 186–187
intermarriage, 86–87
Jewish assimilation in Christian Europe, 87, 148, 227
Jewish resistance to Christian missionizing, 84
Jewish-Islamic relations (see: Judeo-Islamic civilization)
Jews for Jesus, 128 (see also: Messianic Jews)
Jews of African descent, 144
Jews of color, 144, 150
Jonas, Hans, 210
Josephus (ca. 75–94 CE), 27, 93, 99, 110, 112, 115
Judah the Patriarch, 9
Judaism
  anti-Zionist, 189
  Conservative, 66–67, 217–218
  conversion to, 83–85, 91, 153, 161
  crypto-, 102–104
  cultural, 78, 81, 186–187, 192
  Hasidic, 16, 51–52, 66
  Karaite, 71–73
  Messianic, 127–129
  Modern Orthodox, 66
  and the modern State of Israel, 185–186, 192–194
  as a non-Jewish term, 154
  Orthodox Judaism, 66–67
  postethnic Judaism, 91
  Rabbinic, 3–4, 65
  Reconstructionist, 46, 66–67
  Reform, 65–67
  as religion or ethnicity, 153–154, 160
  Renewal movement, 67
  ultra-Orthodox, 51, 66–67, 189–190, 193
Judea, ancient, 112, 115–116, 153, 156–157
Judeans, ancient, 27, 153–154
Judeo-Arabic, 74–76 (see also: languages, Jewish)
Judeo-Christian, 125, 210
Judeo-Islamic civilization, 133–135
Judeo-Islamic tradition (see: Judeo-Islamic civilization)
Judeo-Spanish (see: Ladino)

Kabbalah, 15–17, 60–61, 103
Kaplan, Judith, 46
Kaplan, Mordecai, 46, 66–67, 78 (see also: Reconstructionist Judaism)

Karaite Judaism, 71–73
Karaites (see: Karaite Judaism)
kashrut, 31, 33–34, 36–37, 145, 205
Kaye/Kantrowitz, Melanie, 208
Kellner, Menachem, 81
Kertész, Imre, 178
Khazar hypothesis, 159 (see also: ancestry, Jewish)
kibbutz movement, 189
Kinzer, Mark, 129 (see also: Judaism: Messianic; Post-Missionary Messianic Judaism)
Knesset, 23 (see also: Israel, modern State of)
kosher (see: kashrut)
*Kristallnacht*, 165, 174 (see also: Germany, Nazi; Holocaust)

Ladino, 69, 74–76 (see also: languages, Jewish)
Langer, Lawrence, 177 (see also: Holocaust)
languages, Jewish, 9, 10, 15, 55, 68, 74–76, 128, 131, 136, 223–224
law, Jewish (see: halakhah)
Law of Return, 92, 193 (see also: Israel, modern State of)
Levi, Primo, 58
Lilith, 13
*limpieza de sangre* (blood purity), 102 (see also: Iberian Peninsula)
Litvaks (Misnagdim), 52
Luria, Isaac (1534–1572), 16, 103 (see also: Kabbalah)

Maccabee, Judah, 27 (see also: Maccabees, Books of the)
Maccabees, Books of the, 27, 28, 36, 121
Maimonides, Moses (1138–1204), 21, 24–25, 61, 80–81, 100, 134, 136–137, 205
Manuel I, King of Portugal (r. 1495–1521), 103 (see also: crypto-Jews; Iberian Peninsula)
*Marrano*, 37, 102 (see also: crypto-Jews)
marriage, 86, 156, 165, 169, 193, 232–233
  interfaith, 77, 86–88, 91, 156
Martínez, Ferrant, 102 (see also: crypto-Jews; Iberian Peninsula)
matrilineal lineage, 156–157
medieval period, 10, 13, 24–25, 36–37, 40, 68, 71–72, 91, 100, 102, 134, 201–202
*Mekhilta de Rabbi Ishmael*, 12 (see also: midrash)

*meshichiyim* (messianists), 127 (see also: Messianic Jews)
Messiah, 16, 96–98, 104, 109–110, 122 (see also: messianism)
Jesus as, 10, 109, 113, 119, 122
*Messianic Jewish Manifesto*, 128 (see also: Messianic Jews)
Messianic Jewish New Testament, 128 (see also: Messianic Jews)
Messianic Jews, 127–129
messianism, 96–98, 119 (see also: Messiah)
and anti-Zionism, 189–190
and Zionism, 187, 192, 197, 230
mezuzah, 4
Middle Eastern Jews (see: Mizrahi Jews)
*middot*, 202 (see also: ethics, Jewish)
midrash, 12–13, 24, 61
migration, Jewish, 52, 74–75, 147 (see also: immigration, Jewish)
*minyan*, 46
*miqra*, 71, 131 (see also: Karaite Judaism)
Mishnah, 3–4, 9–10, 21, 24, 33, 71, 134, 157
*Mishneh Torah*, 21, 136–137 (see also: Maimonides, Moses)
Misnagdim (Litvaks), 52 (see also: Hasidic Judaism)
missionizing (see: proselytization, Jewish resistance to Christian)
Mizrahi Jews, 31, 46, 68–70, 145, 154
Modern Orthodox, 66 (see also: Orthodox Judaism)
and sexual orientation, 217–218
*mohel*, 43 (see also: circumcision)
Monotheism, 80, 86, 109, 134, 137
Moses, 3, 6–7, 86, 113, 130, 156, 196, 220, 232
Moses de León, 16 (see also: Kabbalah)
Muhammad, Prophet (570–632 CE), 130 (see also: Judeo-Islamic civilization; Qur'an)
music, 127
Muslims, 69, 103, 133–135, 160, 186, 193 (see also: Islam; Judeo-Islamic civilization; Qur'an)
*mussar* (see: ethics, Jewish)
mysticism (see: Kabbalah)

Nahmanides, Moses, 61
name of God, 60–62
National Conference of Christians and Jews, 125
National Day of Remembrance (see: Yom HaShoah)

nationalism, 189, 193–194, 230 (see also: Zionism)
nation-state (see also: Israel, modern State of)
emergence of, 22
Israeli, 186
Jewish emancipation, 160
Nazi Germany (see: Germany, Nazi)
Nazis, 165–166, 168–172
Jewish resistance to, 171–173
racial discourse of, 145, 160, 168–170
Nazism (see: Nazis)
New Testament, 30, 109–110, 112, 115, 118, 121–122
1948 War, 186–187, 193, 196 (see also: Israel, modern State of)
1967 War, 187, 190, 196 (see also: Israel, modern State of)
*nokhri* (foreigner), 90 (see also: non-Jews)
nonbinary identities (see: trans and nonbinary identities)
non-Jews, 86–89, 90–92, 110, 119, 193
conversion of, 83–85, 91
nonreligious Jews (see: secular Jews)
*Nostra Aetate* (*In Our Time*), 125
*nozrim* (Christians), 127

*olam ha-ba* (the world to come), 93 (see also: death)
Old Testament (see: Hebrew Bible)
Oral Torah, 3–4, 7, 9
oral traditions, 7, 9, 12 (see also: Mishnah; Oral Torah; Talmud, Babylonian)
Orthodox Judaism, 22–23, 66–67
bar, bat, and b'mitzvah, 45–46
LGBTQ+ advocacy groups, 214
ordination of gay and lesbian rabbis, 25–26
ordination of women, 25–26
rabbis in, 25
trans and nonbinary identities in, 214
ultra-Orthodox, 51, 66–67, 189–190, 193
Ottoman Empire, 23, 69, 103, 186

Palestine, 186–187, 193, 196, 230
Palestinians, 97, 145, 186–187, 190, 193
*pareve* (neutral), 33–34 (see also: kashrut)
*parzufim*, 16 (see also: Kabbalah; *sefirot*)
Passover, 30–31, 34, 39, 128, 174–175, 205, 208, 232–233
patrilineal lineage, 156, 157

INDEX 247

Paul, the Apostle of Jesus, 112, 118–120
Pentateuch (see: Torah)
Pesach (see: Passover)
*peshat*, Jewish school of, 72 (see also: Karaite Judaism)
Pharisees, 3, 113
Philistines, 43
Philo, 115
Pilate, Pontius, 115–116
Pittsburgh Platform of 1885, 190 (see also: anti-Zionism)
Plaskow, Judith, 13
pogroms, 180 (see also: antisemitism)
Polish–Lithuanian Commonwealth, 104 (see also: Hasidic Judaism)
pork, 36–37
Portuguese Jews, 103 (see: Sephardi Jews)
postethnic Judaism, 91 (see also: non-Jews)
Post-Missionary Messianic Judaism, 129 (see also: Judaism: Messianic)
post-Zionism, 190 (see also: anti-Zionism; Zionism)
Prohibition (see: Christian temperance movement)
proselytization, Jewish resistance to Christian, 84 (see also: Jewish-Christian relations)
Purim, 39, 214
purity, 34, 102, 145 (see also: impurity of death)

Qur'an, 130–131, 134

Rabbinic Judaism, 3–4, 65, 205, 210 (see also: rabbis)
  Karaite rejection of, 71–72
rabbis, 3–4, 12–13, 16, 21–22, 24–26, 31, 39–40, 46, 55, 61, 65, 229, 236
  ordination of, 25–26
  ordination of gay and lesbian, 25–26, 217
  ordination of people in intermarriages, 88
  ordination of women, 25–26
  rabbinic literature, 9–10, 21–22, 24
  rabbinical courts, 22
race, 144–145, 147–148, 151, 159
  in the Americas, 145
  in early twentieth-century Europe, 168
  in the Holocaust, 168–170
racism
  and feminism, 208–209
  idea of a race of "Semites," 141
  against Mizrahi Jews, 69, 145
  against Palestinians, 97, 145, 186–187, 193
  racial discourse of Nazis, 145, 168–169
Rainer, Peter, 177 (see also: Holocaust)
Rashi (ca. 1040–1105), 24, 40, 57, 61
*rebbes*, 51, 66 (see also: Hasidic Judaism)
Reconstructionism (see: Reconstructionist Judaism)
Reconstructionist Judaism, 46, 66–67
  gender egalitarianism, 46, 66
  and halakhah, 217
  on intermarriage, 87–88
  Mordecai Kaplan, 46, 66–67
  ordination of women, 25–26
  on sexual orientation, 218
Reform Judaism, 65–67
  on angels and demons, 100
  and anti-Zionism, 189–190
  bar, bat, and b'mitzvah, 46
  gender egalitarianism, 46, 66
  and halakhah, 22, 65–66, 217
  on intermarriage, 87–88
  ordination of gay and lesbian rabbis, 25–26
  ordination of women, 25–26
  Pittsburgh Platform of 1885, 190
  on sexual orientation, 217–218
  social justice, 66, 202
  on tattoos, 57
Renewal movement, 67
  on intermarriage, 87–88
  and Kabbalah, 16–17
resistance, Jewish
  to Christian missionizing, 84
  to Nazi Germany and the Holocaust, 166, 171–173
*responsa*, 21–22, 25, 223
resurrection
  of Jesus, 109, 112–113, 121
  Jewish ideas about death, 93
Revelation, 3, 4, 131, 221
  of Christ, 124 (see also: supersessionism, Christian theology of)
  Qur'an on revelations of Torah and the Gospels, 130–131
rituals
  alcohol, 39–40
  bar, bat, and b'mitzvah, 45–46
  circumcision, 42–43, 214
  commemoration of Holocaust in, 174–175

rituals (continued)
  conversion, 83, 91, 214
  and halakhah, 21–22
  Hanukkah, 27–28
  impact of feminism on, 208
  impurity of death, 93
  innovation, 66, 211, 221
  objects, 4
  Passover, 30–31
  Sabbath, 54–55
  slaughter, 33–34
  tattoo, 58
  Temple, 3
  trans-and nonbinary-specific, 214
  wine, 34, 39–40
Roman Empire, 9, 36, 96, 109–110, 112–113, 115–116
Rosen, Moishe, 128 (see also: Jews for Jesus)
Rubenstein, Richard, 180

Sabbath, 39, 54–55, 113, 221–222, 232
Sabbath, The, 54 (see also: Heschel, Abraham Joshua; Sabbath)
Sabbatianism (see: Zevi, Sabbatai)
Sadducees, 93
Sasanian Empire, 9
Satmar Hasidim, 52 (see also: Hasidic Judaism)
Schneersohn, Menachem Mendel (1902–1994), 97 (see also: Chabad Lubavitch; messianism)
Scholem, Gershom, 97
scripture (see: Jewish texts)
Second Temple period, 27, 36, 43, 83, 99, 153
Second Vatican Council (1965) (see: Nostra Aetate)
second-wave feminism, 207–208 (see also: feminism)
secular Jews, 77–78, 81, 153–154, 205
  cultural Judaism, 78, 81, 186–187, 192
  ethnic identity, 77
sefirot (divine attributes), 15–16 (see also: Kabbalah)
Seidenberg, David, 205
"Semites," idea of a race of, 141 (see also: antisemitism; race; racism)
Semitic languages, 141
Sepharad, 68
Sephardi Jews, 65, 68–70, 154
  belief in angels and demons, 100
  contact with Dönme of Salonica, 103
  Edict of Expulsion (1492), 69, 103
  Ladino, 69, 74–75
  settler colonialism, 145, 185–187, 196–197 (see also: colonialism)
sexual orientation, 216–218 (see also: gender; trans and nonbinary identities)
sexuality (see: gender; sexual orientation; trans and nonbinary identities)
Shabbat (see: Sabbath)
Shapiro, Meir, 10
Shekhinah, 15, 211
Sheol, 93 (see also: death)
Shimon bar Yohai, 15–16
Shoah (see: Holocaust)
Shulḥan Arukh, 22, 66
siddurim (prayer books), Messianic, 128
Sifra, 12 (see also: interpretation, biblical; midrash)
slavery, 230, 232–234
social justice, 66, 202, 204–205
socialism, 78, 189–190, 227
Someck, Ronny, 134
Soviet Union, 28, 166, 169
Spain (see: Iberian Peninsula)
Spanish Jews (see: Sephardi Jews)
stereotypes, 69, 77, 116, 145, 148, 151, 226–228
Stern, David, 128
Sukkot, 27
supersessionism, Christian theology of, 122, 124 (see also: interpretation, biblical; Jewish-Christian relations)
synagogue, 24–25, 55
  and alcohol, 40
  bar, bat, and b'mitzvahs, 45–46
  circumcision, 43
  and disability, 221
  and gender, 45, 208, 214

Talmud, Babylonian, 3–4, 7, 9–10, 21, 24, 25, 27, 93, 100, 134, 136–137, 195
  and abortion, 235–236
  commentaries, 13, 21, 24
  and conversion, 84, 86, 91
  Daf Yomi (reading practice), 10
  and disability, 221
  and gender, 49
  and halakhah, 201
  and Jewish ethics, 201–202

Karaite rejection of, 71
and kashrut, 33
and labor justice, 204
and the Sabbath, 54–55
and sexual orientation, 216–217
Tanakh (see: Hebrew Bible)
tattoos, 57–58
Taubes, Jacob, 119–120
*tefillin* (phylacteries), 46
temperance movement (see: Christian temperance movement)
Tetragrammaton (see: YHWH)
texts (see: Jewish texts)
*tikkun olam*, 202, 205 (see also: ethics, Jewish; social justice)
Tisha B'Av, 174 (see also: Holocaust)
tomb, family, 94 (see also: death)
Torah, 3–4, 6–7 (see also: Hebrew Bible; Jewish texts)
 in bar, bat, and b'mitzvah, 45–46
 changing identities in, 213–214
 on death, 93–94
 and disability, 221
 as divine revelation, 3, 221
 and gender identities, 213
 in Kabbalah, 15–16
 kashrut in, 33
 and labor justice, 204
 and Messianic Jews, 128
 and midrash, 12–13
 and name of God, 61
 Oral, 3–4, 7, 9
 Passover in, 30
 and the Qur'an, 130–131
 and the Sabbath, 55
 and tattoos, 57
 Written, 3–4, 6–7, 9
trans and nonbinary identities, 26, 213–215 (see also: gender; sexual orientation)
trauma, post-Holocaust, 58, 175, 177–178, 180
*tzadikim*, 16, 51
*tzedakah* (almsgiving), 201
*tzedeq hevrati* (see: social justice)
Tzvi, Shabbatai (see: Zevi, Sabbatai)

ultra-Orthodox Judaism, 16, 51, 66–67, 189–190, 193
US Civil War
 use of biblical texts in, 230, 233

Vermermacher, Hannah Rachel, Maiden of Ludmir (1805–1888), 52 (see also: Hasidic Judaism)
Volstead Act, 40 (see also: Christian temperance movement)

war, 165–166, 168–169, 172, 174–175, 186–187, 229–230
 Cold War, 28, 125
 Jewish traditions about, 229–230
 1948 War, 186–187, 193, 196
 1967 War, 187, 190, 196
 US Civil War, 230, 233
 World War I, 125, 169, 186, 230
 World War II, 58, 125, 165–166, 168–169, 172
Warsaw Ghetto Uprising, 172 (see also: Holocaust; Jewish resistance to the Holocaust)
White, Lynn, 210–211 (see also: climate crisis)
White Jews, 144–145, 150–151
Whiteness, Jewish, 144–145, 150–151
Wiesel, Elie, 177–178 (see also: Holocaust)
wine, 34, 39–40, 55
women, Jewish (see also: gender)
 and abortion, 235–236
 *conversa*, 102
 and feminism, 207–209
 feminist midrashim, 13
 and halakhah, 48–50
 and intermarriage, 86–87
 and kashrut, 34
 matrilineal lineage, 156–157
 ordination, 25–26
 and Talmud, 49, 216–217
World War I, 125, 169, 186, 230
World War II, 58, 125, 165–166, 168–169, 172
Written Torah, 3–4, 6–7, 9

Yahweh (see: YHWH)
Yakubi Dönme, diaspora of, 104 (see also: crypto-Jews; Dönme of Salonica)
yeshiva, 25, 195
YHWH, 3, 7, 60–62
Yiddish, 68, 74–76, 223–224
Yizkor books, 175 (see also: Holocaust)
Yom HaShoah, 174 (see also: Holocaust)
Yom Kippur, 124

*Zaddik* (see: Hasidic Judaism; *tzadikim*)
Zevi, Sabbatai (1626–1676), 16, 103–104 (see also: Dönme of Salonica; Kabbalah)
*Zimzum*, 16 (see also: Kabbalah)
Zionism, 66, 69, 71–72, 97, 145, 148, 185–197, 230
    anti-Zionism, 189–191
    David Ben-Gurion, 186–187, 195–196
    Christian, 125–126, 186–187, 197
    as form of assimilation to join European nations, 148
    Theodor Herzl, 185, 192, 196
    as response to antisemitism, 185, 187
    as settler colonialism, 145, 185–186
    ultra-Orthodox rejection of, 66
Zohar, 4, 15–16 (see also: Kabbalah)

www.ingramcontent.com/pod-product-compliance
Lightning Source LLC
Chambersburg PA
CBHW051633230426
43669CB00013B/2287